And another book for you

1990

(Although it might explain
my bouts of temper, intemperance
and jealousy)

LOVE AND THE SPANISH

LOVE
AND THE SPANISH

BY NINA EPTON

CASSELL · LONDON

CASSELL & COMPANY LTD
35 Red Lion Square . London WC1
and at

MELBOURNE . SYDNEY . TORONTO . CAPE TOWN
JOHANNESBURG . AUCKLAND

———

© *Epton Books Ltd* 1961
First published 1961

Made and printed in Great Britain by
C. Tinling & Co, Ltd, Liverpool, London and Prescot
F.761

Contents

I

II

Illustrations

I

1. *Arabesques and Slave-Girls*

'YOU won't find much about love in here,' observed the professor—a retired art historian—with an ironical smile. I was standing in one of the large, cool, nearly empty halls of the archaeological museum in Madrid, brooding over archaic statues of Iberian votive goddesses. 'You won't find much about love in here,' he repeated. 'Come. Let us go and drink an *horchata* in the Prado.'

Behind a sceptical exterior, the professor was curious to know how I was proceeding and what—if anything—I had found out about love in Spain. The subject is still taboo and therefore tempting. Nearly all the Spaniards to whom I had been given introductions were eager to help, from university professors to doctors, from elderly Don Juans to mocking students, so long as they remained anonymous. Only a small, bigoted, frightened core had waved me aside, exclaiming: 'We know nothing whatsoever about this subject—nothing. Consult our literature!' But the Spaniards have written better about divine love than about human love.

Over our iced *horchata* in the Prado (the rendezvous of lovers ever since Madrid became the capital of Spain) the professor dropped a few crumbs about Iberian civilization and its contribution to love.

'You have seen from their vases,' he remarked, 'that they were a flamboyant people, given to decoration and not very interested in the human figure.'

'Then it is wrong to say,' I interrupted, 'as so many people have done, that Roman Catholic bigotry accounts for the fear of the nude and the human figure in Spanish art. The Spaniards have been innately prudish ever since their Iberian beginnings, long before the advent of Christianity.'

The professor nodded. 'It would seem so, from the remains unearthed to date. The only vase depicting human figures is the famous one from Liria, portraying four women and three men led by a woman playing a double lute and a man playing a single

3

lute, holding hands in the steps of a round-dance similar to the one described by Strabo as characteristic of the tribe to which the Iberians of Liria belonged.'

'Women must have been fairly free,' I said, 'if they were allowed to hold hands and dance with the men. Freer than in later ages. And they were very conspicuous. What complicated head-dresses they wore! There is nothing quite comparable to them in any other European art. They remind me of Balinese dancers.'

'They were interested in feminine appearance,' said the professor. 'We know, from two fragments left by Ephorus, that the Iberians held a yearly festival during which women showed off materials woven by themselves for which they received prizes. On this occasion, too, their waists were measured by a belt of standard size—those whose waists were found too large were greatly despised. We have always admired small waists,' he said, 'but that is a universal trait; I would not attach too much importance to such a detail.'

'Waist-measuring *competitions* are not a universal trait,' I exclaimed. 'That sounds typically Iberian—and Spanish!' The professor smiled faintly. 'Are you going to study love in Spain chronologically?' he enquired. I shook my head. 'I do not think so. There is so little unity about Spain. There are several Spains. I suppose I must start from the beginning and that means. . .' 'Andalusia,' said the professor, with a gesture of inevitability. 'Romantic Andalusia! How I wish you would explode that myth once and for all!' 'Let us meet again when I come back from the south,' I suggested. 'When I have spoken to a great many Andalusians.' The professor laughed. 'They will keep their mouths shut,' he said. 'Andalusians don't talk about love. They sing it and make up poetry about it but they would never think of analysing it. Indeed, few Spaniards do. I shall be interested to hear how you get on.' The professor was from the north and inclined to be contemptuous of his guitar-playing countrymen in the south.

Most northern and even central Spaniards share this contempt, this feeling of separateness from the more indolent and flamboyant Andalusians, the 'real Spain' of tourists, the Spain of 'blood, death and voluptuousness' dear to the Romantics. Is it because, in their inner consciousness, they feel that Andalusia is dangerous, represents a national weakness, too close a contact with the senses, too great a drain on virility and inventiveness, to which they do not wish to succumb?

'We absorb everybody,' an Andalusian poet told me. 'Many races have come here and they have stayed, weighed down by languor. At first the Caliphs of the Omeyad dynasty from Damascus were homesick for their camels and their sand dunes, but later they too fell in love with Andalusia and made it the centre of the most brilliant courts outside Baghdad. This is where the voluptuousness of the Arabian nights ended. Andalusia was responsive to that warm, sensuous atmosphere as no other region of Europe, and Andalusia alone was capable of seducing an easterner. It is not surprising that the Arabs were the first people in Spain to write about love, and their theories eventually inspired the amorists of Provence. East first met West on love's threshold.' That is what a poet said; scholars still disagree about Arab influence on the troubadours.

A significant legend attributes the first Moorish invasion of Spain to Count Rodrick's desire to avenge his outraged daughter. The typical Spanish conflict between love and honour appears at the dawn of their history. But it is not until the tenth century that the first great writers on love appear in Andalusia, the most original of whom was the poet, scholar, theologian and statesman, Ibn H'azm, whose best known work, *The Dove's Necklace, or of love and lovers*, was written in his old age, as an exile in Jativa.

The son of a minister, Ibn H'azm spent his early years, as he tells us himself, upon the laps of the women of the harem in the palace of Córdoba. It was they who instilled in him a love of poetry and refinement, it was they who initiated him into their wiles and intrigues 'so ingenious as to be almost unbelievable'. If we had to depend upon the other Arab-Andalusian poets for our glimpses of love-life during these times there would be little to say, for they are stilted and repetitive. Ibn H'azm, on the contrary, writes in brisk, personal prose studded with anecdotes about the lovers of his day.

These are the lovers for whom the fountains played and the orange-trees blossomed in the gardens of Córdoba, Granada and Seville. These are the lovers, sultry and confined, who lay among piled cushions in the great halls of mosaics between walls decorated with the geometrical rhythms and endless arabesques of the kufic alphabet. The Alhambra and the Alcázar still exhale the perfume of their endless intrigues, idle day-dreams and effeminate *caprices*. This is not a romantic illusion, or if it is, it has affected countless travellers from every part of the world, including the least susceptible, that is to say Spaniards from other provinces. Andalusia absorbed voluptuousness like a sponge and the effect is intoxicating. St. Teresa complained that she could not pray in Seville as effectively as elsewhere: 'I did not recognize myself,' she wrote. 'The devils there have more hands with which to lead one into temptation.' George Borrow, who distributed Bibles in Andalusia to no apparent effect, did not blame the inhabitants for singing continually about love. He excuses them by explaining: 'We were in sunny Andalusia and what can its black-eyed daughters think, speak or sing of but *amor, amor?*'

'Love,' wrote Ibn H'azm in his opening chapter of *The Dove's Necklace*, 'begins with badinage and ends in all seriousness. Its diverse aspects are of such subtlety that they defy all description. One can only grasp the reality when one has been subjected to love oneself.'[1]

Lovers! He has known countless lovers in all ranks of society, especially among princes. The most recent case of which he was a witness was that of the passion of Abd el Malik b. Abi Amir for Wa'hid, the daughter of a cheese merchant. He was so much in love that he ended by marrying her.

As to the nature of love, he accepts the neo-Platonic view: it is a property of the soul. This true form of love can only end with death—it is a state of spiritual complaisance, a fusion of souls. It is true that love attaches itself nearly always to external beauty but that is because the soul itself inclines towards perfect figures. But if, behind this image, it does not distinguish a corresponding quality, affection will not progress beyond this external form and will not surpass mere physical desire.

Among the many symptoms of being in love, which have varied so little through the ages, Ibn H'azm lists lovers' quarrels. 'You see them attain a degree of discord,' he writes, 'which would in normal cases be taken for irreparable except after a very long time in the case of a temperate and non-vindictive person. But when lovers are involved they quickly become the best friends in the world—there is no more question of mutual reproach,

[1] The author's translations are from the French edition, *Le Collier du Pigeon,* by Léon Bercher (Bibliothèque Arabe-Française, Editeur La Typo-Lytho, Algiers, 1949).

discord evaporates and they are all smiles and cajolery. This same scene may be enacted several times at short intervals. When you have witnessed this attitude on the part of two persons you may be sure that a secret love unites them. . . .'

Ibn H'azm devotes a whole chapter to persons who fall in love at first sight but he has little faith in the duration of such passions. To him it is a sign of impatience, an indication of inconstancy and instability. 'It is the same with everything,' he says, 'the more rapid the growth, the quicker its disappearance.' On the other hand, there are people whose affection does not ripen until after many long exchanges, frequent interviews and a prolonged familiarity. This is the kind of love which has the best chance of enduring and resisting time. 'I cannot but be astonished when I hear somebody assure me that he fell in love at a first glance. I have difficulty in believing him and I take his love for concupiscence.' Twentieth-century students whom I interviewed in Santiago de Compostela expressed themselves on this point in similar terms.

When carnal desire has been surpassed and a spiritual union achieved, then this is love. 'This is the cause of the error made by people who pretend to be in love with two different persons at the same time. What they feel is merely a physical love; in this case love is a mere metaphor. When you are really in love your passion takes hold of you to such an extent that you do not have enough energy left to deal with your own spiritual and temporal interests. Therefore, it is obvious that you do not have the leisure to devote yourself to a second love.' In other words, Don Juan can only be a mock lover, as Tirso called him in his *Burlador de Seville*. Ibn H'azm introduced us to Don Juan long before Tirso, in his account of the Vizir Abu' Amir, who could not be constant to his loves. 'He told me that he wearied of everything and that whenever he was sure of vanquishing a beauty his love turned to apathy and his anxiety to possess her turned to anxiety to get rid of her, so he would sell her off at a low price.'

From time to time, however, Ibn H'azm neglects the soul and devotes a number of pages to the physical aspects of love and to scabrous anecdotes, passing with polished ease from one to the other. He observes, in a chapter upon people who fall in love with a specific physical attribute, that he fell in love with a blonde slave when he was young and since then he has never been able

7

to become enamoured of a brunette. His father had the same predilection for blondes and so did the Caliphs of the Banor Marwan family, all of whose members ended up by being blue-eyed blondes. The same thing can happen with a defect. One of Ibn H'azm's friends fell for a woman with a short neck and all her successors in his esteem had short necks too. (This phenomenon has been frequently observed by modern psychologists.)

Whatever Ibn H'azm may have thought about love at first sight, there is no doubt that the eye played—and still plays—an important role in love, particularly in countries where intercourse between the sexes is jealously restrained. The eye-play of present-day Andalusians has had a long past. Ibn H'azm describes some of the more significant eye gestures in a chapter devoted to this important subject. A lowering of the eyelids signifies consent; a prolonged stare indicates suffering and despair; a wink signifies joy; to touch one's eyelids is a warning. A discreet glance from the corner of the eyes implies a question. An inward glance means a refusal. The vocabulary is endless.

Love-letters, for people of a literary turn of mind, wrote Ibn H'azm, are a form of amorous enjoyment, even when they visit each other frequently and there is no obstacle in the way of their meeting. Although there were women poets in Córdoba and Seville, the examples of love-letters given by Ibn H'azm chiefly concern male lovers. Whoever they were sent by, there was a danger of discovery: since so many loves were secret and sinful, most letters had to be destroyed or dissolved in water. Ibn H'azm composed a poem on the subject:

How painful it is for me to have to destroy your letter.
But at least, nobody can destroy our love.
I prefer that our affection should remain and the ink be
                                                    obliterated. . . .
How many letters have caused their author's death although he
    was far from thinking so when he penned the beautiful lines!

Some lovers had perverse epistolary habits. One wetted his ink with his tears and his beloved replied by diluting the ink with her saliva. A third, a pervert, was in the habit of pissing on his love-letters. Quite a few lovers wrote their letters with their blood. 'The writing looked like red lacquer,' comments Ibn H'azm.

The fate of these furtive love-letters has followed their

successors. No Spanish love-letters have ever been published, few Spanish love-letters are ever kept. Lovers invariably burn and destroy them. This seems to be due to innate Spanish reserve and to their fear of mockery. The idea of a love-letter ever being divulged fills them with horror, although boastful young men have been known not to respect the convention. This does not mean, of course, that they do not write love-letters. They do, and those I have been allowed to see—but not to describe— were excellent specimens of the genre.

An ex-Republican told me that he arrived at Teruel during the 1936 Civil War before the inhabitants had had time to evacuate all their belongings. In the house where he was billeted he found several parcels of love-letters neatly tied with pink ribbon. He read them and shed tears over them—irrespective of their writers' political opinions. When he had finished he destroyed them with a Calderonian sense of honour.

The delivery of early love-letters presented lovers with a delicate problem: the choice of a trusted messenger. This point, stressed over and over again by French and English medieval writers, was considered at some length by Ibn H'azm. In Spain, long before the advent of *La Celestina*, 'pious-looking old ladies who recited the rosary and wore two red cloaks' were often used as messengers. 'I recall that in Córdoba our cloistered women were warned about these crones,' writes Ibn H'azm. Lovers also used women whose profession allowed them to enter houses freely: women doctors, blood-drawers, public criers, hairdressers, mourners, singers, fortune-tellers, teachers, weavers, etc. 'How many calamities have fallen on protected veils, thick curtains, well-guarded apartments and locked doors, by people of this sort! I would not have mentioned them but I feel that I should draw attention to their evil doings. One should never confide in anybody. . . .'

Nevertheless, some lovers are excessively discreet because they wish to conceal their feelings from the rest of the world, in the belief that love is the hallmark of idle and frivolous people; they fly from love and defend themselves against it. 'This way of thinking is not justified. To revel in beauty, to allow oneself to be overcome by love is natural. Since when has Mohammed forbidden love? And does this prohibition appear in the Koran?'

The same questions, replacing the name of Mohammed by Jesus Christ and substituting the Bible for the Koran, would still be pertinent in present-day Spain. 'Too many people are convinced that the Universe has been created for the benefit of the Ursuline nuns. . . . Love is taboo,' wrote José Ortega y Gasset in his prologue to the Spanish translation of the *The Dove's Necklace* by E. García Gómez in 1952.

Most of the feminine beloved referred to by Ibn H'azm were slave-girls. This is not to be wondered at, since they were carefully chosen for their beauty and talents and were more accessible than the ladies of the harem. A number of captivated masters married their slaves and in some instances the wily slaves made fools of them. Ibn H'azm quotes the 'dreadful case' of an imam from the mosque at Córdoba who was so passionately in love with one of his young slaves that he proposed to free her and marry her. But, as he wore a long beard, she said to him mockingly, 'I find your beard is horribly long; shorten it and you will obtain what you desire.' He immediately took up a pair of scissors and shortened his beard; then he called upon witnesses to come and sign the paper by which he agreed to free the slave. After they had signed it, he asked her to marry him. But she did not consent. Among the witnesses was the imam's brother who exclaimed: 'In that case I shall ask her to marry me!' He did so, she accepted him and he married her on the spot. Sa'id accepted this terrible affront. Yet he was a pious and scholarly man.

Abd-er-Rahman V complained to a fickle lady who broke her plighted troth: 'Ah, weary are the nights since thou left me! O graceful gazelle, breaker of vows and faithless one, hast thou forgotten the hours we spent together on a bed of roses while the stars glittered above us like pearls in the blue vault of heaven?'[1]

The great Almanzor was generous when he discovered that the slave-girl of whom he was enamoured preferred his vizier Abu'l Moghira ibn Hazm. During a drinking party in the gardens of Zahira, the slave-girl had the temerity to declare her love for the vizier in the veiled allusions of a song: 'Alas, my kinsfolk, I love a youth who avoids my affection though he is near me. Ah, that I could throw myself into his arms and clasp him to my heart!' The vizier replied, also in verse: 'How, alas, can I approach loveliness that is hedged about with swords and spears? Ah, if I were sure in my heart that thy love were sincere, gladly would I risk my life to possess thee! No perils daunt a man of noble heart,

[1] E. García Gómez: *Poemas Arabigoandaluces* (Espasa-Calpe, Buenos Aires, 1940).

when he determines to reach the goal.' Almanzor, in an access of jealousy rose, drew his sword and forced the slave-girl to tell him the truth. Acknowledging her love for the vizier, she concluded humbly: 'I am in thy power, O Lord, but thou art gracious and lovest to pardon a fault confessed.' The vizier invoked the fatalism of the east: 'Every man is a slave of his destiny; no man can choose his own fate but must submit; mine has decreed that I must love where I ought not.' Almanzor, touched by their love for one another, relented and gave the vizier his slave-girl.

In 903 Ibn Hajjaj of Seville brought a cultured and outspoken slave-girl singer from Baghdad called Kamar, an ardent feminist, with a poor opinion of Spanish Arabs. 'The most shameful thing in the world is ignorance,' she exclaimed, 'and if ignorance were a woman's passport to Paradise I would far rather that the Creator sent me to hell!'

These ladies were not only outspoken, they could on occasion be gross. Wallada, who kept a salon in the eleventh century and had affairs with several poets, including Ibn Zaydun, stimulated highbrow productions on the one hand but gave her poet lovers their *congé* in very unladylike verses when she had tired of them.

In Córdoba, the slave-girl poetess, Rumaykiyya, who married Prince Mu'tamid, saw snow for the first time in her life. The snowfall was a freak and the lady was so bitterly disappointed not to see any more that her husband planted the sierra of Córdoba with almond trees so that their blossoms, which appear soon after the winter frosts have passed, might give her the illusion of snow.[1]

A touching case of submission to the beloved was that of a lover known to Ibn H'azm who had spent many sleepless nights on account of his passion. 'He ended by the conquest of his beloved. She did not refuse him but he soon realized that she did not like his advances. So he left her and went away, not from fear or modesty but simply to please her. He could not find it in him to do something which was not to the taste of his beloved. And yet, God knows what flames consumed him!'

The torment of separation was a theme that inspired poets and caused the death of lovers. Ibn H'azm relates one instance and then goes on to describe his own sorrows over a young slave called Nu'm of whom he was passionately fond in his youth. 'One could not dream of anything more desirable. She was perfect—

[1] R. Dozy: *L'Espagne Musulmane* (1913).

physically and mentally. We understood each other. It was I who had had her virginity and we loved each other dearly. Destiny took her from me . . . when she died I was not yet twenty and she was even younger. For seven months after her death I did not take off my clothes and tears did not cease to fall from my eyes which as a rule do not moisten easily. I swear that I am still not consoled. If a ransom were possible I would buy her back with all my fortune. I would sacrifice a member of my body. I have never tasted real happiness since she died; I have never forgotten her. I have never been satisfied in the intimacy of other women. My love for her obliterated all my previous loves and rendered all that followed sacrilegious.'

Among his rare accounts of conjugal love, Ibn H'azm mentions the love of his sister-in-law Atika for his brother Abou Bakr, who died at the age of twenty-two. He had never known another woman—she had never known another man, and her only desire was to be reunited to him in death. 'What she wished for happened soon afterwards—may Allah have mercy upon her!'

As a stern Muslim of the puritanical Wahabi sect, Ibn H'azm ends his book by reminding his readers of the punishment meted out by the Prophet to the impure and he repeats the words which Abou Sa'id said to him in the great mosque of Córdoba: 'Beware! meditate on what I am about to tell you: Allah has indicated the path to be followed by women: for the virgin who fornicates with a virgin man, flagellation and a year's banishment. For the deflowered woman who fornicates with a man who is no longer virgin, one hundred lashes and lapidation.' Men and women adulterers were stoned to death.

In love, concludes Ibn H'azm, 'the most meritorious attitude to adopt is that of continence and abstention from sin'. He writes highly of a young Cordoban who went to visit a friend. The latter was absent and his beautiful young wife began to make advances. The young man was tempted but he thought of Allah the all-powerful. Putting his finger in the flame of the lamp, he exclaimed: 'O my soul endure this suffering but what is it compared to the fires of Hell?' These young Saracen ladies appear to have been as forward as the Celts and Anglo-Saxons. Yet another friend og Ibn H'azm's was approached by a brazen belle, but he replied: 'No! The gratitude for the gift of Allah who has granted a union with you, my dearest desire, obliges me to renounce your love in order to obey his commandments. I swear that this is a rare attitude to find in the old annals. What shall I say then about the present time, when good has given way to evil?'

Lovers, if one is to judge them by the poets, followed either one of two currents: that of passion, represented by descriptions of orgies: wine, women and poetry, 'when the nipples of the slave-girls pierced our breasts like sharp lances', or self-imposed chastity, a notion imported from the Arabian tribe of the Udri, via Baghdad and Damascus.

Love-feast poems are not highly original. There are hundreds of them in the vein of Ben Ammar, vizir of Mutamid of Seville, who wrote in 1086: 'How many nights have I spent enjoying myself in the shade of Silves in the company of women with opulent hips, rounded as sand dunes, and tiny waists! Blondes and brunettes who produced in my soul the effect of refulgent swords and sombre spears. How many delicious nights have I spent by the river with a damsel whose bracelet emulated the curve of the current! I spent the time savouring the wine of her glances, her vase and her mouth. . . .'[1]

Sa'id ibn Judi declared that 'the sweetest moment in life is when the wine-cup rattles; when, after a quarrel, one is reconciled with one's lover; or yet again, when we mutually embrace and are once more at peace'.

Lovers are notoriously inconsistent and in another poem Ibn Judi exclaims: 'I traverse the circle of pleasures as a frenzied war-horse that taketh the bit between his teeth; I leave no desire ungratified. . . . Steadfast when the angel of death hovers over my head in the day of battle, a pair of bright eyes can sway me at their will.'[2]

When a new and modest beauty was brought to him from Córdoba, he improvised the following poem: 'Why, fair one, dost thou turn thy glance from me to fix it on the ground? Can it be that I am unpleasing in thy sight? By Allah, that is not usually the sentiment I inspire and I dare assure you that I am better worth thy regard than the pavement!'[3]

'You came to me a little while before the Christians began to peal their bells,' wrote Ben H'azm in 1063. 'The beauty-spot on your cheek made you look like a rose-garden kept by an Abyssinian.'

[1] R. Dozy: *L'Espagne Musulmane.*
[2] ibid.
[3] ibid.

13

Aben Guzman, the fair, blue-eyed poet whose only friends in life were 'a beautiful face and golden wine', mocked those who were content with a kiss on the cheek. 'That is not my way,' he exclaimed. He thought little of idealists who died of love and he boasted of being an adulterer and a sodomite.

Ben Farach was made of sterner stuff. 'Although she was ready to give herself to me,' he wrote of his beloved, 'I refrained from taking her and I did not succumb to the snare laid for me by Satan. She appeared in the night without a veil. Her very glance tormented my heart, but I remembered the divine precept that condemns luxuriousness and I subjugated my passion. I spent the night with her like a young camel whose muzzle prevents him from suckling his mother.'[1]

In the twelfth century, Safwan ben Idris of Murcia wrote in the same vein: 'My chastity prevented me from kissing her mouth. . . . Marvel at him who can feel his entrails boiling and who complains of thirst though water be at hand!'

This was the doctrine already taught by Ibn Sina in his *Treatise on Love*, the doctrine of the Sufis and of the Brethren of Purity. 'If a man loves a beautiful form with animal desire,' wrote Ibn Sina, 'he deserves reproof, even condemnation and the charge of sin, as for instance those who commit unnatural adultery and in general people who go astray. But whenever he loves a pleasing form with an intellectual consideration . . . then this is to be considered as an approximation to nobility and an increase in goodness. For he covets something whereby he will come nearer to the influence of that which is the First Source of influence and the Pure Object of love and more similar to the exalted and noble beings. For this reason one will never find the wise—those who belong to the noble and learned and who do not follow the way of those who make greedy and avaricious demands—free from having their hearts occupied with a beautiful human form.'

A little further he goes on to say that conjugal union is permissible only in the case of a man either with his wife or his female slave. He guards against the dangers of kissing and embracing, actions which 'are not in themselves blameworthy but which are liable to arouse lust'.[2] His recommendations coincide with those of the early Christian church. 'Men and women

---

[1] E. García Gómez: *Poemas Arabigoandaluces*.
[2] Ibn Sina: *A Treatise on Love*, trans. E. L. Fackenheim (Pontifical Institute of Mediaeval Studies, Toronto, Vol. VII, 1945).

commit a venial sin,' declared Pope Alexander VII, 'if they experience carnal pleasure when they kiss one another; they commit a mortal sin when the kiss is the prelude to ulterior actions.'

Long after these early Arab poets and philosophers had been laid in their plain Muslim graves, long after the ankle-bells of the slave-girls had ceased to tinkle through the gleaming palace halls, the thoughts that had inspired them lived on, adapted and transmuted by the feudal society of southern France where the troubadours revolutionized the European world with a new conception of love, or better still, a new dimension, that distance between the lover and his beloved which leaves room for the flowers of the imagination.

The idea that lovers could and did die for love, the principle of lovers' submission to their mistresses, the theory of lovers' embraces stopping short before physical consummation, the recommendation to be constantly in love with a beautiful form, even details like the advice on the choice of a messenger—all these themes reappear in medieval European poetry and treatises on love; all of them had already been put into practice on the banks of the Guadalquiver and in the scented orange groves of Córdoba and Granada.

The orange, rather than the apple, became the symbol of love in Spain. The expression 'half an orange', the equivalent of our 'better-half', is an image from the Baghdad poet Ibn Dau'd who reflects Plato's idea of sister souls, which he represented as two perfect spheres. They were puffed up with pride until Zeus clove them in two, since when the two halves spend their lives searching for each other.

In one of his plays, Lope de Vega described a bridal dance on the banks of the Manzanares in Madrid, during which the performers stick coins into a cut orange for the benefit of the newly wedded pair. In the northern regions of Spain, a similar type of dance is performed with an apple.

2. Moors and Virgins

IT would be an over-simplification to say that the love legacy of Andalusia transmitted to the rest of Europe (through still undetermined channels) was a purely Muslim one. It represented much more than that—an amalgam of the many civilizations that flourished in the Mediterranean and even beyond it, in Persia.

Nor were the last pleasure-seeking, over-refined Caliphs of Granada averse to Christian representation of human passions; in the Hall of Justice of the Alhambra, a Christian artist painted a typical medieval scene: the siege of the Castle of Love, with Saracen protagonists enveloped in turbans and almond-eyed beauties riding postilion who closely resemble the figures of Persian miniatures.

From the fanatical Christian minority of Córdoba in the middle of the ninth century comes the spiritual love story of Eulogius and Flora. Eulogius was a priest and fiery preacher. Flora was the child of a mixed marriage and passed for a Muslim but her mother, who died when she was a child, had instructed her in the Christian faith. After a time, she left her home with a younger sister and hid herself among the Christians of the town. When she was discovered her brother had her brought back and scourged by the cadi. Again she escaped and took refuge in a house where she met Eulogius. 'Holy sister,' he wrote to her years later, 'time was when thou didst vouchsafe to shew me thy neck, all torn with the lashes, bereft of the lovely and abundant tresses which once veiled it. It was because thou didst look upon me as thy spiritual father and deem me pure and chaste as thyself. Tenderly I laid my hand upon thy wounds; fain would I have sought their healing with a kiss but I dared not. . . . When I departed from thee, I was as one that walketh in a dream and my sighs ceased not.'

Flora was determined to become a martyr. She insulted the Prophet in front of the cadi and had to be imprisoned. The cadi, loth to sentence such a young girl, called for her brother and asked him to try and calm her. Eulogius happened to be in the same prison, however, and he encouraged Flora in the path of martyrdom. When he visited her in prison, 'methought I looked upon an angel, a celestial light shone about her; her countenance was radiant with joy; already she seemed to taste the bliss of heaven; and with a triumphant smile she related the cadi's questions and her replies. As I heard the words fall from those lips sweeter than honey, I strove to confirm her in her resolve by pointing to the crown which was laid up for her.' Five days after Flora's execution Eulogius was set free. He attributed this to the intercession of the new saint.[1]

The horrible cruelty—the sexual cruelty—of these martyrdoms and the deeply ingrained religious eroticism of the Spaniards are vividly expressed by García Lorca in his 'Martyrdom of St. Eulalia':

> The Consul asks for a platter
> For the breasts of Eulalia.
> A jet of green veins
> Spurts from her throat.
> Her sex trembles, imprisoned
> Like a bird among thorns. . . .
> From the red holes
> Where her breasts had been
> Show little heavens
> And streams of white milk. . . .

Women were considered as part of the loot during the many battles between Moors and Christians. The Christian kings of the various Spanish provinces were not averse to keeping a discreet harem but legends of the heathens' demand for maiden tributes helped to keep up the fighting spirit. In the following translation of an ancient Spanish ballad by J. G. Lockhart, the romantic spirit of the nineteenth century mingles with Victorian-Puritan righteousness:

> If the Moslem must have tribute, make *men* your tribute
>   money
> Send idle drones to take them within their hives of honey;
> For when 'tis paid with maidens, from every maid there
>   spring
> Some five or six strong soldiers to serve the Moorish king.

[1] R. Dozy: *L'Espagne Musulmane.*

It is but little wisdom to keep our men at home,
They serve but to get damsels who when their day is come
Must go like all others, the heathen's bed to sleep in;
In all the rest they're useless and nowise worth the keeping.

In actual fact, the Muslims themselves were hard put to it to protect their womenfolk from their own predatory men; the rules for the administration of Seville compiled by Ibn Abdun in the twelfth century abound in precautions to preserve the virtue of women from lawyers, bachelors, policemen, hawkers and soldiers. Women were frail and Abdun forbade them to expose themselves by washing their clothes in the orchards where they might be seen and spoken to by strange men. They should not even go to church, since most priests, he said, were rakes and adulterers. Christian writers were equally outspoken about their own priests. On the question of virtue, there seems to have been little to choose between them.

The battles between Christians and Moors are still recalled at many a Spanish fiesta, when priest and people actually relive in their imagination incidents real or legendary that took place hundreds of years ago. At one fiesta which I attended in Galicia, the Blessed Virgin—the *dame par excellence*—is involved in the fray and I was nearly lynched for appearing to slight her. A curious example of religious eroticism. This is how it came about:

Of the many fiestas celebrated in honour of Our Lady on 8th September one of the most original in Galicia is to be seen in the mountain village of La Franqueira, off the main road from Vigo to Orense. One of its main features is the ancient 'Dialogue between the Christian and the Moor' which I wished to record for a B.B.C. programme.

This is declaimed before the statue of the Virgin of the Franqueira, brought out for the occasion upon an ox-cart. Before she is installed upon the cart, an auction takes place in the church porch; the peasant who makes the highest bid is entitled to lead the cart with its precious burden round the tiny church to a *plazuela* at the side, where the people assemble to hear the Dialogue.

My guide and mentor, Señor Carrera, owner of the Castle of Villasobroso, had kindly obtained permission from the parish priest, with whom he had quarrelled since the last fiesta, for me to place my recorder upon the performers' platform. After some initial difficulty, Señor Carrera had overcome the priest's reluctance to my presence as a heretic, on the grounds that through me and my recorder La Franqueira's fame would be broadcast to the outside world. It was the first time that any foreigner had evinced any interest and Señor Carrera was all excitement and ready to write several columns upon the event in the local paper.

Trestle tables had been mounted outside the church and a banquet was held in the open air before the proceedings. Señor Carrera had brought an immense pie and various bottles of wine. Three peasant women from Pontevedra sat down at our table to drink their own red wine from their long-necked earthenware pitchers. The youngest of the three startled me by leaning against the church wall and reciting, quietly but incisively, a *risqué* rhyme about a hen that met a Portuguese pilgrim on the way to Santiago and pecked off his trouser buttons.

At last the statue of the Virgin was borne from the church shoulder-high, resplendent in her golden crown, upon which the peasant women had hung old and extremely rare Gallegan earrings which I had sought for in vain in the antique shops of the towns and upon which I cast covetous eyes.

The priest, a gaunt tall man with grey hair and flashing black eyes, brandished a bullock whip and opened the auction. Fifty pesetas, one hundred, two hundred pesetas . . . five hundred pesetas and the whip was handed to a perspiring little man in a snow-white shirt and black waistcoat who advanced towards the cart looking dazed and overpowered. The excitement was at fever-pitch. A great shout went up from the crowd, led by the priest: '*Viva la Señora de la Franqueira, viva, viva!*'

'Isn't she beautiful?' the woman next to me cried ecstatically. 'How happy she looks!' exclaimed another and they alternately wept and sang the *Salve* as the cart was set in motion.

I walked through the now empty church and on to the little side platform where a local radio commentator was exhorting the crowd to be quiet and decorous, for the Moor and the Christian were about to begin their recitation. The statue of the Virgin was brought to a halt and the priest swooped on to the platform to spur the Moor and the Christian to action. Dutifully the two peasants began to bawl the Dialogue which would end with a declaration of the Moor's conversion to Christianity through the grace of the Virgin of La Franqueira. They shouted so loudly and

raucously that I had to move the microphone back, because my
recorder was peaking wildly.

Suddenly the priest pushed his way past the Moor and the
Christian—who began to fluff their lines at this untoward interruption—raised his arms threateningly towards me and rolled his
eyes in unmistakable anger. 'Stop! Stop! You must stop all this!'
he cried. I stared at him, amazed and uncomprehending. 'No—
go on—record the Christian—bring the microphone back!' he
went on. My host, Señor Carrera, white with rage, bent over and
murmured in my ear: 'The silly fool thinks that you are only
recording what the Moor is saying and not the Christian. He
does not understand. I'll make him apologize. It is scandalous to
behave like this to a guest!'

While my host was having an acid altercation with the priest,
the Dialogue resumed and came to its triumphant end with an
exultant cry of '*Viva la Virgen de la Franqueira!*' from both Moor
and Christian, echoed with fanatical fervour by the crowd. The
priest, to whom the technicalities of radio recording had now been
satisfactorily explained, came up to beg my pardon for the
'regrettable misunderstanding'. He was now back in the twentieth
century. Nobody, he now realized, had wished to offend the
precious Virgin of La Franqueira or doubt her powers and
influence. There was no need for a Don Quixote to defend the
celestial Dulcinea. He was prepared to bless us all, even my
recorder.

The transfer of erotic impulses to religious images is a form
of delusion which often gives rise to ludicrous incidents. Henry
Inglis described how, during the Holy Week procession in
Seville in 1831, the statues of the Virgin Mary and of St. John the
Baptist had to be hurriedly withdrawn during a rainstorm and
sheltered in the cathedral. 'The statues had been dressed in their
best clothes and those who know Spain will realize just how
splendid and spoilable these can be. As the rain did not subside, it
was decided that the statues should remain in the cathedral for
the night. And now came the problem: could the Virgin and St.
John the Baptist be left in the cathedral all night by themselves
with any propriety? The canons were sent for and the difficulty
was stated. One said, "It is not decent to leave her and St. John
together." Another said, "When fire is put to the hemp the devil
comes and blows it." The result was that a message was actually
dispatched to the captain general to request a guard; and a

captain's guard with torches did accordingly keep watch upon the Virgin and St. John till morning. These facts I learned from the lips of a lady who had taken refuge in the cathedral and who herself heard the consultation.'

3. *Medieval Mosaic*

A T the time that the Caliphs of Andalusia were organizing love-poem competitions in their courts of Córdoba, Seville and Granada, King Alfonso X of Castile was laboriously compiling his *Siete Partidas* and laying down rules for his knights, who obviously lacked poise and polish, since he felt obliged to tell them not to crack jokes (he probably meant bawdy ones) and not to eat garlic and onions and so foul their breath. The illustrations to this cultured monarch's *Cantigas a la Virgen* provide us with a series of eloquent medieval strip-cartoons on the prevalent loose-ness of morals.

These uncouth knights, particularly the northern ones, never-theless developed a gift for poetry. The songs of their trouba-dours fill the thick *cancioneiros* of Galicia and Portugal. The Castilians showed no comparable lyrical powers. They were better at battle epics like *The Cid.*

Santiago de Compostela became an international centre of pilgrimage, culture and amorous pleasures. From the first efforts of the native poets, we find ourselves in a special atmosphere, influenced but never wholly absorbed by foreign contributions to the 'gay science'.

The inhabitants of this green and well-watered region gather round wood fires in the long winter evenings. In the morning they open their doors to contemplate the mists curling up the long sea-lochs, swaddling the pine trees and the great boulders of granite that top the hills like prehistoric monsters. In the sierras of the centre, whole villages are snowed up in the winter and the men in their round snow-shoes tread softly between the circular thatched dwellings where men and beasts crowd together in the fug and warmth.

Smoke, mist, rain and snow encourage family life, domesticity and the cult of the mother, who presides over the ceremonies of the hearth like a tutelar deity. Smoke, mist, rain and snow—mysterious, incalculable, dream-inducing. Men and women born among these elements dream, sing, roam and write lyrical poetry.

Their feeling for solitude is in sharp contrast with the gregarious-
ness of other Spaniards, as well as their Celtic oneness with the
soil and propensity to enjoy melancholy. They are slower, more
inclined to brood, and more sentimental.

In the north-west corner of Spain, love—and its oracular
medium, the poet—have necessarily differed from those of the
rest of the peninsula. There are no arabesques here, no hyperbole
and little ornament; frank pleasure replaces Oriental voluptuousness, women are permitted to sing boldly of the pains of
separation from their beloved, mothers play an important role.
The girl who says 'no' is roundly insulted. Men and women are
closer to one another. There are no poems about slave-girls and
none about continence. There are no palaces and no queens,
except in the *cantigas de amor* written by polished troubadours at
the court of Santiago, influenced by their counterparts in
Provence; peculiar to Galicia are the popular *cantigas de amigo*
put into the mouths of young women, usually in the form of love
laments for an absent lover.

Galicia has never known the satirical songs of the *malmariés*
which were so popular in France. As a matriarchal people with a
Germanic strain, their idea of woman and of love relations has
been more egalitarian, more human and more natural than those
of austere Castile and half-sensual, half-frigid Andalusia. In no
other European country have poets made women sing of love as
the Gallegans did in their *cantigas de amigo*. Susceptible as they
are to feminine influences, is it because they understood that
man's first teacher in amorous matters—not excluding the Garden
of Eden—has been woman?

These *cantigas*, as opposed to those dedicated to courtly ladies,
spring from the simpler classes of society and describe rural loves.
They tell of lovers' meetings in the woods or by the stream
where the maiden goes to bathe or wash her hair. In the background is the ever-vigilant mother who wants to know why her
daughter has been away from home so long. The symbol for the
lover is a stag and the daughter replies that she was startled by a
stag up in the hills. Sometimes the meetings take place during a
local pilgrimage or *romería*, on a rock by the sea, or in a chapel
surrounded by trees.

The lover is often absent, on the high seas or in the service of
the king. The beloved laments on the seashore or she stops a
wayfarer to ask for news of her *amigo*. One girl prepares to elope

with her lover; another washes her clothes in the stream and wonders whether her *amigo* will pass that way during the chase. The mother accompanies her on the pilgrimages and on the whole makes herself a nuisance. She scolds, advises and sometimes buffets the daughter whose fate is in her hands. These loves end in marriage and are alien to the adulterous liaisons sung by the court troubadours.

In the *cantigas de amor* the tone is melancholy and lyrical. It is never passionate. There is not one instance of a kiss being mentioned. On the other hand, the troubadours of the Compostelan courts, and even the king, could be coarse; the scurrilous *cantigas de escarnio* show them up in primitive, rollicking mood banished from their lady's boudoir. Arab ladies too, as we have seen, were not above composing gross verses. Women poets are not alluded to in Galicia's Middle Ages but gay dancing ladies accompanied armies and crusaders to battle and inspired palace troubadours in times of peace. They were called *soldadeiras*; the best known one was María Pérez, 'La Balteira'. She was a singer as well as a dancer, supposedly of good extraction. She was popular at the court of Alfonso X and Menéndez Pidal believes that he may have used her charms for political ends, to soften the Muslims with whom he negotiated. The troubadour Pedro d'Ambroa, one of her many lovers, wrote an obscene poem about her, probably during an access of jealousy. In the year 1287 María Pérez was preparing to accompany Alfonso X on an expedition directed against the King of Tunis. Her return was sung in sarcastic vein by the troubadour Pere da Ponte who wondered whether she had actually been as far as Tunis and whether she had brought back sufficient indulgences from Rome to compensate for the looseness of her life. In her old age, La Balteira confessed her gay sins and retired to the convent of Sobrado to which she left all her money.

The theme of adulterous love and of a lover who dies for his beloved centred on the legend of the troubadour Macías who was killed by an enraged husband for sending love-letters and songs to his wife. Versions of this legend vary, but Macías's infatuation and death is the constant core of them all. 'To be more in love than Macías' is still a current expression in Spain.

In the fifteenth century, when it was fashionable to argue in print about the defects and qualities of women, a Gallegan championed them in a treatise entitled *El Triunfo de las Doñas*.

His arguments in defence of the fair sex are a curious forerunner of sixteenth-century efforts to hoist women on to a Platonic pedestal. Woman, he wrote, is the last and most perfect of all creatures. She was formed in Paradise, among the angels, not among the animals and from the earth, like Adam. She is more beautiful—and also cleaner than man—more moderate in her eating and drinking habits; she is more chaste and more prudent. She has more of a prophetic nature than man. Wild beasts do not attack her. She was the first to be tempted by Satan, which is a proof that in his eyes she was the more important of the two and she is not responsible for original sin, since the eating of the apple was forbidden to Adam and not to her! If a woman were to be raised into the atmosphere she would lose consciousness, because this is her element. She was made to live in a higher sphere. The author, Juan Rodriguez of Padrón, rather overdoes it.

In his 'Ten Commandments of Love' he propagates troubadour theories of courtly love, with few original additions of his own. He counsels love only in those cases when a lover is sure that his sentiments will be reciprocated, advocates constancy, a sense of measure, truthfulness, frankness, a strict avoidance of solitude and melancholy, and stresses the importance of riches, since 'love and poverty cannot endure together'.

A glance at contemporary laws and decrees shows that 'bought love', i.e. prostitution, was an accepted part of life confined to specific areas of every important town. The ownership of *mancebías* (bordels) was a lucrative position. The Catholic King Ferdinand and Queen Isabella had no scruples about rewarding a gentleman who had distinguished himself in the wars against the Moors, Yanez Fajardo, by granting him the exclusive proprietorship of the *mancebías* of Málaga, Ronda, Marbella, Alhama, Granada, Baeza, Guadix and Almuñécar. They stipulated that his sons and daughters were to succeed him as proprietors and furthermore they were to build more *mancebías* as the occasion presented itself.

In Valencia, the main thoroughfare into the town led straight through the *mancebías* and attracted adverse comments, especially from foreigners. A new gate was started in 1390 but it was not finished until 1431.

During Holy Week and other religious feasts, the girls were taken to the House of Repentants to undergo a purifying course of sermons and devotions. In 1395, the Town Council decided to allocate certain small sums of money to be used as dowries for the truly repentant, but there were so many cases of fraud that the scheme had to be abandoned.

Another sidelight on medieval morals is provided by a decree published by Juan I in the year 1387, forbidding married men from having a public concubine; those who possessed one were to pay a fine of one-fifth of their revenue up to the sum of ten thousand *maravedís*; another decree condemned bigamists to be marked on the forehead with a red-hot iron.

The prostitute and the procuress were particularly well described by Castilian authors. It is not so much the lover in Juan Ruiz's *Book of Good Love* whom one recalls so vividly, as the artful, scheming figure of Trotaconventos, the procuress, a descendant of Ibn H'azm's meddlesome old women who 'profaned the sanctity of the harem'. Trotaconventos is the ancestor of the even better known and more minutely described procuress who has made a niche for herself in classical Spanish literature, *La Celestina*.

Juan Ruiz, the Archpriest of Hita and author of the *Book of Good Love*, was born in Alcalá de Henáres, not far from Madrid. He wrote his book, soon after 1280, for the *juglares* of whose company (as well as that of Moorish dancing-girls) he appears to have been fond. He is the Castilian Chaucer, but he writes in autobiographical vein and gives us an account of various love affairs, prosecuted with the help of Trotaconventos and the goddess Venus, who give him advice which he cheerfully passes on for the benefit of future lovers.

The archpriest appears to have been familiar with the Oriental pharmacopæia introduced into Europe by the Arabs, half of which consisted of sex stimulants, and he mentions in particular such aphrodisiacs as ginger, sandalwood, cummin seed, candies, citrus fruits, marigolds, cloves and 'large quantities of vile carrots'. The latter, according to Elisha Kane, is one of the oldest and most widely disseminated remedies for impotence, and is known even in the U.S.A. at the present time.

The archpriest distinguishes between two kinds of love: *buen amor*, or true love, which comes from God, and *loco amor*, or mad love, which is the worldly love of women. The latter, he freely admits, is delightful even though it may not always be attended by success. 'Is it not pleasant to sit in the shade of a pear tree, even when one is unable to taste the pears?' Women are delicious creatures in spite of all that has been said against them. 'If God, when He created man, believed that woman was evil, He would not have made her man's companion.' Love makes an uncouth man subtle and ugly people appear beautiful.

After an unsuccessful love affair in which the archpriest made the mistake of offering his lady-love songs and verses instead of more tangible gifts, Love appears before him to rebuke and advise him. He has gone after the wrong sort of woman. He must henceforth choose those who are 'discreet in the house and wild in bed'. Lower-class women know nothing about love. It is important to have a good go-between, one of those old women who lurk in the shadows of churches selling powders and knick-knacks and have an entry to the best houses in the town.

The lover must be 'like a pigeon, clean and moderate; like a peacock, gallant and self-possessed. . . . Be cautious, not violent, nor sad and irritable. Serve love and love will increase, with sweet words, amorous gestures. Do not forget to sigh; do not talk too much or your mistress will take you for a liar—do not hesitate to use a little force occasionally, for fear and modesty prevent women from giving in to your desires.'

Physically, a woman should be tall, with a smallish head, fair hair, widely separated eyelashes, large eyes, small ears and wide hips. But there was a lot to be said for short women too. The Archpriest of Hita's poem on the subject was translated by Longfellow in the *North American Review* of 1822:

A pepper-corn is very small but seasons every dinner
More than all other condiments, although 'tis sprinkled thinner.
Just so a little woman is, if love will let you win her;
There's not a joy in all the world you will not find within her.
And as within the little rose you find the richest dyes,
And in a little grain of gold much price and value lies,
As from a little balsam much odour doth arise,
So in a little woman there's a taste of paradise.

Widows fall easily: 'little light is needed to kindle a candle a second time', and so the archpriest resolves to pursue a rich young widow, Doña Endrina. He secures the services of the old bawd Trotaconventos, who speaks so highly of the archpriest that the widow ends by visiting her house where she is seduced. This scene has been cut by a prudish Castilian copyist.

He then endeavours to seduce a young girl but he does not reward Trotaconventos sufficiently; she gives his scheme away and all falls through. Disappointed and low in spirits, the archpriest sets out across the sierra—an episode which allows him to make fun of courtly pastorals. On his way he meets four *serranas* or girl cowherds who make love to him in their coarse way and he is glad to escape from their amazonian clutches.

Making allowances for literary exaggeration, one wonders whether these invectives against *serranas* did not correspond to reality? They are certainly truer to life than the insipid, arcadian *serranillas* describing Dresden-china types of shepherdesses. *Serranas*, loud-voiced, strong, wine-drinking and lusty, actually exist. At least, they did until the nineteenth century, when one comes across references to their sexual habits in the scientific annals of folklorists.

The strange goings-on in the mountains have been compared by the well-known ethnologist J. Caro Baroja to similar practices among agricultural communities of north-east Melanesia. In the province of León, he informs us in *Los Pueblos de España*, girls and boys paired off from May to October and slept together in huts outside the village.

Now for a lover who was more of a philosopher: Auzias March was born at the end of the fourteenth century in the orchards of the beautiful province of Valencia, which had only recently been freed of the Moors. Auzias March took part in various expeditions, was put in charge of the king's falconry and finally retired to his estate in Valencia—some say because of some scandal over a girl—where he wrote poetry and made love. He married twice, had two or three concubines and several illegitimate children of whom he appears to have been very fond. 'My sin is to love madly,' he admitted in one of his poems.

Auzias March boasts of his uniqueness in analysing love and exclaims that very few people know anything about it: '*Oh, quant son poce qui d'amor han saber!*' It is difficult to understand love, to know what it is, where it goes, what it does and how it can make its adepts so happy. There are three kinds of love: mad or bestial, angelical and mixed. Harmony can only be achieved when the soul and love of the flesh combine. Carnal passion is like those strong summer showers accompanied by thunder and lightning which in so short a time cause the rivers to rise and the fields to be flooded. Auzias March confesses that he has fallen a victim many a time. He has worshipped Venus more often than Diana, for 'our flesh does not recognize any other deity'. There is a close parallel between love and death; they are similar in that both run after the fugitive and run away from those who seek it. 'I am he who delights in death,' he wrote. He was constantly preoccupied with the theme of his salvation and that of his lady-love. When she died, he became obsessed with the question of her immortality. Was she in heaven or in hell? If she had been condemned, then maybe he is the culprit. Thinking of her, he succeeds in separating the body from the mind, until he approaches her with the reverence of a worshipper at the temple. Is she in heaven or in hell? he asks himself. He realizes that his prayers are in vain, because the sentence has been rendered. If she has been condemned, he asks God to annihilate him.

Is complete union ever possible? In one body, lover and beloved can unite but their separate spirits cry out, for they do not live in one another's body. Then again, love does not find it easy to reside in women, who have no brain and serve only for procreation. Their lack of intelligence is due to their excessively sentimental nature; their appetite is stronger than their reason. Only the mistress of King Alfonso the Magnanimous found favour in the eyes of this morbidly sensitive poet, one of the first to express boredom with life, *enfastijament di viure*, who sought the boundless through human love, conscious that the infinite forces which stirred within him were stronger than the desires of carnal love. His poems reflect an unequal struggle between Spanish asceticism and the Moorish voluptuousness of the Valencian atmosphere, 'this Garden of pleasures', as Alonso de Proaza called it in 1505, 'this rich temple in which Love forever dwells'.

The language and images of religious eroticism in which both Arab and Spaniard have excelled were subtly blended by Ramón Lull: knight, lover, poet, missionary, born in Palma in 1235 and stoned to death by the hostile Muslim populace of Bugia in 1315. In Ramón Lull's *The Lover and the Beloved* one can read with pleasure at both levels, profane and mystic:

'The bird sang in the garden of the Beloved. The Lover came and he said to the Bird: "If we understand not one another's speech, we may make ourselves understood by love, for in thy song I see my Beloved before mine eyes. . . .

' "This is love's contract: the Lover must be long-suffering, patient, humble, fearful, diligent, trustful; he must be ready to face great dangers for the honour of his Beloved. And his Beloved is pledged to be true and free, just and liberal with those that love him. . . ."

'Say, Fool of Love, if thy Beloved no longer cared for thee, what wouldst thou do? "I should love him still," he replied. "Else must I die, seeing that to cease to love is death and love is life.' "[1]

It was the sight of the corruption of the flesh—of his mistress's breasts disfigured by a cancerous growth—that is said to have turned Ramón Lull away from carnal lures. How tragic it has been, this constant battle between the Spanish love of beauty and their Oriental tendency to treat life and the flesh as an illusion, a dream that passes! How sad that a lover could be in love only so long as his beloved was physically beautiful! To wean themselves from this cult, Spanish mystics contemplate the features of death: the skull, the skeleton, the mutilated forms of martyred saints. If they cannot have beauty, then they will court death. There is no alternative.

One must beware—even of holy images. St. Ignatius of Loyola once told a Belgian novice that his sister-in-law gave him a picture of Our Lady before which he used to recite the Hours of the Blessed Virgin. It reminded him so much of the beauty of his sister-in-law Magdalena, that his devotions were disturbed and he had to stick a piece of paper over the face.

Casanova tells the story of the Madonna of the Calle San Jerónimo in Madrid, whose beautiful bosom attracted male visitors. The chapel became rich on their offerings. When he returned from Aranjuez after the carnival of 1768, Casanova was told that the Madonna's bosom had been painted over. He went to the chapel to see for himself and was shocked to find the picture spoiled. It was the work of the new priest, a young man of thirty. 'Don't you realize that St. Luke was a painter and he must be talking about you to the Blessed Virgin very severely indeed?' Casanova said to the priest. 'It is regrettable,' was the reply, 'but I have to say Mass every day at that altar and the voluptuous image disturbed my imagination.' From that day, wrote Casanova, the chapel offerings decreased to a remarkable extent.

In 1955, when I was visiting the Valley of Roncal in Navarre,

[1] Ramón Lull: *Book of the Lover and the Beloved*, trans. E. Allison Peers (1928).

there had been a commotion over a new image of the Virgin, which the villagers had found too modern for their conventional taste. A young professor of literature who accompanied me to the village church with the priest, Don Marcelino, objected that the new Virgin's blue mantle was far too thin and moulded the 'celestial Roncalesa's' thigh a shade too closely to be proper. Don Marcelino was shocked by this remark but I saw him dart a furtive glance at the image as we went out of the church and purse his lips a little dubiously; he was evidently wondering whether more of his male parishioners shared this irreverent view.

The womenfolk, especially those known as *beatas*, whose life is centred in the church, dress images with a solicitude half maternal, half loverlike. 'She has been left to dress images' is a way of saying that a girl has been left on the shelf. The most beautiful burlesques (this sounds paradoxical but it is true) of the vivid images of Spain have been described by García Lorca in his three Romances on St. Michael, the patron saint of Granada, St. Raphael, the patron of Córdoba, and St. Gabriel, the patron of Seville. St. Michael is laden with laces and displays his fine thighs in bell-shaped ruffles:

> Up in his garret in the tower
> In his skirts, cascading finery,
> Where crystals, lace and trinkets shower,
> Saint Michael, ruler of the lamps,
> And of the Offices and Paters,
> Poised in the Berber eminence
> Of crowds and wondering spectators.

St. Raphael is 'The Archangel, arabianized, with gloomy spangles all around, while in St. Gabriel's embroidered jacket the crickets palpitate and sing. . . .'[1]

Auzias March's brother-in-law, Johan Martorell, also a native of Valencia and author of the famous book of chivalry *Tirant lo Blanch*, was a far earthier sort of person; his book was one of the few which Cervantes approved of and which was spared from the conflagration of Don Quixote's library.

' "Good God," quoth the curate, with a loud voice, "is Tiranfe the White here? Give me it, gossip; for I make account to find in

[1] Roy Campbell: *Lorca, an appreciation of his poetry* (Bowes & Bowes, Cambridge, 1952).

it a treasure of delight and a copious mine of pastime. Here is Don Quireleison of Montalban, a valiant knight; and his brother, Thomas of Montalban and the Knight Fonseca, and the combat which the valiant Detriante fought with Alano, and the witty conceits of the damsel Plazerdemivida, with the love and guiles of the widow Reposada and of the empress enamoured on her squire Ipolito. I say unto you, gossip, that this book is, for the style, one of the best in the world; in it knights do eat and drink and sleep and die in their beds naturally and make their testaments before their death; with many other things which all other books of this subject do want." '[1]

Martorell went to England in 1438 and the core of his novel is taken from the romance of Guy of Warwick (whom he calls Varoych). Tirant, the hero of Martorell's book, is protected in London by the beautiful Agnes, a lady whose skin was so white that when she drank a glass of wine the colour suffused her throat with a warm glow.

After this first episode, Tirant travels as extensively as all other medieval knights. In Paris he hears about the siege of Rhodes by the Sultan of Cairo and hurries to assist the Emperor of Constantinople who was being sorely pressed by the Turks; after saving the Byzantine empire, Tirant conquers the kings of Persia, takes over the kingdoms of North Africa, converts hordes of infidels and returns to Constantinople where, after many intrigues he marries Carmesina, the Emperor's daughter. Far from living happily ever after, however, Tirant dies of pneumonia, Carmesina throws herself upon his corpse with such force that her nose bleeds, and laments his death through tears and blood—a typically Spanish combination. She dies of grief and her father the Emperor soon follows them to the grave.

Prudish critics have said that *Tirant lo Blanch* is an obscene book. I do not share their views. It is much better fun than most books of chivalry and certainly more realistic. Cervantes was right on this point, but the chivalrous ideal is stoutly upheld with a few near-lapses in the relationship between the hero Tirant and his lady-love Carmesina. There is material here to please both the readers of troubadour poems and those who favoured the coarser veins exploited by authors of books on prostitutes and procuresses.

The popular type of the procuress is represented in *Tirant*

[1] *Don Quixote*, trans. Thomas Shelton.

The Castle of Love, the Alhambra

THE MADONNA:

From San Clemente de
Tahul, twelfth century

From Solsona, Lerida,
thirteenth century

From the Cathedral,
Avila, by Berruguete

'La Virgen del Rosario'
by Murillo

Tender lovers, fourteenth- to fifteenth-century polychrome

by no less a person than a princess—Plazerdemivida—who assists the lovers and acts as a go-between, but her words are more brazen than her actions, a Spanish feminine trait which has misled many foreigners through the ages. It is true that Plazerdemivida goes a little far for the squeamish in the scene where she hides Tirant in Carmesina's bathroom so that he may see her undress and touches her rather lasciviously pretending to be Tirant. A similar scene takes place later in Carmesina's bedroom. Tirant, however, respects Carmesina's desire to remain chaste and he refuses to do anything of which his lady might disapprove. He is romantic enough to have the stockings and shoes which Carmesina touched embroidered with precious stones as a memento and he kisses the palm of his lady's hand, which the author remarks is a sign of love compared with the courtesy kissing of the back of the hand. Plazerdemivida believes that love, honour and service should always be granted by a lover to his beloved but that in their private bedroom sessions courtesy should be disregarded, and she upbraids Tirant for his timidity.

The average lover must have had restless hands like Calisto, to whom Melibea opposes such scant resistance in *La Celestina*: 'And because you, sir, are the pattern of courtesy and good behaviour, how can you in reason require my tongue to speak, whereas you cannot rule your own hands and keep them quiet? Why do not you forget those tricks and learn to leave them? Lay your command upon them to be quiet and will them to lay aside this offensive custom, and consider, my dearest, that as to thee, whilst thou carriest thyself quietly and civilly, is the greatest happiness that either my heart or my eye can enjoy; so it is as displeasing unto me to see thee handle me so roughly. Thy honest sporting pleaseth me but thy dishonest hands offend me, especially when they are too far out of reason.

'And though love oft-times forget reason, amongst your well-educated and noble and generous spirits kindness keeps a decorum and revels not but with decency; let such, sweetheart, be our embraces, such and so modest be our dalliance, my dearest Calisto, my love, my lord. But alas, silly woman, why should I direct you? No, I will not. Do, Calisto, do what you will and say what you will, I am yours to use; please yourself and you shall please me.'

Nobody seems to know just what Johan Martorell was up to in London but he had powerful friends at court whom he interested in his personal affairs. He behaved with knightly and typically Valencian susceptibility in the matter of his sister's relationship with a certain Johan de Montpalan. This gentleman had apparently given his word that he would marry her, then disgraced and abandoned her. A long correspondence ensued between him and Johan Martorell. Montpalan replied that he could not understand the complex legal terms used by Martorell. The former appealed to Henry VI to settle the quarrel and sent a battle letter to Martorell through the herald of the Count of Huntingdon. There was no battle, however, because Martorell never turned up for the assignment.

The Valencians have always had the reputation of being violent and trigger-happy, quicker to defend their so-called honour and that of their relatives than any other Spaniards, susceptible though they all are: so much so that they made a profession of it and their services were called upon by people of other provinces who wished to dispose discreetly of rivals and opponents. A nobleman in Madrid once called upon a well-known Valencian professional assassin to kill off one of his friends with whom he had recently quarrelled. Terms were agreed upon and all was set for the deed when the nobleman met his ex-friend by chance in the Prado, where a reconciliation took place. He then sent a message to the Valencian, enclosing the stipulated money for the murder and requesting him not to accomplish the deed but to return home. The Valencian called upon him in a rage. 'You have offended my honour,' he cried. 'I never take money for a service I have not rendered. Take it back, I will not have it.' The nobleman insisted—after all, the Valencian had had expenses, he had spent time working out the details of the planned murder, etc. 'It cannot be,' replied the Valencian. 'You must therefore choose. If I take the money, somebody has to be murdered—either you or your friend.' He was finally persuaded to wait until the nobleman engaged in a further quarrel, 'which is bound to occur sooner or later', he assured the honest assassin. (What is honesty? 'My daughter is an honest woman,' said a Spanish gipsy of her daughter, who had just been imprisoned for larceny. By honest, she meant that she was chaste.)

This warlike attitude extended to Valencian courtship customs. It was customary, until the nineteenth century, for a would-be suitor to announce his intentions by firing a rifle at his beloved's feet, usually when she was on her way home after Mass. She was expected not to turn a hair but to walk on with her eyes demurely cast upon the ground. Later, when the suitor turned up to visit and serenade her, he would signal his presence by a further noisy display. (This custom was followed in Ibiza until recent times.) In a courtship dance of Tarragona, the suitor fired at his *novia*'s skirt, a practice prohibited after a bad case of burning. Nowadays little remains of the Valencians' addiction to firearms except their fondness for pyrotechnics. The best firework displays in Spain are to be seen at Valencian fiestas.

What effect does literature have upon young readers? The question is often posed nowadays in relation to books of pornographic or sadistic intent and nobody seems to know the answer. In the Middle Ages, books of chivalry were the target for moralists who really do seem to have had a case. Were readers more susceptible, more easily influenced in those days? There is no denying that they *were* influenced by what they read and that many heads were turned—not only in Spain but also in England and France. The most often cited case in Spain is that of the knight Suero de Quiñones whose brain was quite befuddled by tales of chivalry. He vowed to wear a chain round his neck, in sign of amorous captivity, until he had overcome all those who dared to cross the bridge of San Marcos in Órbigo. He boasted that he took part in seven hundred battles and fought against seventy-eight knights.

Amadis of Gaul, one of the first sentimental novels, appears to have originated in Portugal and was known in Spain by the middle of the fourteenth century. In the University of Seville, according to Amador de los Rios, there is a tomb of a Master of the Order of Santiago, Don Lorenzo Suares de Fugueros, who died in 1409, and whose dog is depicted with a collar on which the name Amadis is written twice in Gothic characters. This book and its numerous progeny was a best-seller in most European countries.

Another sentimental novel, quickly translated into English, was Diego de San Pedro's *Prison of Love*, which got the author into trouble with the Inquisition because of his sacrilegious raising of profane love to divine status. This seems to be the first novel in which letters are exchanged between lovers. Laureola, the haughty heroine, after having been saved from the tower where she was imprisoned, accuses her faithful lover Leriano of having perjured her honour by writing too intimate letters. Leriano goes on a hunger strike. At the point of death he revives sufficiently, when his cousin Tefeo launches on a long invective against women, to present arguments in their favour neatly and logically divided into fifteen clauses and twenty reasons. This is the bit that upset the moralists of the Inquisition: 'Women bestow upon us all the cardinal and theological virtues and everyone who is in love believes in God with greater faith.' Leriano died after swallowing Laureola's letters, which he tore into small pieces and placed in a glass of wine.

In *La Celestina* both lovers come to a sad end. Calisto loses his foothold when climbing down from his lady's garden wall after a secret assignation, falls and is killed instantly. His servant Tristan exclaims: 'O pitiful, pitiful, O horrible sight! Help, Sosia, help to gather up these brains, that lie scattered here amongst the stones, and let us put them again into his head. O, unfortunate master! O unlucky day! O sudden and unexpected end!'

Melibea commits suicide when she hears of her lover's end, but before doing so she addresses her father thus: 'I would fain speak some words of comfort unto you before this my gladsome and well-pleasing end, gathered and collected out of those ancient books which for the bettering of my wit and understanding you willed me to read, were it not that my memory fails me, being troubled and disquieted with the loss and death of my love as also because I see your ill-endured tears trickle so fast down your wrinkled cheeks.'

None of these sentimental books of chivalry were exactly moral. 'What shall we say of the facility with which a born queen or empress will give herself over into the arms of some unknown wandering knight?' as the Canon of Toledo observed to the curate in Don Quixote's library. But most young ladies would probably have agreed with Maritornes: 'I relish hearing these things greatly, for they are very pretty; especially when they describe some lady or another in the arms of her knight under the orange trees, and the duenna who is keeping watch for them, half dead with envy and fright; all this I say is as good as honey.'

Those who pretended to write against worldly love did so with their tongues in their cheeks, like the Archpriest of Hita, and the Archpriest of Talavera, Alonso Martinez de Toledo, in his book called *Corvacho—o reprobación del amor mundano*, imitated from Boccaccio. Like the *Book of Good Love*, the *Corvacho* is written in a racy, conversational style, by a man who knew women—and their dressing-rooms—intimately. There is ample material here for the historian of cosmetics.

People knew a good deal about love, according to the Archpriest of Talavera. In the old days—those often quoted old days that live in the imagination—a man of twenty-five and a girl of twenty hardly knew what love was all about. 'Nowadays it would be shameful to relate what goes on, so much so that it might well bring about the end of the world. This must come about soon if things go on as they are.'

Lovers had to be wealthy. Not only because they had to make presents to the object of their passion, as had been stressed by medieval writers, but also for the purpose of bribing nosy parkers, to make neighbours who see too much close their eyes and to make those who hear too much close their ears. The author stresses too, not without compassion, that women must be particularly careful of their reputation. Their lives can be ruined if they sin but once, whereas luxuriousness is tolerated in men.

When the thought of sin enters a man's mind, the archpriest strongly advises him to cross himself and go in search of someone to whom he can talk and divert his attention from temptation. Let him call a friend or a neighbour and engage in conversation, even if he does not feel like it. 'If you happen to be in bed, jump out at once, cool yourself down, and pray. Do not look too long at other women for fear that their image may bring that of your beloved to mind.'

Passion has caused many deaths and the archpriest quotes terrible examples: one woman castrated her lover, because of her jealousy over another mistress; a wife bit off her husband's tongue because she suspected him of being unfaithful. . . .

A woman's eyes are all powerful: 'With a look she mocks a man, with a look she speaks to him, with a look she makes him enamoured of her, with a look she can kill him . . . why, a woman can play more games with her eyes than a conjuror with his cards.' These tricks have been handed down to their successors. Spanish eyes are the most expressive and the most made use of in the world. I remember, as a child, coming across our maid Pepita practising eye-exercises in front of her mirror. My ten-year-old English boy friend thought that she had gone off her head. 'What are you doing, Pepita, rolling your eyes about like our fox-terrier in a fit?' he jeered. Pepita frowned. 'I am meeting my *novio* tonight at the fair,' she answered, still rolling her eyes. 'Say, am I *guapa*, am I pretty?' she enquired, munching a raw onion; before we could think of a suitably mocking reply she had turned back to her mirror and began darting sidelong glances with the 'flash of lightning' technique used by Indian dancers, into which Pepita introduced a note of Spanish piquancy.

It requires a great amount of physical vitality to be a good or, at least, a popular lover. The Archpriest of Talavera, in his analysis of the various kinds of temperament, expressed the opinion that phlegmatic types were not apt for love-making. 'They are extremely lazy,' he wrote, 'and at the same time cowardly and suspicious. It is necessary that he who wishes to love according to the mode of the times should be nimble, steadfast, amorous, generous, courteous, moderate, daring, ardent and refined. How can a phlegmatic man love and be loved? As soon as he puts his head out of the door, with the intention of visiting his mistress and he sees that it is raining or snowing he begins to have doubts and to ask himself: "Shall I go? Or shall I not? If I do, I shall get wet, I may come across the police and they might take my sword away from me; or I might fall in the slush and get my clothes dirty; I had better put on my galoshes . . . I might be bitten by a stray dog, or I might be overtaken by bandits and stabbed in the back. . . ." '

Once he does reach his mistress's door, he will never dare to climb into her house through the window or up a ladder, not he. He will shuffle inside and look around him fearfully, peering into the corners to see if armed men are lurking there. His mistress tries to encourage him. 'Come now, *amigo*, do not be afraid, that was only the cat.' . . . 'Ah, lady, I want to go,' he cries, 'I could not stay here, my hair is standing on end with fright.' She, seeing the state he is in and realizing that if he were to stay he wouldn't be of any more use to her than a woman, says to herself: 'Well, woman for woman, there is no need of another woman here,' and so she opens the door and lets him out.

After the usual satires against marriages between old men and young girls, young men and old women, the lechery of the clergy, superstitions and black magic (in which he nevertheless seems to believe), the gay clerical author concludes with the following unpriestly sentence: 'Finished writing on the tenth day of September, with Jupiter in the house of Venus and Saturn laid up with a pain in his side. But alas for the unhappy man who sleeps alone with a headache and in whose house no spinning-wheel ever enters from one end of the year to the other; this is the worst lot of all.'

With the exception of the unequal matches referred to by the Archpriest of Talavera and other contemporary writers, young people do not appear to have been coerced into marriages which they disapproved of. Pleberio, the father of Melibea, observes in *La Celestina*: 'In this particular the laws allow both men and women, though they be under paternal power, for to make their own choice.'

Jewish maidens were not allowed such latitude, if we are to believe Rabbi ben Solomon ben Adreth of Barcelona, who wrote in his *Responses*:[1] 'The maidens consent to wed those whom their fathers or relatives may choose for them. Praise be to the Almighty, in these parts the generation is moral and the daughters in Israel are chaste, so as not to take for husbands whom they might fancy without the assent of their father during his lifetime; that is not the manner of the daughters of the land. Whoever heard of such a thing?'

Nevertheless, unscrupulous men achieved fleeting ends by pretending to go through a form of betrothal with a girl. They presented her with coins, fruit and a prayer book in the presence of two hired witnesses who subsequently disappeared. The presentation of a gift of value in these conditions was tantamount to a marriage contract. Rabbi ben Adreth instructed the Jewish girls of Barcelona, as a matter of precaution, to make an indissoluble vow containing such a clause as 'by the permission of the Omnipresent and that of the multitude', and to abstain from making use of any object given for betrothal purposes unless it was received in the presence of persons whom they knew personally. (This form of cheating was also current among the Christian communities of this epoch.)

Bigamy, frequent among the Christians, was equally so in Jewish communities until they modified their laws. The monogamous enactment of Rabbi Gershon was not recognized for several centuries in many parts of Europe. During the first half of the thirteenth century, bigamy was practised by the Jews in Spain, even by scholars and pious men. Parents who desired to ensure their daughter against a rival would require the groom to

[1] Rabbi Isidore Epstein: *The Responses of Rabbi Solomon ben Adreth of Barcelona*, 1235-1310 (Kegan Paul, Trench, Trubner & Co., 1925).

make a declaration on oath prior to the marriage that he would on no account wed a second wife during their daughter's lifetime.

Rabbi ben Adreth felt bound to lament that unruly persons are on the increase and there is no one to reproach his fellow men and to say to one corrupting his place: 'Wherefore hast thou done so? The daughters in Israel are gentle, but the generation renders them uncouth.' Many instances of adultery and of sodomy are recorded in the *Responses* and of Jews who lived with non-Jewish concubines.

4. Love in the Clouds

As we move away from the Middle Ages and approach the sixteenth century of Platonic love theories and the superficial idealization of women, particularly in literature, we find that one of the chief philosophical sources for these ideas, in so far as Spain is concerned, both in the sixteenth and seventeenth centuries, was the posthumous work of a distinguished and persecuted Spanish Jew, Leon Ebreo, whose *Dialoghi d'Amore* were published in Italy by members of the Platonic Academy of Florence.

The *Dialoghi* influenced Montemayor's famous sentimental novel *Diana*, Maximiliano's *Tratado de la Hermosura y del Amor*, and Cervantes, who wrote in the prologue of *Don Quixote*: 'If you deal with love and you know a little of the Tuscan language, you are bound to come across Leon Ebreo. . . .' In *La Galatea*, Cervantes quotes whole chunks from the *Dialoghi* in his dialogue between Tirsi and Lemio, in favour of 'incorporeal beauty—the only beauty worthy of being loved', and the division of love into honest, useful and delectable love.

The *Dialoghi* represent the philosophical meeting-point between the sages of ancient Greece, their Arab interpreters and Jewish successors; between Plotinus, the Alexandrian school, the semitic philosophy of Ibn Gabirol and Maimonides, with the Platonic Academy of Florence. Little is known about the author who was probably born in Lisbon about 1460 and educated by his father, a doctor in medicine, Isaac Abravanel. We find Leon practising medicine and marrying in Seville in 1483. Later, after the expulsion of the Jews from Spain, he went to Naples and became doctor to the king. The *Dialoghi* appear to have been begun in 1495 and were discovered after Leon's death in 1525 by Pico della Mirandola. They are said to have influenced the great Spanish mystics of the seventeenth century. Leon Ebreo's spirit, if not his body, returned to the land of his fathers and took root in the atmosphere to which he really belonged, among kindred spirits of another faith.

The growth of the sentimental novel was deplored by serious-minded sixteenth-century writers like Vives, Cano, Arias Montano and Fray Luis de Granada, but curiously enough the Inquisition was indulgent towards them. Nothing ever came of the petition addressed to the king by the procurators of the Court of Valladolid in 1555 in which it was declared: 'We affirm that the dangers incurred in this kingdom to young men and women from the reading of books full of lies and vanities, such as *Amadis*, are notorious; young people in their idle moments read these and become so addicted to the genre that when a somewhat similar situation confronts them in real life they give free rein to their passions in a way which would not occur if they had not read these books. We therefore beg Your Majesty not to allow any of them to be read or printed and to establish penalties for the same.'

Although *Amadis* was the main target of these various remonstrances, Montalvo's version of this famous book was really quite respectable. Amorous scenes were glossed over discreetly with such innocuous phrases as the following: 'Galaor took his pleasure with the maiden that night in a way which shall not be recounted here, because in similar cases, which are against the laws of virtue, men should pass lightly over such things, holding them in little esteem.' This author propounded a theory which has never been popular in Spain, namely: that love increases with physical possession, and he describes the love of Amadis and Oriana as 'a great love which did not occur by accident, as it does with so many people who, as soon as they have loved and desired, begin to hate the object of their passion, but their love was so deep and based on such honest thoughts, in conformity with a good conscience, that it increased as do all things on virtue'.

This view of physical possession is explained by Leon Ebreo as follows: 'Albeit a lover's appetite is sated by the union of copulation and straightway this desire or appetite of his is thereby extinguished, yet is not his heart's love quenched thereby. Nay, it makes possible a closer and more binding union, which comprises the actual conversion of each lover into the other, or rather the fusion of both into one, every diversity and distinction between them being eliminated as far as possible. Thus the love endures in greater unity and perfection and the lover remains continually desirous of enjoying the beloved in union; which is the true definition of love.'[1]

Luis Vives, the great Renaissance educationist born in Valencia, tutor to Mary Tudor and friend of Erasmus, warned young ladies against the wiles and deceits of suitors. 'He saith he shall die for thee, yea, and that he dieth even straightaway. Believest thou that? A fool; let him show thee how many have died for love, among so many thousands as have been lovers. Love doth pain sometimes, but it never slayeth.' A little further on, he relents somewhat and admits, 'Yet I would not a maid should clearly be without love, for mankind seemeth to be made and shapen unto love.'

Subterfuge was not the prerogative of the male sex. 'And this the maid may be sure of, that she shall never have good life with that husband which she hath gotten by wiles and crafts. Let the maid neither catch and deceive by subtility him that should be her inseparable fellow, nor pull and draw by plain violence, but take and be taken by honest, simple, plain and good manner.'

Vives did not want women to be weak and clinging; on the contrary, he liked them 'somewhat manly and strong'. Although husbands should teach their wives, they 'should not have her as a servant, or as a companion of thy prosperity and welfare only, but also as a most faithful secretary of thy cares and thoughts and in doubtful matters a wise and a hearty counsellor. This is the true society and fellowship of man. . . .' Still, he would be wise not to confide too many of his secrets to his wife.

Vives had little good to say about the entertainments of his day. 'What a custom is this, that a song shall not be regarded unless it is full of filthiness?' As for dancing: 'What good doth all that dancing of young women, holden up on men's arms, that they may hop the higher? What meaneth that shaking unto midnight and never weary, which if they were desired to go but to the next church, they were not able, except they were carried on horse back or in a chariot? If men were brought from a far country and saw our women dance, they would run away thinking they were taken with a strange kind of frenzy.'

Foreign influence—particularly French influence—on morals, was condemned, from medieval times to the present day. During the festivities in Barcelona to celebrate the treaty between France

[1] Leon Ebreo: *The Philosophy of Love (Dialoghi d'Amore)*, trans. F. Friedeberg-Seeley and Jean H. Barnes (The Soncino Press, London, 1937).

and Spain, bigots wrote to Queen Isabella's confessor, the Archbishop of Talavera, giving an exaggerated account of her participation in the gaiety. She defended herself with spirit and dignity, after a preface expressing humble submission.

'You say that some danced who ought not to have danced but if that is intended to convey that I danced, I can only say that it is not true; I have little custom of dancing and I had no thought of such a thing. The new masks you complain of were worn neither by me nor by my ladies; and not one dress was put on that had not been worn ever since we came to Aragon. The only dress I wore had indeed been seen by the Frenchmen before and was my silk one with three bands of gold, made as plainly as possible. This was all part of the festivity. . . .

'As for the French people supping with the ladies at table, that is a thing they are accustomed to do. They do not get the custom from us; but when their guests dine with sovereigns the others in their train dine at tables in the hall with the ladies and gentlemen and there are no separate tables for the ladies. The Burgundians, the English and the Portuguese also follow this custom; and we on similar occasions do this. So there is no more evil in it, nor bad repute, than in asking guests to your own table.'[1]

In Madrid, which had become the capital of Spain in 1561, theologians deplored the lascivious *zarabanda* and *chacona*. In 1597, theatres were closed by order of the king, because it was found that they 'fostered habits of idleness and pleasure-seeking in the people and turned their minds from warlike pursuits'.

These warlike pursuits included the repulsion of English raids on the coasts. One of the few pleasant memories of these episodes is connected with an old love story from which we gather that a Spanish lady forgave our trespasses to the point of haunting an English manor house. The story of the Green Lady of Thorpe Hall is told in Chambers's *Book of Days* and begins invitingly:

'Hard by the neat old town of Louth, in Lincolnshire, which lies nestling at the foot of the famous "Wolds" and is noted for possessing one of the most beautiful parish churches in the kingdom, stands Thorpe Hall, an old mansion, charmingly situated amidst most delightful scenery, and connected with which is an old legend but comparatively little known. . . .'

It seems that Sir John Bolle, of Thorpe Hall, who lived in the reigns of Elizabeth and James, was celebrated for the gallantry

[1] Martin Hume: *Queens of Old Spain* (Grant Richards, 1906).

with which he distinguished himself in the army and especially for his exploits in the 'memorable expedition against Cádiz in 1595, for which Queen Bess knighted him upon his return'. Tradition assures us that amongst the prisoners taken at Cádiz, it fell to the lot of Sir John Bolle to take charge of a lady of extraordinary beauty and of distinguished family and great wealth. This lady the noble knight treated with the care and tenderness which was the right of her sex, by endeavouring to soften and alleviate the heavy hours of her captivity. (We are not told in what this alleviation consisted.) This generous care naturally evoked feelings of gratitude and these ultimately warmed into love. This resulted in her throwing at the feet of the warrior her riches and her person and such was her ardent passion that when released she entreated him to permit her to accompany him to England as his page. . . . But the gallant knight had a wife at home and neither the charms of the beautiful Spaniard, nor the powerful influence of her gold, could prevail. Like a true knight, therefore, he returned whither duty and honour alike called him and the beautiful and inconsolable lady retired to a nunnery, there to spend the remainder of her days in sorrow and seclusion.

The devoted Spanish lady was generous enough to give Sir John several presents for his wife. Among them was a portrait of herself, dressed in green; this picture led to her being called in the neighbourhood of Thorpe Hall, the 'Green Lady'. Tradition further records the belief that the old hall was haunted by her and that she used to take her seat in a particular tree near the mansion. It was also said that during the lifetime of Sir John's son, Sir Charles Bolle, a knife and fork were always laid for her at table, in case she chose to make her appearance. In another account, we are told that the picture was actually a portrait of Sir John Bolle, but that in the upper right-hand corner was a seven-inch-high figure of a Spanish lady in a black mantilla and a green dress. This was mentioned as late as 1857 in a letter from a member of the family to her son. This lady had first seen the picture in 1792 when it was copied and returned to the owner by her nephew, with the figure of the Spanish lady cut out! The aunt was so angry that she did not speak to her nephew for two years after the incident.[1]

[1] Quoted in article by Richard W. Goulding, F.S.A., in *Goulding's Illustrated Household Almanach for* 1925 (Louth).

The romantic story of the Green Lady became the subject of a ballad, first printed in the reign of James I and subsequently published in Percy's *Reliques of Ancient English Poetry*, called, 'The Spanish Lady's Love for an Englishman'.

5. *Don Quixote and Don Juan*

THE seventeenth century had fortunately not finished with books of chivalry, otherwise we should have been deprived of the satirical outburst which they provoked from the pen of soldier, adventurer, civil servant and one-armed writer Cervantes. What did Cervantes have to say about love and sex?

Dulcinea, the heroine with the green eyes, of whom Don Quixote's imagination was enamoured, was loved with a love Platonical, as the knight carefully explained to Sancho, whose vision of the lady had not been clouded by tales of chivalry. 'My love and hers have ever been Platonical, never extending themselves further than to an honest regard and view the one of the other, and even this same so rarely, as I dare boldly swear, that in these dozen years which I love her more dearly than the light of these mine eyes, which the earth shall one day devour, I have not seen her four times and perhaps of these same four times she hath scarce perceived once that I beheld her—such is the care and closeness wherewithal her parents have brought her up.' 'I know her well,' replied Sancho, 'and I dare say that she can throw an iron bar as well as the strongest lad in our parish. I vow, by the Giver, that 'tis a wench of the mark, tall and stout and so sturdy withal, that she will bring her chin out of the mire, in despite of any knight-errant, or that shall err, that shall honour his lady. Out upon her! What a strength and voice she hath!'

Deluded though he was, Don Quixote was a man of flesh and blood and he kept a close watch over his carnal desires. Remember the farcical scene when he is walking about in his bedroom, wrapped in a quilt, wearing a woollen cap and a thick cloth round his neck. Mistress Rodriguez comes in to talk to him. The middle-aged pair delude themselves into believing that they are in mutual danger: 'Am I safe, sir knight? For I hold it not a very honest sign that you are up from your bed.' ' 'Twere fit I asked that question of you,' quoth Don Quixote, 'and therefore let me know whether I shall be free from ravishing.' 'By whom?' quoth she. 'By you,' said Don Quixote, 'for neither am I of marble nor you of brass; neither is it now ten o'clock at day-time, but midnight and something more, I think; and we are in a more secret and close couch than the cave in which the bold, traitorous Aeneas enjoyed the fair and pitying Dido; but give me your hand, mistress, and I'll have no other assurance than mine own continency and wariness.'

The knight had already remarked to Sancho, in one of his lucid moments, that no love adventure is accomplished with more facility than that which is favoured by a woman's desire. Since women were supposed to be reserved, they had to resort to stratagems. This was considered to be a legitimate part of the warfare between the sexes; as Don Quixote declared: 'Love and war are all one; and as in war it is lawful to use sleights and stratagems to overcome the enemy, so in amorous strifes and competencies, impostures and juggling-tricks are held for good to attain the wished end, so they be not in prejudice and dishonour of the thing affected.'

Demonstrativeness in public places was frowned upon and it is Sancho who reproaches Dorothea for her 'billing with her spouse Don Fernando, who would now and then privately steal from her lips some part of the regard which his desires did merit which, Sancho spying, it seemed to him that that kind of wanton familiarity was more proper to courtesans than becoming the queen of so great a kingdom'.

Courtly lovers like Cardenio were reserved in their wooing. This gentleman's presumption did not extend beyond taking his mistress's 'beautiful and ivory hands and kiss them as well he might, through the rigorous strictness of a niggardly iron grate which divided us'. This iron grate, the symbol of Spanish love-making until the nineteenth century, prolonged the medieval myth of woman as a *princesse lointaine*, chaste, protected, a creature to be worshipped in the shadows of night, mysterious and unattainable. A mere touch of her hand would set her lover aflame.

Cervantes, in common with many of his countrymen, divided desire and sentiment into separate, non-communicating compartments. It was a fairly widespread idea, although Leon Ebreo had denounced it, that once a man had satisfied his lust with a woman, he would not be interested in her any more. This characteristic of the seducer was applied to youth in general and Cervantes makes Cardenio say: 'As love in young men is not for the most part

48

love, but lust (the which, as it ever proposeth to itself as his last end and period, is delight), so as soon as it obtaineth the same, it likewise decayeth and maketh forcibly to retire that which was termed love; for it cannot transgress the limits which nature hath assigned it, which boundings are measures nature hath in no wise allotted to true and sincere affection.' In another passage he reaffirms this belief: 'For where there is love, there is never much looseness.' Knowing society as well as he did, Cervantes had no illusions about love in high places: 'Loose desires are as incident to the fields as to cities, and as well in shepherds' cottages as princes' palaces.'

In his opinion two things incite men to love more than all else: surpassing beauty and a good name. All beauties do not enamour, however, for 'some do only delight the sight and subject not the will'.

And why should a beautiful woman be reproached if she fall not in love? To this Marcela, a fascinating shepherdess, who preferred to lead an independent life among her flocks rather than attach herself to one of her innumerable wooers, replies: 'I cannot conceive why, for the reason of being beloved, the party that is so beloved for her beauty should be bound to love her lover although he be foul. But set the case that the beauties occur equal on both sides, it follows not therefore, that their desires should run one way. . . . As I have heard, true love brooks no division and must needs be voluntary and not enforced.'

As for the state of matrimony, this, in Don Quixote's words, 'is a ticklish thing and there is great heed to be taken and a particular favour to be given from above, to make it light happily'. The Christian dogma of 'one flesh' or *henosis* was touched upon by Shakespeare in England and by Cervantes in *Don Quixote*. The former, in *The Comedy of Errors*, makes Adriana say:

> I am possessed with an adulterate blot;
> My blood is mingled with the crime of lust. . . .
> I do digest the poison of thy flesh,
> Being strumpeted by thy contagion.

The Spaniard, more lenient to men, reverses the situation and makes Anselmo say, in the *Tale of the Curious-Impertinent*: 'Hence it proceeds that by reason the wife's flesh is one and the very same with her husband's, the blemishes, or defects that taint it do also rebound into the husbands, although he . . . have ministered no occasion to receive that damage. For as the whole body feels any pain of the foot, head or any other member, because it is all one flesh, and the head smarts at the grief of the ankle, although it hath not caused it, so is the husband participant of his wife's dishonour, because he is one and the selfsame with her.'

As Sancho's wife said, when Don Quixote's ideas of grandeur had affected her husband to the point that he wished to marry his daughter ('as long as a lance, as fresh as an April morning and as sturdy as a porter') to a count: 'Do what you will; for we women are born with this clog, to be obedient to our husbands, though they be no better than leeks.' The sensible woman would have preferred her daughter to marry one of her equals, for then they all would be as one: 'parents, sons and grandsons, and God's peace and blessing will always be among us'. Sancho, be it said to his credit, was touched by his wife's sobs and he comforted her, saying that he would defer their daughter's marriage to a Count for as long as he could. Sancho was attached to his wife. 'She's not really very bad,' he admitted on one occasion and he sent messages to her whenever he got the opportunity during his wild goose-chases with Don Quixote.

Women wear the trousers in many a peasant household, although they are careful to conceal the fact. Even the men recognize the necessity of letting them have their own way once in a while. In Castile, married women are allowed to 'take over' on the feast of St. Agueda. The men disappear for the day while their spouses form a council, elect a mayoress and disport themselves in what appears to be a survival from a remote matriarchal era.

Another Spanish trait referred to by Cervantes is the necessity of confiding one's amorous adventures to bosom friends. As Cardenio remarked about his treacherous friend Don Fernando, to whom he entrusted the secret of his love: 'I thought it was not lawful, by the law of amity, to keep anything concealed from him.' I was reminded of this recently in northern Spain when a young woman, who was having an affair with a married man, told me how embarrassed she felt because her lover had confided their secret to a mutual friend. 'Why did you do it?' she asked him. 'I had to,' he replied. 'Paco is my best friend. We never keep any secrets from one another. The laws of friendship must be respected.'

In the Golden Age of Spain, life, love and adventure were exuberant and intense. It was an age of conquest before the sunset and the gloom. Conquest was not only an occupation, it was a leisure pursuit which extended to women. 'In this detestable age of ours,' wrote Cervantes, 'no virgin is secure, though she be hidden and enclosed as in a new Cretan labyrinth, since here, through the crannies or by the air, with accursedly industrious assiduity, the amorous pestilence comes to them and makes them cast away all their self-respect.'

It was also the age of professional rogues, cheats and picaresque elements of society who mocked law and authority. It was the age of the Inquisition and of repression. Woman's body, worshipped in private, could not be reproduced in painting. (The first and only tolerated nude of the seventeenth century was Velazquez's famous Rokeby Venus, who lies with her back turned in an attitude of haughty modesty.) The Inquisition forbade the making or exposing of immodest pictures and sculptures on pain of excommunication. Ayala censured those artists who exposed the feet of their Madonnas.

This part of a woman's anatomy, which usually leaves northerners cold, inflames Arabs, Spaniards and—curiously enough—the Chinese, who were as circumspect as seventeenth-century Spaniards over their goddess Kwan-Yin. The sign that this goddess is also a harlot is proved by the fact that her shapely little foot peeps from under the folds of her robe, a gross indecency, for even in pornography, in illustrations depicting lovers who have taken off every stitch of clothing, the feet of the women are covered.[1]

In the seventeenth century, Mme d'Aulnoy writes on the subject of women's feet which, incidentally, are very attractive in Spain: 'Spanish ladies hide their feet carefully, more than any other part of their body. I have heard that after a woman has showered all the favours possible upon her lover, it is by revealing her feet that she confirms her tenderness for him. That is known here as "the last favour of all". One must admit that there is nothing prettier: women's feet are so tiny that when they walk they look like dolls—and they fly rather than walk.

[1] F. Skierskma: *The Gods as We Shape Them* (Routledge & Kegan Paul, 1960).

In a hundred years we could never learn to displace ourselves with such grace.' (Martin Hume tells us that when the Extreme Unction was about to be administered to Queen Isabella 'she exhibited a curious instance of her severe modesty, almost prudery, by refusing to allow even her foot to be uncovered to receive the sacred oil, which was applied to the silken stocking that covered the limb, instead of to the flesh'.)

Father Labat, a member of a French Preaching Order, had an embarrassing experience connected with a Spanish lady's shoes. One day, while he was waiting for the wife of one of his Spanish friends in Cádiz in the drawing-room of their house, he spied a pair of new shoes which had been brought for the *señora* and left on the chair next to which he was sitting. 'They seemed to be made in such a peculiar way that, curiosity getting the better of me, and oblivious of *bienséance*, I picked one of them up hardly able to believe that they were destined for a lady's foot, so small were they; nor could they have been made for one of the children, for they were too young. I was still holding it in my hand when Mme Rosa's servant came in. The maid looked so nonplussed that I asked her mistress (in French) what could have upset her. Mme Rosa advised me to replace the shoe where I had found it and to pretend I had thought it belonged to her little girl, so that I could not be accused of having boasted I had seen a *lady's* shoe. This would have been an unpardonable crime.'

Breasts were out of favour and women flattened their bosoms with leaden plaques and bandages. Their belts jingled with medals and reliquaries. A protective measure? Chastity was at a premium—and 'virgin-restorers' much in demand. The cult of the Blessed Virgin was centred in 'the darling dogma of the Spanish church'—the dogma of the Immaculate Conception which became an official article of Spanish faith in 1617. Murillo painted no less than twenty pictures on this theme.

The Blessed Virgin would seem to have been tolerant with sinners, especially male profligates, who paid their devotions to her regularly. Blanco White tells a story of a Spanish soldier who returned from the wars in the Netherlands laden with booty to take up a life of debauchery in his native city of Seville. Over the door of his lodgings was a large picture of the Virgin clad in a black mantle. Every night, as the soldier left his rooms for his rounds of pleasure he would bow before the picture and recite a Hail Mary. This gesture was accompanied by an inclination of his halbert which inflicted many a wound on the canvas. Eventually the soldier met his death in a street brawl and the Devil, who believed him to be a fair prize, anxiously awaited the decision on the future of his soul. At this critical moment, the Blessed Virgin made her appearance in a black mantle similar to that which she wore in the picture, but sadly rent and slit in several places. 'These are the marks,' she said to the affrighted soul of the soldier, 'of your rude, though certainly well-meant civility. I will not, however, permit that anyone who has so cordially saluted me every day should go into everlasting fire.' So, instead of being dispatched to hell, the soul was sent off for a brief spell in purgatory.

Saints were sometimes equally amiable—also in so far as male sinners were concerned. Blanco White describes a picture he saw in the cloister of the convent of St. Anthony in Seville, shewing the hair-breadth escape of a great sinner, a lawless nobleman, whose soul was represented on the canvas. During his lifetime two Franciscan friars lost their way one stormy night and asked for shelter at the nobleman's castle. He bade his servants give them some fresh straw and a couple of eggs. 'In the picture, St. Michael is shown appearing after his death to weigh his good and bad actions on a pair of scales. The newly departed soul, in the puny shape of a sickly boy, is placed naked on one scale, while the opposite side groans under a monstrous heap of swords, daggers, poisoned bowls, love-letters and portraits of females who had been the victims of his fierce desires. It is evident that this ponderous mass would have greatly outweighed the slight and nearly transparent form which was to oppose its pressure, had not St. Francis, whose figure stands prominent in the painting, assisted the distressed soul by slipping a couple of eggs and a bundle of straw into its own side of the balance. Upon this seasonable addition, the instruments and emblems of guilt are seen to fly up and kick the beam.'

Women do not seem to have been assisted in this helpful manner. The nearest approach to compassion for their woes— on this occasion from a living saint—concerns a lawfully wedded Valencian wife whom the idea of approaching maternity kept in a constant state of terror. This lady confided her fears to St. Vincente Ferrer, a native of Valencia 'who possessed the gift of miracles in such a degree that he performed them almost unconsciously and not infrequently in a sort of frolic. The good-natured saint desired the lady to dismiss her fears as, he told her, he was determined to take upon himself whatever inconvenience or trouble there might be in the case. Some weeks had elapsed when the good monk, who had forgotten his engagement, was heard in the dead of night roaring and screaming in a manner so unusual, and so little becoming a professional saint, that he drew the whole community to his cell. Nothing, for a time, could relieve the mysterious sufferings. Only at dawn was the cause discovered, when the grateful husband came to return thanks for the *unconscious* delivery of his consort! Since then, San Vincente Ferrer has never ceased to be one of the invisible accoucheurs appealed to by Spanish women.'

Ecclesiastics, thanks to the confidences of the confessional, if not through more personal means, knew a good deal about the relationships between men and women. St. Vincente Ferrer converted a great many people to a 'better life'. His sermons, as well as the writings of his contemporary, Fray Antonio de Guevara, throw interesting sidelights on the ways of the times. Fray Antonio in his *Familiar Letters*, castigates a number of lovers, particularly the very old and the very young, but he does so in a pleasant, good-humoured way far removed from the fulminations of English Puritans who were attacking sensual pleasures about the same time with a vehemence which must have been a disservice to their cause. Fray Antonio writes in the avuncular vein of a family spiritual advisor who knows life and people intimately and is aware of the power of love.

In his letter to Governor Luis Bravo, who fell in love in his old age, the friar points out without undue severity—one feels he is smiling indulgently as he writes—that the Governor is too old to compose motets, strum guitars, climb walls and go serenading in the streets; at his age it is not seemly to wear a lover's outfit, namely, silk embroidered shoes, an elegant knee-length cape, golden medals on one's cap and the colours of one's lady-friend. He should avoid looking up at windows and speaking to procuresses; if one of these should approach him the best thing is to run home and shut the door upon her and not to go out into the streets after the angelus. These remedies may not suffice to eradicate love but they may help.

It is difficult to know anything about love, the friar admits; all trades and all sciences can be learned, excepting that of love, about which not even Solomon knew how to write, nor Asclepius heal, nor Ovid teach, nor Helen of Troy recount, nor Cleopatra learn—all one can ever know comes straight from the school of the heart and discretion must be our guide. For love to be true, constant and fixed, it must be allowed to develop little by little in one's heart. The friar is no believer in love at first sight.

He deplores early marriages, such as one which he had witnessed between a boy of seventeen and a girl of fifteen; for 'at this young age they do not know anything about the duties they are taking upon themselves and do not realize what freedom they are losing'. Parents should not force their children into marriage but at the same time young people should not engage themselves secretly after too brief an acquaintance.

There were not many happily married couples. For every ten who were happy, the friar knew a hundred who regretted having entered the marital state. He had witnessed many violent domestic scenes and in his *Familiar Letters* he offers a few words of sensible, down-to-earth advice. 'If only the wife would keep her mouth shut when her husband begins to scold he would not have to eat a cold supper and she would not have indigestion; what usually happens is that the husband begins to complain, then the wife begins to shout and this leads to a free fight and even to an appeal for help from the neighbours.' The friar knew a number of irate husbands who had 'combed their wife's hair with their fingers'.

Women, wrote the friar, should not only *be* good but appear to be so. They must watch their deportment carefully. They are changeable creatures and the husband should not be surprised if after thirty years of wedded life he still finds contradictions in his wife's manners and conversation. Husbands should not be too severe, particularly when they are newly wed. They should be indulgent with a woman's faults and proceed cautiously on the basis of 'bite once and lick the wound a hundred times'. A wise husband will praise, give presents and show himself amorous of his wife. Nor should he be too jealous. Of course there are times when he will find it necessary to close the door behind his wife, lead her away from the balcony overlooking the street, forbid her going out of the house and prevent her from receiving bad company, but all this must be accomplished with the greatest discretion because women are made in such a way that they desire nothing more than that which is forbidden them.

There are bound to be domestic quarrels but there is no need to tell the neighbours about them. And finally, in the matter of jealousy, the law of goodness as well as of Christianity decrees that the fidelity which the wife owes her husband should be equally observed by him. Women are so suspicious, observes the friar in an aside, and when stung by jealousy they are so shrewd, so inquisitive, so anxious to know where their husbands have been and to whom they have spoken, that they will go to any lengths to find out, corrupting the living with their money and calling up the dead with incantations.

St. Teresa would have agreed with him. She was fully aware that women were liable to cause scandals when their marital suspicions were aroused. In a letter to a relative, she had commented: 'As for my sins, the matter has been made public, no doubt you have heard of the violent jealousy of Don Gonzalo's wife on her husband's account, and that people say, as coming from her, that a guilty love exists between him and my sister's daughter, Doña Beatriz. This is affirmed by Don Gonzalo's wife with such publicity that most people must believe her. The girl's good name must have been lost beyond recall, but I am deeply grieved that a relation of mine should have occasioned such offences against God. I have implored my niece's parents to send her away from Alba. . . . Common prudence would teach us to fly from the tongue of a passionate woman as from a wild beast. Other people tell the parents that this would make the scandal seem true and that they ought not to leave the place. The husband and wife are said to have separated.'[1]

The seventeenth century was an age of mystics, libertines and repentant profligates. The two extremes were typified by the idealistic wanderings of Don Quixote, inspired by a misty Dulcinea, and by Don Juan Tenorio of Seville, created by Tirso de Molina, the *burlador*, the mocker of women and all ideals— including the religious. Don Juan knew as little about love as the heroes of the picaresque novels, who were nearly all born in what we would nowadays call 'broken homes'. Don Juan, the nobleman, is the *sexual* picaresque hero. He represents the lax side of sex life prevalent in seventeenth-century Spanish society, especially in the leisured classes.

One of the many possible historical prototypes of Don Juan was Don Miguel de Mañara Vicentelo de Leca, of Seville, a Knight of Calatrava, duellist, rake and roisterer who abandoned his life of profligacy to become a sincere pietist. It was said that his

The Letters of St. Teresa (Thomas Baker, 1924).

conversion took place after a vision he had had when he was staggering home after a night of debauchery. He met a funeral procession in a dark and narrow street, one of these sinister processions with draped figures carrying lighted torches peculiar to death-loving southern countries; stopping to ask who had died, one of the mourners stepped up to the corpse, drew back the shroud and revealed—his own face! It was his own funeral! Don Miguel later became responsible for the restoration of the Hospital La Caridad and he commissioned many pictures from Murillo, as well as the cadaverous compositions of Valdés Leal.

'It is a pity,' wrote Maurice Barrès, 'that one cannot obtain a copy of his death mask from the sisters of La Caridad, but they refuse to give their permission. What an ironical revenge! He whom the most passionate women were incapable of keeping at their side in spite of their tears, is today the prisoner of cold virgins. They and they alone forbid the reproduction of Don Juan.'

Who is Don Juan? Is he a slave to sexuality, a man forever in search of love, or a man who does not want love but merely seeks for physical sensations at the expense of a woman's dishonour and mental anguish, a sadist, in fact? Is he a rebel against the father-image, as psychiatrists argue, incestuously attached to his mother and anxious to prove that all other women are harlots? Is he simply emotionally immature, or perhaps even impotent, anxious to prove and to boast about his virility? In real life there are endless variations of Don Juan and he is not peculiar to Spain.

Dr. Gregorio Marañon believed that the Conde de Villa-mediana, Don Juan de Tassis, was a more likely prototype of Tirso's *Burlador de Seville* than Don Miguel de Mañara. (This gay lover, who was alleged to have had a liaison with the queen, was implicated in a scandalous affair, discovered in 1622, which proved that he was a homosexual, a piece of evidence found in the archives of Simancas by Alonso Cortés in the twentieth century.)

Dr. Marañon protests that Don Juan is un-Spanish and that few of the type are to be found in Spain; I am more inclined to agree with Pio Baroja that 'it is part of the Spanish and Latin heritage to believe that in matters of love it is permissible to deceive and mislead. I have heard Don Juan Valera (the famous Andalusian writer) laugh himself sick over stories about ways in which women had been deceived by men. Spaniards keep their word to men but not to women.' I believe this is true of Latins in general and remarked upon this characteristic in *Love and the French*.

Closely allied to Don Juan's chase after illusions is the Castilian concept of love as a hoax, as Unamuno described it in his *Tragic Sense of Life*: 'Love is the son of deceit and the father of disillusion. Love seeks furiously through the beloved something which is beyond him and as he does not find it he despairs. . . . Love is carnal even in spirit. . . . Perhaps the supreme pleasure of procreation is but an anticipated taste of death, a wrenching of the vital essence. . . . Love is a struggle. The lover and the beloved are both tyrants and slaves. Is it strange that the deepest religious feeling has condemned carnal love and exalted virginity?' He goes on to extol compassion, the love of one's neighbour, of God, love universal. This is the true Castilian conception of love, of a people too imbued with ideas of honour, grandeur and spiritual conquest to wish to stoop to carnal love; a people too individualistic to be interested in personal relationships, a people eager for single combat: man to man, man against bull, man against the devil and, finally, man confronting God.

What other role can a woman fill in such a man's life but that of mother, a pale shadow of the Mother of God? 'In woman, all love is maternal,' wrote Unamuno, who could not bear his novelist friend's (Felipe Trigo's) outpourings in favour of sensuality. He could not understand them. 'At bottom,' he wrote to Trigo, 'you come from Estremadura and I am a Basque; every day I am more convinced than ever that the problem of Spain is an ethnical one. A flood of sensuality would only incapacitate our people.'

Felipe Trigo wrote highly coloured novels at the beginning of the twentieth century. Nobody remembers him, or his efforts to 'make Venus shine with the splendour of the Immaculate Conception'—but he meant well and some of the things he said were sensible. He lamented the *malentendu* which had dogged men and women since they left the woods of Eden, the harmony of bodies and the disharmony of minds; he deplored the Spanish extremist views of love: brutal vice or absurd chastity. 'Love will be possible,' he wrote, 'when woman is educated and has the same freedoms as man. Woman will be free when she no longer needs a man to support her.' Pio Baroja did not have so many illusions about his countrywomen: 'They want to obtain the advantages [of emancipation],' he wrote, 'but they do not appear to be disposed to give up "the eternal feminine". So long as they do not sacrifice this it will be impossible to get on with men. This eternal feminine is merely an affectation. . . . Woman is hypocritical and the Catholic religion has complicated it,' according to Pio Baroja. 'The confessor is like a squid who, after having made the water black all round him, proceeds to analyse it with a microscope. . . .'

Don Juan was born in Andalusia, the province which is said to have produced the greatest number of homosexuals; it is also the part of Spain where love has been sung and put to music more than in any other. It is the land of guitars and serenades which treats sentiments as transient rhythms, where sex is stamped out of the system in fiercely erotic dances. In this climate love becomes a theatrical pastime, a conventional ritual, or the pretext for a duel. It is decorative and superficial, like the patterns on Iberian vases.

The devil—in Spain as elsewhere—was the sexual scapegoat of this volcanic, fanatical age. Grave discussions took place as to how he should be represented in paintings. The right of the devil to his horns and tail underwent strict examination, with the result that the first were fairly fixed on his head—on the authority of a vision of St. Teresa—and the second was allowed as a probable, if not exactly proven, appendage of the fallen angel.

The Inquisition discovered witches who sold their young daughters and said that they were married to the devil. The feasts of St. John, St. Peter, St. James, and even those dedicated to the Blessed Virgin, were made an excuse for orgies, particularly in remote areas where paganism was still rife. According to Bernardo Barreiro, the association of the devil and prostitution was taken advantage of by local *seigneurs* who dressed up for the purpose and sampled many a young village virgin in satanic disguise. Several cases of this nature are described by Barreiro who alleges that 'marriages between the devil and young villagers were very prevalent in Galicia'. The victims of these orgiastic scenes nearly always became prostitutes and later, when they were unlucky, fell into the hands of the authorities and were branded as witches.

Witchcraft found its way into convents. Two nuns of the Royal convent of St. Clara de Allariz in Galicia were in trouble with the Inquisition in 1637 for having made use of incantations and expressed the wish to abandon their cloister. The cause of the trouble was a young girl, the niece of one of the nuns, who was being brought up in the convent prior to her marriage. Who was the *novio*? Nobody knew—not even the young girl, since the marriage was being arranged for her by her parents—but she was so anxious to find out that she persuaded the nuns to enlist the support of a reliable local witch. According to official documents, the crone told Sister Bernarda de Novoa y Taboada that she was to pray to St. Peter while another nun immersed her foot in a pail of cold water and recited the following words: *Revela oculos meos*. A second nun was to walk round exclaiming: *Abincola Sancti Petri*, while a third held a lighted candle. All this was done, but nothing happened until, after nearly a whole night spent in this uncomfortable exercise, Sister Bernarda and her companions saw, or thought they saw, 'a white face on the surface of the water, accompanied by a sound of drums'. The apparition also wore a strange kind of hat.

After several months had elapsed, an ensign came from La Coruña, wearing the same kind of hat as the nocturnal aquatic apparition; moreover, he took the nun's niece away from the convent and married her. All this appears to have impressed the nuns so much that they were heard to declare 'the married state is preferable to that of a nun', and they called for two witches to help them get out of the convent without being seen. Somebody having denounced them, two of the nuns were arrested on 23rd October 1636 and taken to Santiago. They were interrogated by the tribunal of the Inquisition on a site now occupied by the modern Hotel Compostela. The case was heard *in camera* and the nuns were eventually sent back to their convent with the obligation to fast for six Fridays in succession and beat themselves every Friday from then on. The fact that the convent was so well-known and frequented by such high-ranking ladies no doubt explained the lightness of the punishment and the desire to avoid awkward publicity.

It was the age of the 'Illuminated' or erotic pseudo-mystics, and of sexual licence.

In his play, *No hay peor Sordo*, Tirso de Molina alludes to the difficulty of finding a *doncella* who was still a virgin. In *La Tia Fiugida*, Cervantes gives a list of current 'virgin-restorers'. There were Doña Juanas as well as Don Juans, and feminine adultery was referred to by Villamediana, Lope de Vega, Góngora,

Zabalete, Quiñones Benavente, Salas Barbadillo and, of course, the highly satirical Quevedo. (He is always pointed out as a woman-hater, yet he was gallant enough, on one occasion, to come to the help of a lady in the church of St. Martin in Madrid. She had been praying devoutly when all of a sudden a man came up to her and for no apparent reason gave her a sound buffet on the cheek. Quevedo rushed forward, seized the aggressor and dragged him outside the church. In no time swords were drawn and Quevedo had run his opponent through. He died of the wounds several hours later. When it was discovered that he was a personage of some note Quevedo retired discreetly to the palace of his friend Osuna, Viceroy of Naples.) Hurtado de Mendoza wrote 'In Praise of Horns' and Quevedo, 'From One Horned Man to Another'.

6. Blood and Honour

ROJAS ZORILLA, in his plays on upper middle-class life in Madrid, describes people with no other occupation in life than flirting, each sex regarding the other as its main means of diversion. In the play, *Sin Honra no hay amistad*, Doña Juana opens letters from six of her many suitors, making scornful remarks about every one of them. Marriage she considers as a purely commercial undertaking. Duels were prevalent and fought on the flimsiest pretext; in the passions aroused by the conflict between love and honour, love was rarely triumphant. Calderón was the greatest exponent of 'honour'. He made a virtue out of what was in real life a puffed-up sense of self-importance. For him human love halts the quest after the religious ideal, the temptations of the flesh are man's greatest affliction. His women are almost Wagnerian and they could rival men even in the military field.

This ultra-developed sense of honour which amounts to self-pride appears to be a narcissistic trait peculiar to Spaniards. It is not yet extinguished, although other seventeenth-century traits—such as an exacerbated sense of jealousy—seem to have been eradicated from their character. There is a curious example of this *amor proprio* in a book on Navarre, written by a Navarrese only a few years ago.[1] Iribarren relates how intolerable it is—in the region of Tafalla—for anyone to be called *fato* or boastful. One day a lad who had been taking part in a fiesta rushed into the main house of his village to escape from a band of youths who were chasing him; he had stabbed one of their companions. 'What has happened?' the owner of the house asked him. 'I have killed someone,' the boy replied, laying a blood-stained knife on the table. 'And what are you going to do now, *desgraciado?*' 'I shall give myself up to the Guardia Civil as soon as I can.' 'But you were never a quarrel seeker!' 'No, but he asked for it. We had an argument about whether or not we should invite a band to next year's fiesta instead of bagpipers. We got worked up. He began

[1] Manuel Iribarren: *Navarra* (Madrid, 1956).

to insult my father, I kept silent. He said I don't know what about my mother and I didn't utter a word. He libelled my sister in front of everybody and I bit my nails and still remained silent. And then, Don Ventura, he called me *fato*—and the blood rushed to my head.'

The sight of blood as a sexual stimulant is a matter for scientific investigation. Seventeenth-century Spain appears to have realized the connexion although people were probably not conscious of it. Brothels were situated in the vicinity of the bullrings to which *aficionados* repaired after the spectacle in the lustful frenzy which it had aroused in them. (In ancient Rome, brothels were built over the circus where gladiatorial combats took place.) Flagellant penitents in the course of processions during which their thoughts were supposed to be directed towards God, struck themselves with such violence when they met a handsome woman that their blood splashed on to her. This was taken to be a great compliment for which the lady thanked the *caballero* with Spanish grace.

In the eighteenth century, the Chevalier de Bourgoing saw a young woman in a town of Estremadura one Good Friday dressed in a gown of gleaming whiteness. 'She was awaiting the Flagellants with impatience. She went up to the window which was on a level with the street and separated from it only by a grating. The Flagellants stopped before her and struck themselves. In an instant she was covered with the streams of blood that gushed from their wounds. She seemed to take delight in seeing her clothing drenched in their frightful dew. The riddle of her white dress was solved. . . . I suppose the young woman's lover was among the performers.' The royal order forbidding these practices had to be repeated in 1799 and in 1802.

In Galicia (as in southern France), menstrual blood was used by women as a love charm. A few drops of blood sprinkled on ham, prepared by the girl's mother and consumed by a recalcitrant young man, was a recipe guaranteed to make him lovesick within twenty-four hours.

Spanish wit and repartee in amorous dialogue was—and still is —a constant source of astonishment to foreigners; segregation and dragon-like duennas did not prevent them from finding opportunities to make use of their voluble gifts. 'They lock up their women,' observed Bodine, 'and will not suffer them to be near men, so much as in the church, but with a partition between.'

When he was Ambassador in England, he heard Mendoza, the Spanish Legate, finding fault with it 'as a filthy custom for men and women to sit promiscuously in churches together; but Dr. Dale, the Master of the Requests, told him again that it was indeed a filthy custom in Spain, where they could not contain themselves from lascivious thoughts in their holy places, but not with us'.

Jealous Spanish husbands, furious at the audacity with which gallants hovered round holy water fonts in the churches of Madrid, petitioned the Nuncio, who thereupon issued a decree forbidding men from presenting holy water to women on the tips of their tingling fingers, under penalty of excommunication. This presentation of holy water was invariably accompanied by profane remarks and compliments which the ladies replied to in a few well-chosen words because, as Mme d'Aulnoy observed, 'One must admit that they know just what to say—their wit provides an immediate answer.'

Men were expected to be bold in their language. The Marquesa d'Alcanizes is reported to have said: 'I must confess that if a gentleman after half an hour's private conversation with me had not asked me all that one can ask of a woman, I would be so indignant as to stab him if I could.' 'But would you grant him all the favours that he asked?' interrupted the Marquise de Liche. 'That is a different and quite irrelevant question,' replied the Marquesa d'Alcanizes. 'I have reason to believe that I would not grant him anything at all, but then I would not have occasion to reproach him, whereas if he had left me in peace I would have taken his attitude for a sign of disdain.'

At the theatre, women sat in a reserved box called *cazuela*, forbidden to men, where their loud voices were heard making the most outspoken comments, to the delight of the rest of the audience. 'Their vivacity,' wrote Madame d'Aulnoy, 'is not inhibited by any convention or sense of propriety; besides, they know about everybody's amorous intrigues and their remarks often make one die of laughter.'

It was not unknown for high-born ladies to put white lace mantillas on their raven-black hair and walk along the Prado incognitæ in search of intrigues; gentlemen on horseback would alight to engage in verbal combat, well aware that the defence would be as sharp as the attack.

Those ladies who rode in their carriages, accompanied by the orthodox escort of duennas, received discreet adulation from cavaliers in the form of flowers and perfumed water thrown in the windows. If they had the temerity to start a conversation, the duennas would soon draw the curtains with a remark to the effect that 'the most respectful form of love is discreet', so that the dialogue had to be pursued by means of eye-language and sighs.

Jealous husbands were permitted by law to kill their wives' lovers but the women were as volcanic as the men. One of the most beautiful courtesans of Madrid disguised herself as a man and stabbed her unfaithful lover. He recognized her and tore open his shirt in a gesture of defiance. The lady wounded him seriously and then, repenting of her action, exclaimed that she wished to be killed. She was brought before the king, who observed: 'I do not believe there is a more miserable state to be in than to love and not be loved in return. Go, you are too much in love to be guided by reason; try to be wiser in the future and do not abuse the freedom I have granted you.'

'Their love,' wrote Madame d'Aulnoy about Spanish women, 'is a furious kind of love; they are never moderate and they go to the greatest lengths to revenge themselves upon a lover when he leaves them without a motive, so that great attachments usually end in some terrible catastrophe.'

A faithless lover, cited by Madame d'Aulnoy, accepted the situation stoically. Confronted by his ex-mistress with the choice of death by sword or poison, he chose the latter, which was presented to him in a cup of chocolate. His only comment when he had drunk it was, 'You really should have put a little more sugar in the mixture; the poison makes it very bitter. Do remember, won't you, for the next occasion?'

On the other hand, there were liaisons which lasted for years on such a Platonic footing that the lovers scarcely ever exchanged a word! Madame d'Aulnoy was so impressed by all the accounts she heard of Spanish love affairs that she wrote: 'We have never known how to love like that in France and apart from the attentions, the devotion, the delicacy, what I find so charming is their fidelity and discretion. The men speak of their mistresses with the respect and consideration due to sovereign ladies; the latter are entirely absorbed by their passion; they spend several hours a day writing to their lover, speaking about him with their friends and looking out from their balcony to watch him pass in the street.

In brief, from everything that has been said to me I could easily believe that love was born in Spain.'

Marriage was a different proposition. During the first year of their marriage, high-ranking ladies could not leave their house alone; they could go out only in the company of their husband in their carriage and they sat opposite one another as stiff as candles, without exchanging a word. Most husbands had a mistress—very often an actress—and natural children were brought up with the legitimate offspring. 'It is rare to find couples separating,' wrote Madame d'Aulnoy. 'Most men have a wife, a *mancebada* and a mistress; the latter is nearly always a lady of quality; she is the one he goes to meet at night and for whom he risks his life. Both men and women are surprisingly bold and take the greatest risks sometimes for only a quarter of an hour of conversation.'

It was not easy for foreigners to have an affair with a Spanish woman of any standing—Spain has never been a good country for facile amours, least of all where strangers are concerned, but ladies of easy virtue were up to their universal tricks. One of them took in the famous English nobleman Sir Kenelm Digby, who was travelling abroad to forget his lady love at home, from whom he had been separated by hard-hearted relatives.

One night when he was sauntering through the streets of Madrid he heard a woman singing at a window. He approached and found that she was standing in her nightdress. As he walked nearer he was ambushed by a gang of fifteen armed men whose leader, the lady's lover, had forced her to act out the scene. Sir Kenelm took on the gang but in the middle of the fight he began to think that it was rather silly to be combating a band of unknown men for an unknown cause. He told the leader as much but the ruffian replied, if we are to believe Sir Kenelm's account, 'Villain, thou liest; thou hast done me a wrong which cannot be satisfied with less than life.' Sir Kenelm dispersed the gang, killing a number of their members; his feat is said to have spread through Madrid and to have reached England, 'where it caused grief to his lady love'.

Sir Kenelm indulged in a flirtation with Doña Ana Manrique, sister of the Duke of Maqueda. 'He waited on her in courtly manner (whensoever she went abroad, he was the next to attend her chair; if she went to any place of devotion he went too but behaved there as if she were the only saint that he came in pilgrimage unto; if she were a spectator to any public entertainment, as of tilting or the like, he would there make himself known for her servant by wearing the livery of her colours and by clothing his servants correspondently) and at any comedy or masque at the court where she was present he would teach his eyes in their dumb language to beg her favours so effectually, that many times in public conferring them upon him she did exceed that reservedness which is practised among the ladies of those parts.'[1]

This poor lady appears to have been misled by Sir Kenelm's casually flirtatious attitude. She must have thought that he meant business; Spanish Don Juans seduce, they do not leave their victims in mid-air. Doña Ana wrote to Sir Kenelm via the British Ambassador, but apparently received no reply and she ended her days in a convent.

A Spaniard was not considered to be a man until he had had a mistress and his sexual life began at the age of twelve or fourteen, as in many Oriental countries. Not infrequently he neglected his studies for his concubines.

A number of books appeared on the subject of venereal disease, an all too common affliction which was openly discussed even at court and among ladies of the aristocracy. 'This is the wedding present which a Spanish husband gives his wife,' observed Madame d'Aulnoy.

'Why should foreigners come to Madrid?' asked Madame d'Aulnoy. 'The most beautiful and amiable objects—by which I mean the ladies—are always hidden from view and those whom one can see are so dangerous for one's health that one must be prompted by a great curiosity to take such a risk. Nevertheless the only diversion and pleasure of the Spaniards is to have an attachment of this nature.' The situation had not changed in the eighteenth century, when Tomas de Yriarte, himself stricken, devoted a poem to venereal disease, from which Goya also suffered. Lord Chesterfield, in a letter addressed to Francis Hastings, the tenth Earl of Huntingdon, warned his friend: 'I cannot help repeating to you, my dear Lord, the volunteer advice, which I took the liberty of giving you when I had the pleasure of seeing you last, with regard to Spain. There *Venus rarius colatur* is not sufficient, but *Venus nunquam colatur* is absolutely necessary; at least *inermis*. Pray do the reverse of Achilles and provide solid and proof armour for the only vulnerable part. I must observe that the

[1] R. T. Petersson: *Sir Kenelm Digby* (Cape, 1956).

blunder of a hero's arming himself everywhere but on the vulnerable part would not have been so easily passed over in any modern poet, unless an Irish one. Let not air, probability or even attestations of health, nay of untouched virginity itself tempt you. Their vestal fire is hereditary and inextinguishable.'

According to Ballesteros there were more than eight hundred brothels in Madrid. To be able to enter a *mancebía* a girl had to be twelve years old, no longer a virgin, an orphan or child of unknown parents. To exercise her profession she had first to appear before a magistrate who would try to persuade her to abandon the idea; if she persisted then he gave her a document authorizing her to become a *manceba*. With so many shrewd Celestinas about, one can hardly believe that the acolytes had much choice in the matter.

Brunel, the French Ambassador to Spain, said that they painted their private parts red as well as their face and that they displayed a curious mixture of sensuality and mysticism, often taking part in religious processions.

In Seville (where small rooms called *boticas* could be hired daily) the inmates of bordels were taken to Mass on Sundays; a pious woman founded a special chapel for this purpose. Archbishop Pedro de Castro had an altar and crucifix raised at the door of a bordel which he ordered to be closed on the feast days of the Virgin. Moreover no woman by the name of Mary was to exercise the profession of *manceba*.

7. Majos, *Fandangos and Flagellants*

DURING the eighteenth century, when a foreign dynasty—the House of Bourbon—was on the throne, and French manners threatened to swamp all that was genuinely Spanish, it was the people who reacted—not the aristocracy or the intellectual *élite*—but the people of Spain, with their fierce pride, their boastful swagger, their love of violence. What they wished to preserve was nothing more profound than a picaresque way of life close to banditry and the romance of the highway. It was bound to be swept away eventually by material progress. While it lasted, this colourful display against things foreign, it gave rise to the popular image of a vivid, romantic Spain: the Spain of *majos, majas* and *chulos* immortalized by Goya.

'The individuality of the *majo*,' wrote Blanco White, 'is due to a mixture of Andalusian boasting and wit, Valencian gaiety, Castilian severity and grandiloquence; he had an accent and gestures peculiar to himself, an air of grave and frigid pomposity, of threatening severity which is not softened even in the presence of his mistress. He wore a distinguishing costume; close-fitting breeches, buckled slippers, a short jacket, a large sash and a folding knife concealed in it. His long hair was gathered in a net round a hat which was sometimes high and pointed. A large cape and a black cigar completed his theatrical appearance. His companion, the *maja*, wore a full skirt, a low-necked embroidered bodice, a scarf or a lace mantilla and a high comb. She often carried a poniard in a sheath held by the garter of her left stocking as she was quite ready to share in the quarrels provoked by the *majo* inflammatory code of honour. The *majo* and *maja* lived together without any form of wedding ceremony. Their distinguishing features were an aversion to foreign influence and brazen conduct that made their quarter of Madrid—the Lavapies—a place apart.' Although the *majo* was said to be a jealous husband, the *maja* sometimes had a *majo* for a lover and a wealthy gentleman friend from the upper classes who paid her bills. The young gentlemen of the aristocracy liked to go slumming among the *majos.* There always was a certain familiarity between them. The people of Spain never tried to imitate the grandees; it was the other way round.

(The Empress Eugénie had herself painted in *maja* dress. An English traveller, commenting upon the little dagger in an ornamented sheath that was stuck in the *maja's* belt, wrote: 'I saw one the other day, sent from Seville to a young lady, with an inscription on it in pure Andalusian, saying: "You do not need me—your eyes do execution enough." ')

While the *majos* upheld traditional Spanish personality in the humble and vivid quarters of the capital, the upper classes aped the French and produced precious *petits-maîtres*, or the Italians and their *cicisbeos*. These gallants accompanied married ladies everywhere and presumably gave husbands leisure for their clandestine amours. French manners and styles of dress and toilet preparations were adopted, masked balls were introduced from Paris and prohibited for a time by the Archbishop of Toledo (theatrical performances were forbidden in various cities: in Calahorra in 1700, in Pamplona in 1729, in Valencia in 1748 and in Andalusia in 1734).

Were the Spaniards still so jealous? The Reverend Edward Clarke, writing in 1760 and 1761, found that 'jealousy, ever since the accession of the House of Bourbon, has slept in peace. It is observable that, in proportion as manners become more civilized, that furious passion always loses its force.'

Jardine, an English officer, writing twenty years later, observed that 'though the jealousy of husbands seems now out of fashion, the spirit of it is preserved among the lovers and love is still an object of the first importance in Spain'. In the same year, Henry Swinburne declared that 'the very mention of horns is an insult and the sight of them makes their blood boil. As their constitutions may be said to be made up of the most combustible ingredients and prone to love in a degree that natives of the more northern latitudes can have no idea of, the custom of embracing persons of the other sex which is used on many occasions by foreigners, sets the Spaniards all on fire. They would as soon allow a man to pass the night in bed with their wives or daughters as suffer them to give them a kiss and indeed I believe the ladies themselves would look upon that favour as a certain prelude to others of greater consequence.'

Most writers agree not only on the subject of Spanish warmth and passion, but also on the women's lack of delicacy which seems to be in such an unaccountable contrast with their puritanical upbringing. Bourgoing, a French Minister Plenipotentiary at the Court of Madrid, observes: 'I have heard them hold such discourses as few men, though not very scrupulous would make use of at their most dissolute banquets and have heard them sing some of the most indecent songs imaginable; I have been more than once shocked at the abominable stories of some *women of the town*. I have heard them relate without blushing the most secret details of their amorous scenes; and they were astonished that their auditors should discover any embarrassment . . . these women are neither for that more seductive nor more easy to seduce.' Bourgoing believed that these manners would disappear 'with more refined civilization' and a better education. Young people of all classes were left to the servants.

The German traveller, Christian Augustus Fischer, shared this view: 'The Spanish women are very far from delicate in objects of this kind. With a warm imagination and burning passions, they are ignorant of those charms, those sweet illusions, which the fair sex derive from delicacy. Hence the most unrestrained language and the most lascivious looks are incapable of making them blush. They speak on these subjects with the freedom of men; their lips, eyes and their ears are alike strangers to chastity, but their pride prevents them from going further. The most timid and the coldest of men are often more successful with them than the most enterprising and impassioned lover.'

Spanish women were believed to be constant in their attachments. Bourgoing said that 'the infatuation which they occasion and which they experience, so different from all extreme situations that do not last long, is often prolonged much beyond the ordinary time; and I have seen in this land of ardent passions more than one lover die of old age. May not this apparent contradiction be accounted for from their religious scruples? The conscience of a Spanish woman, though complaisant enough to permit only one choice at which her duty murmurs, would it not be frightened with a succession of infidelities? I have known many women, abandoned to an attachment of which their duty disapproves, surrounded with relics and scapularies, bind themselves by the most insignificant vows and fulfil them with scrupulosity. The impetuosity of desire leads them to effrontery and it is not rare to receive advances from that sex destined by nature not to provoke but to await them. The younger females, however, though less reserved in their behaviour, grant much less than their exterior promises and it is very seldom that they anticipate marriage.'

Many a foreigner was swept off his feet by this display of beauty and spontaneity. Fischer found that Spanish women 'have a character of energy and sublimity that would carry you away in spite of your better judgment and of all your philosophy. The physiognomy of a Spanish woman bears the stamp of sensibility. Her slender form, her majestic step, her sonorous voice, her black and brilliant eye, the vivacity of her gesticulation; in a word the whole action of her person shows the temperature of her soul.' He believed that the down upon their upper lip, which made them have recourse to *velleras*, or women whose business it was to pluck out hairs, was a sign of the warmth of their constitutions.

'Attached to her religion, this sacred tenderness certainly opens her soul to the attacks of love. To love saints naturally awakens a sense of her sexuality and thus a voluptuous devotion becomes from sixteen years of age the most important occupation of her life. In this view alone can the contradictions of her conduct be explained. Divided between religious duties and the pleasures of sense, a Spanish woman seems to be in a state of continual warfare between her conscience and her constitution. It is by no means rare to see a beautiful woman quit the arms of her lover to kneel before a Madonna and, being reconciled by this act of devotion, again hasten to give herself up to pleasure.'

'No Spanish woman, however loose she may be,' wrote Casanova, 'will forget to cover the image of Christ or of the Virgin in her apartment before she yields to the desires of her lover.' What was the Holy Inquisition doing? It was as severe, and as ineffectual, as ever. 'What is the Holy Inquisition so interested in?' asks Casanova. 'Everything,' he tells us. 'It wants to know if you eat meat on lean days, if there are several people of both sexes in one room, if women sleep alone or with men and when they do, whether the men are their legitimate husbands; they lead them into prison if they cannot produce the requisite certificates. If you dine alone with a lady in a private room in a Madrid tavern, the waiter will remain constantly on guard to be sure you do nothing else but eat and drink. In spite of this luxury of precautions, there is a great deal of *libertinage* in the capital.'

Typical of the Spaniard's disgust for women who yield to carnal lust—even though in this instance it may have been provoked by personal feelings—are the women in Goya's *Disparates*: in one plate, a hippogriff is taking off into the air with a sneer on its face. He carries with him a man in black holding a woman in white. The hippogriff is the symbol of creative activity—the woman in white struggles; she does not wish to be borne away on the wings of the spirit. In another plate, a white stallion has seized a woman's white dress in his teeth and is bearing her away. There is a smile of voluptuous ecstasy on her face.

'In Madrid,' wrote another German traveller, 'there is a great scarcity of amusements which are therefore supplied by devotion and its sister passion love.'

The mingling of the two is still found at the present time. A Spaniard told me that a colleague of his, during the Civil War of 1936, had an affair with a Navarrese girl who made her lover kneel down in a village church and pray to the Madonna with her before they made love at the back of the altar!

It was the wit and gift of repartee of their women that made them particularly attractive to men, even more than their beauty. As Udal ap Rhys commented in his *Travels*: 'Nor are their women less distinguishable for their Vivacity and Politeness, their Beauty and their Wit, which renders them so charming and amiable that the Passion of the Spaniard is little less than adoration. And as there is no danger which he will not encounter, to see his Mistress, so there is none to which she is not ready to be exposed in order to receive him. And when they have mutually pledged their Faith, there is nothing which they will not suffer rather than violate it. Such is their Sense of Honour, that there is something heroic even in their Gallantry.'

In Andalusia Jardine found that 'the native graces, more than the beauty of the sex here, may be said to be too powerful for the devil himself; for in spite of a constant and well-cultivated dread of him and all that their ghostly and ignorant fathers can say, they are perhaps the gayest, the most lively and agreeable women in Europe....' And he admires 'the romantic force of their passions, their strong and inviolable attachments, especially when heightened by the difficulties of intrigue'.

Francis Willoughby, travelling through Andalusia in 1737, was more severe. He wrote that 'for fornication and impurity they are the worst of all nations, at least in Europe; almost all the inns in Andalusia, Castile, Granada, Murcia, &c., having whores who dress the meat and do all the business. They are to be hired at a very cheap rate. It were a shame to mention their impudence, lewdness and immodest behaviour and practices. (In Catalonia, Guipuzcoa and some other places they are not so bad.)'

Major Dalrymple was less puritanical. When he discovered a servant sleeping with her master in an Andalusian inn, he jotted down in his diary: 'Sport on, ye amorous Castilians! Nor let the ill-judged caution of a gloomy Englishman deprive you of those transports he cannot enjoy.'

Of course, there were prostitutes in the other provinces as well. Major Dalrymple saw fifteen prostitutes at the Ferrol in Galicia being drummed out of town for their malpractices: 'They were placed on the steps of ladders, carried horizontally upon men's shoulders, with the hair of their heads and eyebrows shaved off.'

In Madrid, after dark, according to Augustus Fischer, 'Third-class courtesans threw their arms round men's necks and covered their mouth with kisses, asking "do you want to see my little bed", &c., to which they add gestures that would make you blush even in the dark. And yet those women are frequently not destitute of wit and talents and often have their heads full of verses which they recite.' Love of poetry—or should we say of rhyme and hyperbole?—is inherent in all Spaniards, and always has been. In Arab-occupied Spain of the tenth century, a Moorish author observed that even the labourers in the fields composed verses, and in a recent novel (*La Colmena* by José Maria Cela, 1942) a Madrid prostitute asks her lover to recite his poetry to her.

Fischer thought that the Andalusian climate had a lot to do with their fiery temperament. 'In Andalusia, everything bears the stamp of a burning climate, every sensation is strong and impetuous, everything tends to extremes, everything is immoderate and without restraint and above all in what regards the sexes. But it is when the *solano* blows that this impulse (in no part does the influence of the climate so easily disarm the severest of moralists) becomes most impetuous; for then the very air they breathe is on fire and all the senses are involuntarily inebriated; the imagination is bewildered and an irresistible instinct becomes authorized by example and is excited by solicitation. If anything could moderate this ferment of the blood it would be sea-bathing, of which both sexes make frequent use.' Women bathed in a separate part of the sea, guarded by cavalry, but lovers, according to Fischer, were quick at deceiving the guards. He saw young people of both sexes bathing in the nude at low water. This is difficult to believe, in view of traditional Spanish modesty.

In Cádiz, too, ladies were high-spirited and fond of adventure. Father Labat, whose curiosity in feminine affairs led him into various indiscretions, relates in his *Travels* that the women took advantage of a hood which only left one eye uncovered 'to behave with great effrontery in the full knowledge that nobody would recognize them or dare to remove their veil. In this disguise, they believe that everything is permitted them. They speak to passers-by who take their fancy, start conversations and even intrigues; one could write volumes about this. As they are witty, their conversation is agreeable, delicate, gay.'

The Father began to suspect his own landlady when he too was accosted by a female *tapada*, as the veiled ladies were called, and he had her followed to make sure. 'It was useless, because what these women usually do is to walk into the first church they find on their way. They join the other animals of the species at their devotions and after having prayed a little, or gossiped a little, they rise five or six at a time, talk to each other, change places, sit down again, get up, so that what with these various movements the uniformity of their dress and the darkness of the churches, one soon loses trace of the person whom one wishes to follow.'

The Father finally succeeded by a stratagem: when his landlady was not looking, he picked up her mantilla and made a little mark on it. Later on that same evening she accosted him in the street—not for the first time, as he had correctly guessed—and he was able to reveal her identity. At first the irate lady believed that her maid had given her away. 'She would have eaten her servant out of anger if I hadn't told her it was my own doing,' wrote the mischievous Father.

Henry Swinburne was less enthusiastic than other English writers on the subject of Spanish women and less enamoured of their external charms. 'Their tempers, having never been fashioned by polite intercourse nor softened by necessary contradiction, are extremely pettish and violent. They are continually pouting for something or other and put out of humour by the merest trifles. They are never without some sort of sugar plum or high-priced comfit in their mouths. As soon as they come out of the convent and before they have fixed upon a lover to fill up their time more agreeably they rise late and loiter away the remains of the morning among their attendants or work it out at church in a long bead-roll of habitual unmeaning prayers; they dine sparingly, sleep, and then dress to saunter for a couple of hours on the Prado.'

This description tallies with the confidences of Count Fernán-Nuñez preserved in his correspondence with a German friend, in which he describes his Gallegan wife and her deficiences: 'If my wife had been born in a country where people are brought up with a certain amount of education, she would be perfect,' he wrote, 'but she has not had this good luck and I am afraid that being so accustomed to doing nothing will make it very difficult to remedy this defect. This habit of never concentrating on anything and of doing as she likes without any consideration for others is an obstacle for one who would like to suggest a different mode of life. To this must be added a great self-pride and a no less greater propensity to take offence easily.'

French travellers were frankly bored with Spanish women. 'They have *tertulias* or gatherings,' wrote Morel-Fatio, but these are not *salons* in any sense of the word. 'Dancing and gallantry are the only objects of these meetings. The great ladies of the end of the century arranged readings or declamation sessions, but one never *talked* there.' Charles Pierre Coste, writing from Pamplona in Navarre, commented on the dull parties during which men rolled their eyes at the ladies seated at the far end of the room; nor did he think much of the custom of the serenade: 'Lovers scrape an untuneful guitar all night under their mistress's window and were it to freeze enough to break stones he won't think of leaving until dawn, when the sun jealously arrives to interrupt this delicious pastime.' He added that many young students or seminarists served as pages in the best houses and that lovers often introduced themselves in this guise—although their boldness nearly always ended in some terrible catastrophe.

'Nothing can be more burdensome than the restraint attached to the title of lover,' wrote Fischer. 'It is one uninterrupted succession of minute cares and attentions. At the Prado, at Mass, at the theatre, at the confessional, never must he quit her, and the whole weight of her affairs of every kind rests upon his shoulders.

Never must he approach her empty-handed, especially on feast days; in a word, he must in all things be the passive agent of a woman. From being a slave he becomes a master at marriage, hence hostilities and *cortejos*.'

It was the age of the fan, and the manœuvring of this beautiful object became an art in the agile hands of Spanish women. In the words of Blanco White: 'A dear friend at the furthest end of the public walk is greeted and cheered up by a quick, tremulous motion of the fan, accompanied with several significant nods. An object of indifference is dismissed with a slow, formal inclination of the fan, which makes his blood run cold. The fan now screens the titter and whisper, now condenses a smile into the dark, sparkling eyes, which take their aim just above it; a gentle tap of the fan commands the attention of the careless; a waving notion calls the distant. A certain twirl between the fingers betrays doubt or anxiety—a quick closing and displaying the folds indicates eagerness or joy.'

Other movements of the fan—demonstrated to me by my Andalusian grandmother—were the quick, nervous 'come to me, come to me' of the disengaged girl who was free to accept a lover, and the slower, gentler movements of the lady who implied 'he has come, he has come'.

Fans are still in use, but not for amorous purposes. The gentle feathery rustles of black fans in churches during the summer and the gay snapping of coloured fans at the theatre is one of the characteristic sounds of Spain; the fan shops of the Plaza San Jerónimo in Madrid display gorgeous wares in silk and satin, ivory and lace, which are eagerly sought and bought by tourists. No woman can wield a fan as gracefully as the Spaniard or with such variety of gesture. With the fan and the rosary she expresses the whole scale of her emotions.

8. Southern Fire: Carmen and her Sisters

ALTHOUGH flamenco and Andalusian dances were not to become a European craze until the following century, their powerful effect was commented upon by several eighteenth-century travellers, who did not always know what to make of the eroticism. Joseph Townsend describes the fandango with Anglo-Saxon caution: 'It is banished from genteel assemblies and justly so, as danced by the vulgar it is too disgusting; as refined in higher life, covered with a most elegant yet transparent veil, it ceases to disgust and from that very circumstance excites those passions in the youthful breast which wisdom finds it difficult to curb. The music of it has such a powerful effect in young and old, that all are prepared for motion the instant the instruments are heard, and from what I have seen I could almost persuade myself to receive the extravagant idea of a friend who, in the warmth of his imagination, supposed that were it suddenly introduced into a church or into a court of judicature, priests and people, judges and criminals, the gravest and the gay, would forget all distinctions and begin to dance.'

Casanova learned the fandango in three days and danced it at masked balls in Madrid with a young beauty to whom he made love—prudently, for she wished to 'remain pure for her husband'. He admits that it was a dance that 'set one on fire'.

In the nineteenth century, the fame of the fandango reached England and became the subject of a ballad which was sung in the eighties by Charles Leybourne:

SHE DOES THE FANDANGO ALL OVER THE PLACE

I've seen many beauties whilst travelling around
The world, but in Spain there my fancy I found;
She'd hair black as coal, eyes bright as a star,
And I fairly felt gone when she twanged her guitar.
Chorus:
She sang like a nightingale, twanged her guitar;
Danced the Cachuca, smoked a cigar;

Oh! what a form! Oh what a face!
And she did the Fandango all over the place.

To England I brought her to make her my bride,
And when my friends saw her they laughed till they cried,
And the buttons flew off from a dozen white vests
When at breakfast she somewhat astonished the guests

(*Chorus*)

But she carries her Spanish ways slightly too far,
I, at times, think she'll have to destroy her guitar;
For she sits at the window, and sings long and loud,
Until in the streets she collects a large crowd.

Spoken: And horrid boys cry out, 'Chuck it out, Sarah!' Dreadful!
And when I insist on her concluding her performance she rushes into
the garden, mounts the summer house and won't come down till she's

Sang like a nightingale, twanged her guitar;
Danced the Cachuca, smoked a cigar;
Dev'lish bad form, quite a disgrace,
She will do the Fandango all over the place.

The German, Christian Augustus Fischer, was subjugated by
the bolero, of which he gives a fascinating description. The
bolero, he explains, portrays the mysteries of love and is often
danced at the end of a play, 'when the stage is converted into a
magnificent apartment, the orchestra again strikes up, the
castanets are heard and a dancer and his partner come forth from
opposite sides, each in the graceful Andalusian costume, which
seems invented for dancing, and dart towards each other as if they
had been seeking each other.

'The lover seems about to embrace the object of his passion,
who appears ready to throw herself into his arms; but she
suddenly turns round, her partner half-angry does the same, and
immediately the music stops, generally in the middle of a bar.
The art of the dancers consists in a rapid, equal and neat poise and
stopping as accurately together as to seem at once rooted to the
ground opposite to each other.

'They now appear undecided but presently the music, which
begins again, reanimates and quickens their motions. The lover,
now grown more ardent, endeavours to express his desires and
his beloved receives him with more tenderness, her looks

becoming more languishing, her bosom palpitates with more force, and she extends her arms towards him. Vain hope! Too timid to meet him, she flies off again till a new pause gives them fresh courage.

'The music, now more lively, gives wings to their feet and inebriated with passion the lover again darts towards his mistress who, transported with similar sensations, flies with ardour to meet him. They join their arms, the lips of the fair dancer open, and she seems ready to surrender at discretion. The music now gives louder and stronger sounds, a more rapid melody and the motions of the dancers are redoubled. 'Tis a kind of intoxication of delight and the same sensations seem to animate them both; each muscle is alive and every pulsation accelerated, when suddenly the music stops and the dancers at the same instant become motionless and disappear, for the curtain falls and the illusion of the spectators is dissolved.

'The climate, the vivacity, the beauty and the agility of the inhabitants render Andalusia exclusively adapted to this dance. You should see it performed by a well-assorted couple, whose persons are only exceeded by their talents, and then you would forget everything of the kind you had seen before as tame and inexpressive. How can such a dance, which refers so strongly to a passion that animates the whole of nature and which alone can counterbalance the selfish principle, not be preferred to all other amusements?'

As the Victorian Mr. Baxley observed many years later: 'The condemnation of Spanish popular dances, as voluptuous *in-decencies*, by *fastidious foreigners, silent as to their own sins and fanciful about those of their neighbours*, is unfair and without foundation in the customs of the reputable.'

Another Victorian, Miss Matilda Betham-Edwards, forgot all about decorum and prudery under the influence of a guitarist from the Albaicin in Granada: 'It was music as one had never dreamed of before. His fingers but touch the cords and all at once your breath is taken away, your blood is warmed as if by strong wine, your brain whirls, your eyes see visions, your ears hear marvellous voices, your senses are all mastered by a power that seems to shake the very spheres . . . you are indeed for the nonce a gipsy and know what the gipsy's world is, above, below, in heaven and in hell; your pulses are quickened to gipsy pitch, you are ready to make love and war.'

A medieval wedding, Valencia

A jealous husband kills his parents, taking them for his
wife and her lover, Navarre, sixteenth century

St. Liberata, the bearded female saint, eighteenth century

'The Lovers of Teruel' by Muñoz Degrain

When the music stopped and the spell was broken, Miss Matilda Betham-Edwards returned to reality: 'We were a company of ladies and gentlemen, whose utmost vagabondage had not exceeded boiling a picnic kettle in Epsom Forest or, more likely, taking tea on our own lawns. We felt thankful to Señor Antonio for having given us so full an experience of wild life in the space of a few minutes.'

This must indeed have been a glimpse of 'wild life' to a lady who believed in travelling with the greatest number of Victorian impedimenta imaginable. Miss Betham-Edwards and her companion journeyed through Spain in a ladies' coupé which they nearly always had to themselves, 'and very comfortable travelling we found it'. She gives intending travellers to Spain a few tips: 'Always travel in your best clothes and with half a dozen trunks at least. Luggage and good clothes take the place of a train of servants. Luggage and good clothes ensure you good places, general civility and an infinity of minor comforts. It is all very well for savages to travel without luggage . . . but if anyone wants to travel pleasantly and profitably, let him carry a well-stored portmanteau. Surely in no country but patient Spain would two ladies have been allowed to fill the first-class compartment as we did. Under the seats, on the seats, above the seats, were piled an infinite variety of packages, a box of medicines, a folding india-rubber bath, a basket of provisions, two or three parcels of books, two or three bundles of rags, a leather bag of sketching materials, sketching blocks of various sizes, a silk bag of needles and threads; lastly an odd bag, containing notepaper, opera glasses, passports, a teapot, a water-bottle, an etna, an air-cushion, slippers and sundries without number. We breakfasted, we dined, we wrote letters and diaries, we read all our books from beginning to end, we mended our clothes, we made sketches, we made tea, we might have refreshed ourselves with a cold bath but for want of water. Not a bit of our precious luggage could we have spared. . . .'

The Spaniards' reaction to this invasion of their country by British matrons does not appear to have entered into their literary annals but it has been embodied in a 'giantess' that figures in the carnavalesque procession at the feast of St. James on 25th July in Santiago de Compostela. Blonde, florid, full-bosomed and yet strangely sexless, the 'giantess' pirouettes coquettishly in the wake of older and more distinguished figures, African and

Asian kings. '*La turista inglesa!*' cry the street urchins delightedly. Whenever I see her, I think of Miss Matilda Betham-Edwards and wonder whether she inspired the first 'giantess' of Santiago.

9. *Black Eyes and a Siege of Nuns*

In the nineteenth century, more than ever before, Andalusia continued to be the magnet of foreign visitors. We have seen how it affected Miss Matilda Betham-Edwards. Male visitors sampled Andalusian charms at closer quarters, not so much because of their advances to the fair sex as of the latter's advances to them.

Byron spent only three days in Seville, staying at the house of two unmarried ladies, but he made such an impression upon the elder that at parting she cut off a lock of his hair and presented him with one of her own, three feet in length. This trophy is now in the Murray collection of Byronian relics at 50 Albemarle Street, London. Byron said that the young lady offered him a share of her apartment, which his *virtue* induced him to decline. The lady, incidentally, was on the point of marrying an officer in the Spanish army.

The ladies of Cádiz were still irresistible with 'their long black hair, dark languishing eyes, *clear* olive complexions and forms more graceful in motion than can be conceived by an Englishman used to the drowsy, listless air of his countrymen'. Intrigue was the business of life and 'if you make a proposal, which in England will bring a box on the ear from the meekest of virgins, to a Spanish girl, she thanks you for the honour you intend her and replies: "Wait till I am married and I shall be too happy." '

Lord Byron appears to have been taken in by the Andalusian sense of humour, their habit of putting people off and of saying 'yes' when they mean 'no', and 'no' when they mean 'yes'. The Andalusian prefers to leave his interlocutor guessing. This, he thinks, adds spice to life. An Andalusian lady who had to follow her husband to Burgos a few years ago complained in a letter to a Sevillan friend: 'In this part of the country, my dear, people really mean 'yes' and 'no' when they say so. This makes life utterly boring and it is one of the things I simply cannot bear about this place.'

Nor would an Andalusian woman reply to an amorous proposal by a straight 'yes' or 'no'. She would refuse her suitor at least three times before accepting him. This ritual is also observed with food. It is vulgar to accept a second helping straight away. This attitude reminds one of the Oriental love of bargaining, which comes from a similar attachment to ceremonial etiquette.

The love-game was pursued with particular zest on St. John's Eve, when young ladies waited behind their *rejas* or iron bars, usually in the company of a sister or friend of their own age, to banter with the young sparks who walked the streets—mostly in disguise—from midnight until dawn. The girls often disguised themselves, too, and changed characters to puzzle their out-of-door visitors. The latter, provided with sweetmeats and flowers, pretended to be farmers just arrived from the country, or poor mechanics, or foreigners speaking broken Spanish or Gallegans making love in their own language—anything to give rein to the Andalusian love of jest.

One wonders how many abductions there would have been— principally by ardent foreigners—had Spanish girls not been protected by their *rejas*. 'I do not believe,' wrote the Italian traveller, Edmondo de Amicis, 'that there exist in any country women who are so thoroughly fitted to suggest the idea of abduction as the Andalusians, not only because they arouse the desire to commit all sorts of devilries, but because they really seem created on purpose to be seized, bundled up, and hidden away, so small, light, plump, elastic and soft are they. Their little feet could easily be got into your coat-pocket; with one hand you could lift them by the waist as you would a doll, and by pressing them lightly with your finger you could bend them as you would a reed.'

The women of Cádiz, wrote Henry Inglis in 1831, 'are the first in Spain'. They are also coquettish. 'Presuming upon their charms, the ladies of this city indulge in some curious whims. Every family of any consequence has a state-bed, highly orna-mented, and placed in an elegantly fitted-up apartment and the use made of it is this: at a particular time of the year, generally after Lent, the *señora* of the house, or her daughter, if she has reached and her mother has passed a certain age, feigns sickness. Having previously made all the necessary arrangements, she takes to her bed; there she lies in an elegant nightdress, under em-broidered sheets, her head resting upon a rose-coloured silk pillow, and a tablestand near her with silver candlesticks and wax lights, a little silver bell, and several vases containing choice perfumes. There she receives company; there all her male and female acquaintances resort, and there, attired to be seen and bent upon admiration, she listens to the language of mock condolence, pleasing flattery and undisguised gallantry!'

Cautiously, this same early Victorian writer leads us into a boudoir secret: 'I was informed that the ladies of Cádiz are adepts in the manufacture of the female person; that in looking at them, we may frequently apply with truth the well-known proverb "all is not gold that glitters", and that the most experienced dressmaker of the British metropolis would be "all in amaze" at the various and subtle uses to which the cork tree is put in the City of Cádiz.'

Morals, according to this author, whom one suspects of bias, were at a low ebb. 'Female virtue is a thing almost unknown and scarcely appreciated. It is with difficulty and with pain we can bring ourselves to believe that in a civilized country there should exist a state of society in which that purest gem, female modesty, bears no price. . . . I could give innumerable examples of the depraved state of morals in Cádiz; I have at this moment before me a closely written page of notes full of these; and even the names of individuals are mentioned; but I have turned the leaf and will not sully my page with details which might indeed gratify curiosity but which could add nothing to the truth of the statement I have made.'

Mr. Inglis did not always hesitate to satisfy his own curiosity. After telling us that only strangers may enter shops where curtains are drawn during the siesta hour, on the pretext of ignorance, he goes on to say: 'Sometimes, during the hour of sleep and silence—in Madrid—I have ventured, in passing along the street, to draw aside the curtain that is meant to secure an interrupted siesta to the inmates of the embroiderers', perfumers' or dressmakers' shops; and I have more than once interrupted a *tête-à-tête*.'

Sir Arthur de Capell found that the 'finely-rounded limbs' of the ladies of Cádiz 'contrast very agreeably with those sharp, angular points which one is so apt to come in contact with in our country, resulting from coldness of climate, constitution, or other causes'.

The author of *The Attaché in Madrid*, after declaring that 'nowhere can such eyes be seen as in Spain, whether for size, colour or expression', goes on to say: 'As an Englishwoman advances in years, she generally grows thin; the Spanish *señora* is apt to become unwieldy. The one contracts, the other expands; and the expansion system, though it must be inconvenient, preserves the beauty of the face to a later period of life.' He also remarked that 'the race of old dowagers, with rouged cheeks, false ringlets and shaking pendants, forming so prominent a feature of London society, is almost entirely unknown in Madrid'.

Even nowadays, elderly Spanish ladies are in general more attractive than their English counterparts, not only because they are less angular and neat-footed, but because they carry themselves so much better. Their faces seem to be less lined, their expression more mellow. The fact that they do not wear hats makes a difference too. What could be more pathetic than an old, heavily lined face quivering under a girlish, gaudy hat adorned with inappropriate spring flowers, bunches of vernal fruit, or multi-coloured feathers? The elderly Spanish lady, with her wavy, well-groomed hair, her black lace mantilla, dignified deportment and soulful eyes, knows how to display old age gracefully.

The warmth and spontaneity of Spanish belles distinguished them from their Gallic neighbours, thought Blanco White: 'Were their charms the effect of that cold twinkling flame which flutters round the hearts of most Frenchwomen they would only be dangerous to the peace and usefulness of one half of society. But, instead of being the capricious tyrants of men, they are— generally—their victims. Few, very few Spanish women and none, I will venture to say, among the Andalusians, have it in their power to be coquettes . . . there is more of that vice in the men than in the females.'

A Frenchman with considerable experience of high society, the Marquis de Custine, found, on the contrary, that Spanish women were too coquettish, too anxious to please; moreover, they lacked nobility. What the Spaniard looked for in a woman was, above all, *sal*—a gift of repartee combined with native audacity of expression and good humour. The marquis commented that many a grandee of Spain chose his mistress from among the market women, who have always been particularly rich in *sal española*. Nevertheless, in Spain he found the last refuge of romantic and passionate love. 'In France, love is intrigue, conversation, vanity—in Spain, it is felicity; everything here is the result of surprise and spontaneity in attachments, everything is involuntary from the first seduction of the senses to the summum of happiness. Love is life for those who find it in Spain.'

One does not hear so much about Spanish men, from the point of view that interests us. Andalusians, from the little one can glean, seem to have been divided into two groups: on the one hand effeminate and blasé like those of Cádiz (a town which is still famous for its great number of homosexuals) whom Henry Blackburn described as 'over-dressed in modern costume, with a profusion of rings and a partiality for fancy umbrellas'. To his insular eyes, 'They have not either the dignity or the repose of the well-bred European.'

The Spanish word for 'pansy' is *maricón*. Last time I was in Spain, I heard that the wife of the English consul in Cádiz (not the present one!) who did not know the niceties of the language, asked her servant whether she could recommend a gardener. 'I'll send you our *maricón*—he will do it,' she said. The consul's wife, believing that this was the lad's name, received him graciously, as she thought, by saying brightly: 'Good day, *Maricón*,' and then proceeding to give him orders. She could not understand why he blushed so violently.

On the other hand, there was the wild type of young man, half-bandit, half-Don Juan, like the one who entertained Blanco White in the village of Olbera, near Seville. The entertainment took various forms and at times degenerated into rowdyism. 'One night the dance was interrupted by the hoarse voice of our worthy friend Don Juan, who happened to be in the kitchen on a visit to a favourite jar of brandy. The ladies, though possessed of strong nerves, showed evident symptoms of alarm and we all hurried out of the room, anxious to ascertain the cause of the threatening tones we had heard.

'Upon our coming to the hall, we found the doughty hero standing at a window with a cocked gun in his hands, sending forth a volley of oaths and protesting he would shoot the first man who approached his door. . . . The assault, however, which he had thus gallantly repulsed, being now over, he soon became cool enough to inform us of the circumstances. Two or three individuals of the adverse party, who were taking their nightly rounds under the window of their mistresses, hearing the revel at Rosa's house, were tempted to interrupt it by setting fire to the door of the entrance-hall. The house might in short time have been in flames, but for the unquenchable thirst of the owner, which so seasonably drew him from the back to the front of the building.'

Serenading, as is obvious from the above and from other more northerly accounts, was often the excuse for quarrels and fights between rival gangs of youths, out for boisterous fun—'kicks', they would be called by present-day youth—rather than amorous pursuits. Love has often been a pretext for, rather than the cause of, aggression.

Jealousy seems to have been confined mostly to the lower orders of society, but love—as Blanco White observed—was not the main instigator of murder among the Spaniards. 'A constitutional irritability, especially in the southern provinces, leads, without any more assignable reason, to the frequent shedding of blood. A small quantity of wine, nay, the mere blowing of the easterly wind, called *solano*, is infallibly attended with deadly quarrels in Andalusia.'

It is of this and of preceding centuries that love in Spain could be described in the words of Salvador de Madariaga 'as spontaneous, as uncalculating, as volcanic as Spanish nature would lead us to expect. At the same time deeply carnal yet strangely chaste. No intellectual or ethical elements come to disturb the free flow of a passion which feels itself in so direct a contact with life's own sources. Love in Spain is often found to act with that implacable strength which made of it an awe-inspiring myth in antiquity.'

I do not believe, however, that this applies to severe Castille, nor to tender Galicia—and certainly not to Spanish love in the twentieth century. Even in the nineteenth century, we find a worldly playwright like Bretón de los Herreros expressing sceptical disbelief in the so-called passionate loves of his countrymen. Herreros's young ladies are shrewd and coquettish, his widows prudent and malicious.

The observant Monsieur Laborde remarked cautiously in his *Souvenirs* that in his opinion the Spaniards were far less romantic than was commonly believed. It was fashionable to equate romanticism and melancholy and he said that 'a melancholy Spanish woman is not to be seen'. The same temperate writer found Valencian women 'sweet-natured but their ascendancy over men inclines them to be imperious and they sometimes take advantage of their superiority. Just as the men in the middle classes are active and industrious, the women of all classes are idle and enemies of every kind of occupation.'

Captain George Carleton, who fought in Spain under the Earl of Peterborough, described life in Valencia at the beginning of the century in very different terms: 'The mildness of the climate seems to contribute to develop their constitutions and their passions very early and I have seen extremely young girls on the point of becoming mothers. In general in Valencia all is amusement and pleasure: promenades, riding in carriages called *taranas*, fishing in the lake Albufera, the theatre, concerts in the *alameda*, pilgrimages to magnificent convents, etc. Everything invites to the enjoyment of life, which the fair sex partake, not indeed with Andalusian licenciousness, but yet with an amiable freedom.'

These visits to 'magnificent convents' were not always innocent and the captain relates a disreputable incident involving two of his officers: 'Valencia is famous for its fine women. Two of our English officers, not caring for the common road, however safe, resolved to launch into the deeper seas, though attended with much greater danger. Amour, the common failing of that fair city, was the occasion of this accident and two nuns the objects. It is customary in that country for young people to resort to the grates of the nunneries there to divert themselves and the nuns with a little pleasant and inoffensive chit-chat. I never saw or heard anything unseemly. ['Nuns' gallants' as they were called, had been satirized by writers like Quevedo and Góngora and a popular sonnet said that the devil had given up wearing a serpent skin, that trick being too well known; now he hid himself in friars' hoods.]

'Our two officers were very assiduous at the gates of the nunnery in this place and having pitched there upon two nuns, prosecuted their amours with such vigour that in a little time they had made very great progress in their affections, without in the least considering the dangers that must attend themselves and the fair; they had exchanged vows and prevailed upon the weaker vessels to endeavour to get out to their lovers.'

The nuns took weekly courses in keeping the keys of all the doors and so it was easy to carry them off. But being ladies of quality the news of their elopement soon reached their relatives, who 'received the news with vows of utmost vengeance and as is usual in that country, put themselves in arms for that purpose'.

The caddish English officers had abandoned the poor nuns, who 'knew not where to fly' and were soon discovered. The nuns were condemned to be immured for life. 'The Earl of Peterborough, though highly exasperated at the proceedings of his officers, in compassion to the unhappy fair resolved to interpose by all the moderate means possible. The nearest of the relatives were the most opposed to his generous mediations.' In the end, with the help of a considerable sum of money, he saved the nuns from the intended punishment.

In Valencia, as in Cádiz, women were bold enough to accost strangers under the protective disguise of their mantillas. The captain described one of them in particular 'whose discourse was always entertaining and full of wit and her enquiries not often improper'. Serenading was much in fashion, often with the same violent results as in Andalusia. (English sailors, by the way, did not think much of guitars; they called them 'the strum-strums'.) 'Yet,' wrote the captain, 'they are perpetually at nights disturbing their women with the noise of them under the notion and name of serenadoes. From the barber to the grandee the infection spreads and very often with the same attendant danger; night quarrels and encounters being the frequent result. The trueborn Spaniard reckons it a part of their glory to be jealous of their mistresses which is too often the forerunner of murders or at best attended with many other very dangerous inconveniences.' In Valencia as in other parts of Spain a sense of personal honour rather than amorous sentiments was the real cause of most affrays.

'Though adultery is looked upon as a grievous crime,' remarked the captain, 'and punished accordingly, yet fornication is softened with the title of a venial sin, and they seem to practise it under that persuasion.'

In the sixties, the ladies dared to bathe, 'amid an immense host of bathers all wearing large straw hats which gave the sea the appearance of being covered with floating, erratic mushrooms. The ladies disport themselves like playful naiads on one side of the bay, while the straw-tiled, hirsute mermen dabble about on the other, smoking cigarettes even in the water. The intervening space is jealousy guarded by armed sentries extending from the water's edge up to the line of timber huts or fixed bathing machines, whither the bathers, wrapped in long winding sheets, repair to dress themselves after their ablutions.'

In San Sebastian, towards the end of the century, René Bazin described the men bathing on the left of the beach and the women in the middle. The latter, upon entering the water, wet the tips of their fingers in the waves and piously crossed themselves. Twentieth-century readers, who flock to Spanish beaches in such large numbers, do not have to be told that whereas armed sentries may have disappeared, vigilant Guardias Civiles nicknamed *La Moral* by Spanish youth, parade up and down most of the beaches to ensure that the regulations on modest bathing attire prescribed by the puritanical Franco régime are not being flouted by shameless foreigners. Our immodesty and corrupting influence are proverbial. In 1960, a case of adultery—the first ever, it was said—came to light in a remote village of Andorra. The President of Andorra blamed the whole affair on 'foreign influence' and threatened to close the frontier.

The Spanish custom of the *piropo*, addressing compliments to an unknown woman in the streets, of which I shall have more to say further on, was a source of astonishment to English lady travellers like Miss Matilda Betham-Edwards who commented: 'Spanish ladies, when promenading the streets *en grande tenue*, are flattered by the admiration, expressed or implied, of passers-by. A notion so opposed to our English sense of delicacy that it is entertained with difficulty. . . .'

Spanish ladies were still notoriously uncultured but a German attaché in Madrid, during a salon conversation on this subject, expressed the view that 'a more learned education might make them more brilliant but I am not sure that it would improve them. You know how charming they are in conversation, how full of wit and vivacity. Give them a knowledge of general literature, and with their quick perceptions and lively imaginations they will become the most remarkable women in Europe. In the meantime, their education fits them to be good wives and mothers and judicious mistresses of their families, and their natural talent supplies the want of knowledge, where this want exists.' 'In short, dear Count,' said the French lady with whom he was talking, 'you must take a Spanish wife back with you to that château of yours with its unpronounceable name; make her go through a course of literature and she will become a formidable blue.'

'The Spanish girls are extremely clever,' remarked a third member of the salon, 'but they get none of their cleverness from books, depend upon it.' 'So much the better—give me anything but a woman who reads that she may talk and talks to show her learning.' 'I adore their black eyes,' said Monsieur de T. 'And I their little feet,' said Monsieur de E. 'They have wonderful hair,' said Count G. 'They are good-natured, unaffected, clever and have no nonsense about them,' said M. 'They never try to show off and no one but a rich bachelor, or one reputed rich, knows what a relief that is,' he added pathetically.

The German attaché affirmed that 'with the exception of a very few fashionable persons, whose lives do indeed seem to pass in one round of dissipation, whose time is spent driving in the Prado, attending the theatre, the opera, the ball-room, precisely as their compeers do in every other great city, the Spanish women are the most domestic in the world, the most devoted to the care of their children, the most truly pious and the best *ménagères*'.

A pretty face is the gateway to most desires in Spain—from railway tickets to government posts, and Spanish husbands, in spite of the reputed jealousy, have not always resisted the temptation to make use of their wives' charms. (In 1588 Philip II was obliged to issue a decree forbidding husbands from hiring out their wives for illicit purposes.) In the nineteenth century Sir Arthur de Capell, travelling in a diligence between Madrid and the north of Spain, met two fat and fortyish Spanish ladies; one of them was a countess who had been despatched to the capital to entreat the favour of a minister on behalf of her husband who had fallen into disgrace and been ordered to retire into a distant province, while her companion had been using her influence to obtain an exchange of command for *her* husband, who was stationed at one of the frontier fortresses and who wished to get nearer to Madrid.

'This is the general system in Spain,' writes Sir Arthur, 'and petticoat influence has in consequence by far the most preponderating weight in affairs. Does a person wish to obtain any situation, post, or office, to be appointed to a certain command, or to effect, in short, any object essential to his interest and of which the government has the disposal, his rib, as a far abler negotiator than himself, is despatched to Madrid and, repairing every day to the minister's levees, brings into play her different points of character and the numberless little tricks which her sex in general, and the Spanish ladies in particular, know so well how to exhibit to the best advantage. A Spanish minister's levee is thus crowded with fair applicants, who bring into play the whole of the artillery with which nature may have supplied them against the crafty courtier. . . . Those who happen to be blessed with any superior share of personal charms and attractions, accompanied with proportionate address, are first attended to and seldom have to wait long, or fail in the object of their mission; the others make up with hard dollars. In the end, they are all sent trotting back to their spouses in the country, tolerably content and not dissatisfied, at least, with the gaieties of the capital which their little trip has thus enabled them to indulge in.'

It is curious to observe that in the inns where they stopped on the long, uncomfortable journey, most of the bedrooms contained four beds and had to be shared by both male and female passengers. The gentlemen drew straws to determine who were to share the ladies' room. The latter, says Sir Arthur, took it all gaily and were good-humoured throughout. No doubt northern Spanish ladies suffered less from scruples of modesty than their southern sisters, accustomed to a life of purdah.

Andalusia absorbs all comers, even the gipsies, who had adopted the chaste Spanish amorous code. They were 'discovered' by half-gipsy George Borrow who observed: 'There is a word in the gipsy language to which those who speak it attach ideas of peculiar reverence, far superior to that connected with the name of the Supreme Being, the creator of themselves and the universe. This word is *lachá*, which with them is the corporeal chastity of the females; we say corporeal chastity, for no other do they hold in the slightest esteem; it is lawful among them, nay praiseworthy, to be obscene in look, gesture and discourse, to be accessories to vice and to stand by and laugh at the worst abominations of the Busné, provided their *lachá ye trupos*, or corporeal chastity, remains unblemished.'

In those days the gipsies kept to themselves and the womenfolk had an aversion to white men. When they were betrothed, they never went out together and after marriage the women generally continued faithful to their husbands. Borrow was the first writer to give us a description of a gipsy wedding: 'After much feasting, drinking and yelling, in the gipsy house, the bridal train sallied forth—a frantic spectacle. First of all marched a villainous jockey-looking fellow, holding in his hands—uplifted —a long pole, at the top of which fluttered in the morning air a snow-white cambric handkerchief, emblem of the bride's purity,

Then came the betrothal pair, followed by their nearest friends; then a rabble rout of gipsies, screaming and shouting and discharging guns and pistols, till all round rang with the din, and the village dogs barked. On arriving at the church gate, the fellow who bore the pole stuck it into the ground with a loud huzza and the train, forming two ranks, defiled into the church on either side of the pole and its strange ornaments. On the conclusion of the ceremony they returned in the same manner in which they had come.

'Throughout the day there was nothing going on but singing, drinking, feasting and dancing; but the most singular part of the festival was reserved for the dark night. Nearly a ton weight of sweetmeats had been prepared, at an enormous expense, not for the gratification of the palate but for a purpose purely gipsy. These sweetmeats of all kinds, and of all forms, but principally *yemas*, or yolks of egg prepared with a crust of sugar (a delicious bonne-bouche) were strewn on the floor of a large room, at least to the depth of three inches. Into this room, at a given signal, tripped the bride and bridegroom, dancing *romalis*, followed by all the gitanos and gitanas. . . . To convey a slight idea of the scene is almost beyond the power of words. In a few minutes the sweetmeats were reduced to a powder, or rather to a mud, the dancers were soiled to the knees with sugar, fruit and yolks of eggs. Still more terrific became the lunatic merriment. The men sprang high into the air, neighed, brayed and crowed, whilst the gitanas snapped their fingers in their own fashion, louder than castanets, distorting their forms into all kinds of obscene attitudes and uttering words to repeat which were an abomination.'

More earthy and not at all romantic, was Thornbury's description of a gipsy girl of Granada: 'She is rather like a sailor's wife at Wapping. She has ropy black hair, drawn back behind her ears, in which dangle heavy gold ear-rings. She wears a large, red, cauliflower-patterned gown. She is stout and thick. I don't believe the harebell would ever lift up its head again if her strong feet had once come on it. . . . As for the recitative gipsy song, it is more fit for Irish wake-singers or Arab serpent-charmers than for festive dancers, who dance to the pulsation of their own heart music and what other extraneous help Heaven may send them.'

Gipsy love, hedged about with all the taboos of Spanish honour and virginity, was hardly the voluptuous madness invented by the Romantics who, confusing them with the Andalusians in general, disseminated the Carmen myth all over Europe, to the accompaniment of a bull-ring fanfare.

Bullfights. What is—what has been their relation to eroticism? After seeing the behaviour of Spanish women at the *toros*, the Marquis de Custine waxed less enthusiastic over their charms. He was shocked by the ferocity which came into their lovely faces at the spectacle of blood, at the cruelty displayed by the beautiful girls wearing bright carnations behind their ear, by their insensitivity; most of them probably did not consciously see blood and entrails, they only saw the ritual fight between man and beast, the victory of man—handsome, brave, sacred as a tribal priest, virile as an Adonis. These are people who must live on the exaltation of the senses, who need the aphrodisiacs of wine and blood. I have already commented on the closeness of bordels to the principal bull-rings.

At the end of the eighteenth century, women 'adopted' bullfighters and picadors, presented them with splendid costumes and the best Andalusian horses, arrayed them, adulated them. Such was the flamboyant Duchess of Alba, immortalized by Goya, and many other ladies whose names have not been recorded. The matadors were not always their lovers—they were sometimes Platonic champions, protected by the fair, to whom a famous name led added interest; they, in turn, gave an added piquancy to the lady whose colours they wore and to whom they bowed in the ring, as a knight before a joust. Here the lady was in a primitive role—the dual, ambiguous role of Eve, the goader of instincts and inspirer of noble deeds, in a desperate game that can lead to death.

At the bullfight young people met, flirted with eyes, hands, and fans. René Bazin recounts a delicious scene which took place in the bull-ring at Vittoria towards the end of the nineteenth century: 'A couple of *novios*, both belonging to well-known local families, were sitting in the front row of the bull-ring one afternoon, in adjacent boxes. The girl happened to place her pretty white hand on the velvet-covered edge of the box, her *novio* immediately made an attempt to seize it and kiss it; laughingly, the modest *novia* withdrew her hand and rapped her *novio* on the knuckles with her fan. The incident was noticed by the spectators who rose as one man and, taking the defence of the *novio*, cried: "To the plaza, the *novios*—let her kiss him and let them dance together in the ring." There was such a tumult that the bullfight was interrupted and the president was obliged to descend from his tribune and beg the couple to comply with the wishes of the crowd. The amorous pair agreed, descended arm in arm into the ring, under the bewildered eyes of the bull, whirled round in a waltz and embraced amid tremendous applause.'

The matador is adored by women, but he must conserve his strength and not allow them to become too predatory—he remains aloof and godlike, chaste as primitive warriors before battle. In the provinces, when a matador is not up to standard in the ring, the angry spectators turn to his mistress and shout: 'It's all your fault—you should let him get more sleep!'

10. *Foreign Romantics and*
Spanish Coplas

In 1838, an exhibition of Spanish pictures took Paris by storm. It was a revelation. Spain became fashionable. The Romantics were thrilled. Théophile Gautier, Prosper Mérimée, Alexandre Dumas (who was slapped by a Spanish dancer for kissing her hand with excessive Gallic gallantry) and others with equally vivid imaginations brought back from their travels that picture-poster impression of Spain which never ceases to ruffle Spaniards and enchant aliens. Carmen was invented and set to music.

Later on in the century, when a little of the glamour had worn off, René Bazin described the tobacco factory in Seville where Carmen was supposed to have worked as 'a horrible place, the floor littered with pieces of tobacco. Clothes and shawls hung in bundles all over the room; the women's faces pale, drawn, poisoned by the vitiated air. Beside many of the tables, swaddled infants sleeping in their cots. . . .'

Majorca began to come into the romantic picture too, although the first famous and illicit honeymooners to that island, George Sand and Chopin, were not welcomed by the prudish population and they spent a miserable winter, minutely described by George Sand in *Un Hiver à Majorque*. 'One more month and we would have died in Spain,' she wrote, 'Chopin from melancholy and disgust and I from anger and indignation.' They returned to Barcelona in a boat full of pigs in February 1839.

A few decades later, a British train was conveyed to Palma from Birmingham. 'A railway arrived in Majorca from Birmingham!' exclaimed a Victorian traveller; 'half the romance of the island seems to vanish at the sound!'

In the rest of Spain, houses were constructed low, for the purpose of courting. No family with marriageable girls would think of living in the upper storey of a house, for how would they ever be able to get married? The whole system of *reja* courtship depended upon life on the ground floor. In Palma, things were different, however, and Mr. Graham Bellingham, travelling through the Balearic islands in 1883, observed that 'it seems strange that the courting should be transacted from the pavement in a town where the houses are as high as at Palma, and where the upper storeys only are inhabited. The tender confidences are, of necessity, not whispered but shouted at the pitch of the voice so that the passer-by is entertained during his monotonous walk. The more bashful ones in Palma, however, hit upon a happy expedient. The lady at her window in the upper storey, or the maid for her benefit, bores a hole at the end of the water-pipe; the gentleman bores a hole at his end, nearer the pavement, and with the assistance of this telephone . . . the conversation is transmitted direct to the one ear for which it is intended.

'When we crossed over to Mahón in Minorca we particularly admired the patience of the lovers in that quiet little town and congratulated them when we found that the ground-floor was inhabited instead of the upper, as unfortunately in Palma. At Mahón the lady sits in the room with her mantilla becomingly arranged and a red rose in her hair, the outspread fan helping the expression of her thoughts, while above it her black eyes flash now defiantly now tenderly at the lover who stands on the pavement with the green shutters sometimes drawn round him, the windows here being made English fashion *à la guillotine*, as though on purpose to decapitate clandestine lovers, so that his legs remain visible—usually, I noticed, cased in uniform with a scarlet stripe. In the middle of the day, when everyone else is enjoying the siesta, the stranger may perceive several pairs of legs adding colour to the dim perspective of the street while waiting for the "upper storey" to allow them to proceed.'

What absurd postures lovers adopted! While the lads of Mahón were standing behind their ladies' shutters, their counterparts in Andalusia were prostrate on the ground before the cat-hole in their front door, and the boys of La Mancha wandered about the streets carrying a 'wooing ladder' on their back. The custom of climbing up a ladder to a *novia*'s bedroom was seen by a friend of mine only a few years ago and it may still be extant in out-of-the-way villages of this province.

In Ibiza, until the first decade of the twentieth century, two or three evenings a week were set aside for courting couples. The ritual here was that would-be suitors assembled in the hallway of the girl's house and chatted with her relatives until she made her appearance. The girl then sat on a chair leaving a vacant one beside her which each suitor occupied for the same length of time. If he stayed longer than his allotted courting time, the boys in the queue threw stones at him until he moved off. But if the girl rejected all her suitors, they threw stones at her when she came out from Mass! The official suitor was allowed to talk to the girl at her window and his public recognition was announced by his placing himself at her left hand as she left church on the Sunday after the betrothal.

In the old Ibizan dance called the *curta*, the woman lowered her eyes and moved round with short, slow steps in a figure of eight, pretending to be oblivious of her whirling and leaping male partner. She was supposed to remain as calm as when her would-be suitor announced his intentions by firing a gun into the ground at her feet as they did in Valencia.

The Spanish fondness for repartee was displayed in Ibiza in duets known as *dos de profedi*, sung by men and women who sat opposite one another with their knees touching and beating a drum held between them. This so-called love duet, which they improvised as they went along, was frequently bawdy and even offensive. It was a more modern and dual version of the medieval *cantigas de escarnio* of Galicia. In these remote, uncultured regions, the peasantry, like their fellows in other countries, were inclined to be blusteringly aggressive in their mode of courtship.

In Andalusia, sexual aggressiveness between partners, restrained by their ritual of *reja* courtship, was picturesquely displayed in flamenco dancing with brio and grace. Love songs were the prerogative of the menfolk whose imagination found expression in the traditional *coplas*—familiar, homely, mocking and tender in turn.

Love was always a singing thing in Spain. Poetry and song appear in every province at every stage of courtship up to the wedding ceremony. *Coplas* were invented for every possible contingency, improvised to meet every situation. There were serenading *coplas* and lamenting *coplas*, there were *coplas* for the bride as she left her home for the wedding ceremony, *coplas* for the newly wed couple as they were presented with fruit and flowers at the wedding feast, *coplas* reminding the groom to treat his new wife gently, *coplas* by wedding guests in praise of the good fare they had partaken of . . . endless *coplas*, many still uncollected and moribund owing to the advent of radio and uniformity.

'How delicious were the soups,' sing the wedding guests of Vellillo de Guarde near Palencia, 'they were neither too salty nor insipid; the calves you killed were plump and tender and there were more sausages than we could eat. To all the cooks who prepared the feast we give our hearty thanks, they have made a brave show; to all the lads we would say, "Don't look at the bride any more now she is engaged for life."' Improvised *coplas* on the people present often continued until four in the afternoon.

'Say good-bye, lovely child,' sing the people of the province of León, as the bride is about to leave for church, 'say good-bye to the house of your parents, for this is the last time that you will go out from it as a spinster. Kneel down, child, on the threshold, for your dear parents to bless you before you go.' The old-fashioned custom of a parental benediction is still preserved in many parts of Spain, and when I was there in 1960 I was fortunate enough to secure photographs of this ceremony from the district of Lagartera, near Toledo, where wedding customs are particularly elaborate. This is the most moving part of the proceedings. The Spanish father, dignified and dramatic, plays his role as splendidly as a Shakespearean actor. In parts of Galicia, the only region of Spain where women are in the ascendant, it is often the mother who blesses the young people who are about to be wed.

In the region of the *maragatos,* also near León, the medieval symbolism of the rose is invoked as the bride leaves her parents' house: 'Now the rose is shedding its petals, the rose from the rose-tree, now the girl is leaving the house where she was born. . . .'

'When you take her home,' chant the wedding guests, 'don't treat her like a broom. She was well treated in her house,' and they conclude by wishing the happy pair 'dozens of children and hundreds of mules'. Sometimes, however, the jokes become too bawdy and cause serious quarrels.

In Guadilla de Villamar, near Burgos, the groom is invited to 'esteem his bride' and to 'treat her with love and reverence; they haven't given her to you for a slave, but to be your companion'.

In Huesca, the boys make fun of the wedding presents: 'They gave them a candlestick without a handle to hang it by—they gave them a jar that won't stand up—they gave them a stewing pot with a hole in it and a knife that won't cut. . . .'

When the bride and groom are in bed, the boys sing under their window *coplas* which are usually too salty to be printed. The chastest I heard was the following: 'Now you have her in your arms, treat her tenderly, she who always will be yours, for all eternity.'

The old custom of the 'three nights of Tobias', whereby the newly wed couple were supposed not to consummate their marriage before three days, is recalled in the following *copla*: 'How pleasant the bed looks—even softer is the mattress—but you will not be able to make use of it tonight with your wife.'

'Don't look for a sweetheart at the fair,' says a popular refrain, 'and less so in a *romería*; look for her nearer home, dressed in her everyday clothes.' Nevertheless, these two sources of supply have always been fully taken advantage of by young people. Among the many attractive songs of Galicia are the *foliadas*, sung to the accompaniment of bagpipes and tambourines by young folk walking home from a fair or pilgrimage across the hills.

In stricter Andalusia, young people were more closely supervised; the suitor was obliged to visit his beloved in imagination: 'Ah, were I but a moonbeam, so that I could pass through your window, draw closer and closer and bestow a kiss upon your face.' The moon is the symbol not only of love and fertility but of death, and the Andalusian lover never forgets the association: 'I should like to be the tomb where they will bury you, to be able to hold you in my arms for all time.'

Eyes play an important role in Andalusian *coplas*, with their Islamic memories of veiled women: 'Tomorrow I shall go to church and confess how your black eyes have led me into temptation. . . .' Freckles were admired: 'The heavens are more beautiful when they are filled with stars. . . .'

'I have as many *coplas* in my body as wasps in a nest, struggling to see which one will come out first.' And the *coplista*'s love of wine is not forgotten: 'The guitar demands wine, the strings spirits, and the gay fellow who plucks them young girls from fifteen to twenty.'

The effect produced by a beauty in church is described in many a 'lover's mass', such as this one: 'Those who sang in the choir, got lost in the middle of the *Credo*, the abbot who was saying Mass mixed up the lessons and the little boys who were assisting him, instead of saying amen, amen, said *amor, amor*.'

A number of *coplas* are on the subject of hair. 'Long live fair tresses,' says one, 'long live fair hair, long live those of my *morena* [brunette] which are naturally blonde.' And another one: 'If you have fair hair, don't dye it black, for it is the colour of Jesus' head when he was a child.'

In Salamanca, a rejected lover sings rudely: 'Show yourself at the window—with your face like a fried sardine, you are capable of frightening away the holy souls.' In northern *cantiga de amiga* mood is the *copla*, 'Ay, Mother, they have broken my . . .' 'Daughter, don't tell me what . . .' 'The jar I took to the fountain, Mother; what *did* you think?'

Is sex really worth it, asks a bitter *copla* from Galicia: 'For one hour of fun, nine months of trouble, three weeks in bed and twins to bring up!' Satirical *coplas* on the married state are to be found in every province, from the jealousy of Andalusian husbands: 'Don't call me *salada*, for that will cause trouble; I am newly wed and my husband is jealous,' to the lament of the Andalusian wife: 'My mother-in-law wants to give me crosses for a rosary, but with her son I have not only a cross but a calvary,' and the earthy Galician: 'When you are a spinster you can wear new clothes; when you are married, you have to make do with patched ones.'

'Marriages,' says an Andalusian *copla*, 'are like melons; in every hundred you will only find one good one.' Southern fruits and tastes are used in Andalusian love *coplas*: melons, olives, cinnamon, roses, jasmine, salt and sweets. 'No doubt your father was a confectioner, since he made your lips of caramel'— 'Blessed be your mother, who emptied a salt-cellar in your mouth when she brought you into the world!'

In wooded Galicia, pine trees and chestnuts are love symbols: 'I fell in love with a chestnut tree, I fell in love with a briar; I fell in love with you, sweet child, because you have curly hair. . . .' In the autumn, chestnut parties were held for the young people with a lot of chasing of the girls by the boys and rough romps peculiar to northern peoples.

The chief originality of courtship customs in Spain consists in the prevalence of conversation, as well as *coplas,* in the art of repartee, practised in various degrees and with varying rituals, from the *rejas* of Andalusia to the knee-touching couples of Ibiza and the *parrandeas* of the Gallegans. The verb *parrandear* means to engage in a lively conversation between unmarried couples.

This conversation is not necessarily amorous; it can revolve round almost any topic, but it is a kind of introduction to a girl, a means of getting into her favour by a verbal 'showing-off'.

Parrandeas used to be a feature of village life and many men (and women) were renowned for their conversational talents. The men would go from village to village at fiesta-time, spending three or four hours talking to a girl on a given theme. A good *parrandeador* was never beaten by his interlocutor and he was not permitted to change the theme of the conversation. There were times, of course, when love came into it and the following *copla* alludes to this by saying that 'where there is fire there is smoke, where there is smoke there is fire, where there are *parrandeas* at night there is bound to be affection'.

Spain seems to be the only country where a woman's tongue is admired, even today. In *Málaga Farm*, Marjorie Grice writes: 'A girl who cannot hold her own and be ready with some pointed retort is thought little of by the men. They admire a woman of spirit who can reduce them to silence if need be.' I remember witnessing a young bourgoise accompanied by her servants replying to a ticket-collector at the Atocha station in Madrid. I missed the beginning of the dialogue, in which he must have accused her of some fiddling with her season ticket; all that I and the whole of Atocha station heard was the woman's magnificent self-defence—a philippic, delivered with haughty gestures in impressive tones. The ticket-collector was so entranced by her performance that he ended by listening in silent admiration. When she had finished and 'reduced him to powder' as the Spanish saying goes, she swept off, followed by the tight-lipped maid. The ticket-collector shook his head as he slowly recovered and murmured to us, '*Vaya*—what a woman! Wasn't she splendid? Her husband won't have a chance, though, will he?' He punched our tickets automatically, still dazed, still shaking his head. They talk, these women, with the vivacity and imagery that was so well captured by such diverse authors as those of the *Book of Good Love*, the *Corbacho*, *Tirant lo Blanch*, *La Celestina* and *La Lozana Andaluza*.

At the lowest end of the scale, comes the famous and much discussed *piropo*, or compliment, which is hardly known in the north of Spain. One can hardly call the *piropo* a conversation, since it is addressed by an unknown male passer-by to an unaccompanied female, but in the south it often amounts to a verbal exchange, for the woman can and does answer back with verve.

The lyricism and love of poetry which is the Spaniard's birthright is nowhere more apparent than at country weddings. Even today the traditional songs and customs are observed in out-of-the-way places—and there are still many out-of-the-way places in Spain.

Although I was not fortunate enough to attend a country wedding myself, I met one of the authorities on the Gallegan aspect of the subject, Don Antonio Fraguas Fraguas, who kindly gave me some details about them in the noisy corridors of the secondary school in which he teaches in Santiago de Compostela. It was examination time—his pupils were about to be examined orally in English—and a bustling crowd pressed through the doors of the examination room. The atmosphere was gaily informal. Knots of anxious relatives, mostly feminine, blocked the corridors and eavesdropped on the examinations. There did not appear to be any rule against the presence of parents and relatives while the children were being examined. Nor did the pupils seem to be at all disturbed.

A friend accompanied me. The porters had disappeared and by the time we found Don Antonio he was in the middle of an examination. My friend advanced calmly and began to make signals to him from the door. 'We can't ask him to come out *now*!' I exclaimed. 'Why not?' said my friend calmly. 'He will probably be glad to have a break.'

Don Antonio came out, sat on a stone bench in the *patio* and began to recall rustic weddings and the toast-verses that accompany them. He had a prodigious memory! 'One of the longest toasts I ever heard addressed to the bridal pair,' he said, 'was in 1931, in the parish of Loureiro. It was recited by a man called Bianor Cavaleiro who had been in Brazil for a number of years. It went on for twelve verses,' and he proceeded to recite them. They were in Gallegan, of course, one of the prettiest languages in the world for lyrical poetry.

Señor de Madariaga has pointed out how very often Spanish popular lyrics invoke the soul in their love poems. So do the French, but to a less extent, and the Anglo-Saxons are even more bashful. Perhaps this is because they feel it is sacrilegious to bring the soul into profane love-songs. But the way in which Spaniards speak and sing of the soul is entirely different. One wonders, indeed, what they have in mind when they refer to the soul. I do not believe that they attach much metaphysical significance to the word. They are not given to abstract ideas. No, the way in which it is used in popular verse inclines one to believe that for them *alma* is the quintessence of their being, an organ that beats and feels like the heart only more intensely. Some popular songs, it is true, make a distinction and claim that the soul belongs to God, but on the whole the heart and the soul tend to become confused.

The Ten Commandments have been versified and transformed into the Ten Commandments of the Lover. This is a survival of medieval poems. The version I heard was collected only a few years ago in the district of Pontevedra. The Commandments are sung by the lover to his mistress; he begins by telling her that he will recite them if she gives him leave to do so. Then the paraphrase continues: 'By the first commandment, I am instructed to love you more than my life. By the second commandment I promise never to forget you or remove your image from my heart; to the third I pay little attention when I am in church, because the thought of you fills my breast entirely; the fourth: to my parents I always paid respect and never disobeyed them except when I came and spoke to you secretly. The fifth commandment enjoins me never to kill but I do not know what I would do if I saw another man speaking with you! As for the sixth, I never desired any other woman but you in all my life, oh loved one of my soul! Seventh: I never harmed anybody or lied to anybody except when I went to see you and did not tell my parents. The eighth—I never was a false witness, but what lies they tell to make us quarrel! The ninth: I never coveted a woman in my life, it is only you I desire. And the tenth: I never coveted anybody's property or belongings; there is nothing on earth worth more than you. Lady, these commandments have been composed for lovers and although it may cost me my life, it is you whom I must marry.'

To return from this digression to country weddings. After the rhymed toast, friends of the bridal pair advance and present them with two branches of myrtle decorated with flowers and sweets and these are accepted in verse speeches by the bride and the groom. When the bouquets are placed before them, bride and groom remove a sweet from each one of them and present them to a couple who are either engaged or known to be 'sweet on each

other'. This presentation is accompanied by a verse to the effect
that it is hoped the young persons in question will join the merry
company of the wedded within a year.

In many parts of Galicia, a dance follows executed by the girl
wedding guests and a song called 'Of the *regueifa*'—the latter being
a large loaf decorated with sweets, which one of the girls places
on her head while she dances a jig or *muiñeira*. This custom,
which had almost disappeared, is believed to be a survival of the
Celtic cake which was distributed to guests during wedding
ceremonies. (The distribution of round cakes is still part of the
Moroccan wedding ceremony and is supposed to bring good
luck.)

A custom which has not yet entirely fallen into disuse is the
waiting with a lighted candle for the bridal pair at the threshold
of their new home. The candle is held by one of the relatives and
is probably a survival of the Roman light of Hymen, the fire of
the new hearth.

This may also be considered as a form of introduction of the
bride to the household gods, or the spirit of the ancestors. In
parts of the Pyrenees and the Basque country, the bride was
expected to assist at a Mass for the souls of her new family's
ancestors on the day after the wedding. This idea of continuity,
of the inevitable death that follows life, was observed in the valleys
of Navarre where brides used to be married in black 'because the
state of matrimony begins in mourning and ends in mourning'.
In the valley of the Ansó the father-in-law presented the bride
with her bridal nightdress, which was carefully preserved and
used as a shroud when she died.

11. *Love and Suicide*

IN cities like Madrid and Seville, nineteenth-century love-life followed the general urban pattern of the Romantic Era: suicides and melodrama on the one hand and philandering on the other.

'Mystery and reserve are the two most necessary conditions of love,' wrote Severo Catalina. 'Remove the palpitating interest of curiosity and uncertainty, and love would be transformed into a very common subject indeed.' There were two or three—perhaps more—sensational suicides for love. José de Larra, who shot himself at the age of twenty-seven for the love of a vapid belle, wrote in *El Doncel*: 'There exists a tyrannical love, a love that kills; a love that destroys like a ray of lightning the heart on which it alights. . . .' In his review of Hartzenbuch's play on the medieval lovers who died for love, *Los Amantes de Teruel*, he wrote: 'Sorrows and passions have filled more cemeteries than doctors and fools . . . love kills, although it does not kill everyone.'

Larra's friend, Don López Guijarro, tried to dissuade him from his melodramatic state of mind and reproached him for wasting his life, but it was no use. 'Some people,' replied Larra, 'think that Quixote would be splendid without his madness. . . . I am just as mad about my passion . . . it has entered into my soul like gangrene. It is incurable, so let me be.' A small room is devoted to Larra in the Romantic Museum of Madrid. Among the manuscripts, accounts and bibelots lies the pistol with which he ended his life; or rather, the pistols, for there are two. There is apparently a doubt as to which one of his two pistols Larra used for his suicide and the scrupulously honest curator has decided to exhibit both of them.

The Romantic neurosis is satirized in two pictures by Leonardo Alenzo. In the first, a 'romantic' commits suicide at the feet of his beloved; he is old and ugly, she is a monster, holding a garland with which to recompense—posthumously—the lover about to offer her his life. In the second picture, the 'romantic', attired in a ridiculous night-shirt, throws himself from a cliff. As

107

an extra precaution this lover has taken a dagger with him in case the fall does not prove fatal. In the distance, another suicide case hangs from a tree and a third lies at his feet in a pool of blood.

Among the more obscure Romantics whose names appear in local annals is Don Antonio Cuervo y Fernandez Reguero, a native of Asturias, who after a four-year engagement to a young lady by the name of Rosa Perez Castropol, lost her at the birth of their first child. The disconsolate husband was on business at La Coruña when she died, but when he returned he disinterred the corpse and cut off a lock of its hair. A few days afterwards the peasantry were woken up in the middle of the night by a mournful song coming from the direction of the cemetery. It was Don Antonio, lamenting his wife in a dirge of his own composition, in very 'romantic' vein:

> Solitaria mansion del sepulcro,
> solo en ti mi esperanza se encierra;
> que, perdido de amor, es la tierra
> un abismo de mal para mi. . . .

Between 1800 and 1824, the populace of Madrid was terrified by the nocturnal apparitions of 'Mortal Sin', a brotherhood of the Virgen de la Esperanza, whose members walked through the streets in pairs, enveloped in long cloaks, carrying a lantern, a bell and a leather purse. From time to time they would stop, face each other and wail in a high-pitched, lugubrious tone: 'Do good and say Masses for the conversion of those who are in a state of mortal sin!' Then, ringing a little bell, they would add: 'I advise you on God's behalf to confess your sins if you do not wish to be condemned. If you conceal but one sin and confess a million, you will not obtain pardon.' These scenes, wrote E. Rodriguez-Solis, struck terror into the hearts of all that heard them until, as time went on and familiarity bred malicious contempt, the Madrilenians gathered on their balconies when the hooded men passed their street, threw a few coins and sang home-composed *saetas* on the sins of their neighbours, entreating the brothers to pray for them. The gossip, the laughter, the angry retorts from the accused, eventually put a stop to the visits of 'Mortal Sin'.

One of the greatest lyrical Romantic poets of the end of the century was the Sevillan Gustavo Adolfo Bécquer, to whom a delicious monument has been erected in the most tropical of all European parks: the Parque Maria-Louisa in Seville. Delicious is the only word for this monument built round the trunk of an immense tree, with its figures of ladies in ringlets and crinolines, wringing their hands in despair at the death of their favourite poet.

I must admit to a prejudice against Bécquer from childhood. My mother and my Spanish aunt were Bécquer addicts and they would frequently recite yards of Bécquer in a mournful voice, always with the same funereal tempo and interspersed with heavy sighs. Being in a marked Anglo-Saxon phase at the time and ready to denounce all manifestations of sentimentality, I found Gustavo's verses positively nauseating.

Lines like: 'This was the time of the year when swallows flew without our initials in their beaks,' and, 'Today the earth and the skies smile, today the sun has reached the bottom of my soul; today I have seen her; I saw her and she looked at me, today I believe in God,' irritated me. Years later, however, I realized that Bécquer was a great lyrical poet.

It is not much use asking Sevillan lady passers-by where the archæological museum is to be found, or the Academy of Painting, but even the women who sweep in the park will tell you where the Bécquer monument is located. The poet's remains are buried in a crypt in the university church. The last time that anybody went down there was about thirty years ago, when the German actress Berta Singerman, a great admirer of Bécquer, gave a poetry recital in Seville and insisted upon depositing a bouquet of carnations at the feet of her idol. Joaquín Murube (now Director of the Alcázar) has described the consternation which this caused among the Sevillans, none of whom had ever thought of visiting the crypt before.[1] Murube went on a scouting mission first, assisted by several beadles, after having obtained permission from the town authorities. The entrance to the crypt was a heavy stone in the middle of the church nave. A ladder was produced for the descent, for there were no steps. Murube climbed down a rickety ladder, holding a lighted candle, and hung desperately on to a projecting piece of wall, which turned out to be none other than the leaden box containing the famous poet's remains. The floor of the crypt was damp and muddy and just as Murube was wondering how the stoutish German lady

[1] Joaquín Romero Murube: *Lejos y en la Mano* (1959).

would manage to penetrate into the crypt, noises from above announced her arrival in the company of her South American husband.

One of the beadles dragged an electric cable and bulb as far as the entrance to the crypt and tied it to the top of the ladder. Murube, on his way up, received the bouquet of carnations upon his head. Berta, helped by an anxious group of Sevillans, had already started the perilous descent. Murube climbed down again quickly and pointed to the leaden box. Just as Berta was contemplating the lugubrious scene with delight, the electric light failed and all was plunged in darkness. This was too much, even for Berta, who shrieked hysterically in true feminine Romantic fashion. Murube slipped and fell into the mud but recovered himself in time to help the lady to ascend, no easy feat, as the actress was heavy as well as hysterical. Before leaving the crypt, Murube hastily re-arranged the flowers, which had been scattered in the excitement. 'It was grotesque, ridiculous, nearly comical....' The incident left the Sevillans shaking their grave heads over Teutonic obstinacy.

At the end of the century the Jesuits, who moved in high circles, condemned the immorality and callousness of Spanish aristocracy. In his book *Pequeñeces*, Father Luis Coloma piled on the melodrama in his denunciation of ladies who neglected their children, took lovers and dabbled in political intrigues. He describes whisky-drinking duchesses reclining on chaises-longues, smoking cigars with a fine leather apron to prevent the ash from falling on to their lace frills, and he loudly condemned the libertinage of Spanish youth, whom he curiously described as the products 'of an antithetical union of an Andalusian bull with a Parisian soubrette'.

In her *Memoirs* of an earlier period, the Duchesse d'Abrantes related how the Marquese of Santiago arrived late at Aranjuez for a royal party, in the company of her *cortejo*; 'The marquese apologized by saying that the beauty of the evening had tempted her to take the air in the calle de la Reina. While she spoke, a titter ran through the room for she had but one eyebrow! Finally, the lost eyebrow was discovered to have accidentallly fixed itself on the forehead of the *cortejo*.'

The gardens of Aranjuez were favoured by the amorous king Fernando VII but when the chief of police, Don Trinidad Balboa, in his desire to demonstrate how vigilant he was, told the king that his subjects were alarmed for fear he might catch cold in the damp night air of the gardens, the king was furious and threatened to send him to Ceuta for a change of atmosphere.

12. Naughty Boys and Nice Prostitutes

CONCERN with the morals of Spanish youth was a theme which preoccupied serious writers at the beginning of the twentieth century such as G. Martinez de la Sierra, Dr. Gregorio Marañon and Dr. González Lafora.

Dr. Lafora pointed out that the early sexual experiences of Spanish youth in bordels rendered them incapable of an idealistic, deeply psychological type of love and of a placid, domesticated life. The Spaniard's wife, the 'innocent companion', very often frigid because brought up to believe that sex is sinful, does not satisfy his awakened need for sensual thrills and so he goes back to prostitutes. (Dr. Marañon believed that most female frigidity was due to 'inexpert males'.)

In the twenties, one could read advertisements like the following in the daily papers:

> *Frou-frou*: rubber goods. Gay photographs. Catalogues sent on request. Syphilis, venereal disease? Cured in three ways. Capsules Armengot. In all chemists' shops.

> Young lady, excellent appearance, would housekeep for single gentleman or priest.

> Foreigner, seeks handsome, dark young lady, preferably Andalusian, to accompany him on holiday. Send photographs.

> Star of my soul, suppose you could not manage last night. How I suffer. I adore you in spite obstacles. Coach in that spot awkward. Better behind church, in front sacristy. You know. Till tomorrow, my heart, I cannot live far from your eyes. Please wear sky-blue drawers.

The lack of warm, family domesticity was commented upon by Martinez Sierra in his *Cartas a las Mujeres de España*: 'Do you know what is lacking in Spain, what has always lacked? Have you ever in your childhood read a book which dealt with family intimacy, with domestic union, with the light of the kitchen, with work by lamplight, with studies, with conversations between parents and children, with busy mothers? Have you ever read anything which deals with these genuine pleasures of life in a book written by a Spaniard? I do not believe you have.'

Dr. Marañon, who thought that one of the reasons for the short stature of many southern peoples is their precocious sexual life, declared himself in favour of juvenile continency. 'Youth is the age of love,' he wrote, 'but not the age of libertinage.' Martinez Sierra deplored the way in which Spanish mothers passed over their sons' peccadilloes. 'They who are so severe with their daughters are criminally indulgent towards their sons. They say that it is necessary for youth to spend itself thus, but youth does not pass, youth remains for ever marked in the character of every human being.'

There is no doubt, as Dr. Marañon pointed out, that part of Don Juan's erotic power over women was due to his caddishness. This is still true, and not only in Spain.

In countries where the sexes are as strictly segregated as in Spain, man's supposed knowledge of an amorous world into which decent women can never penetrate gives them a picaresque aura of sinister romance. A man who had not had such experiences and adventures would most likely be looked down upon by his intended fiancée. It was all a great hoax, of course. Neither partner could ever be really satisfied: neither the woman who discovered brutality in her man, nor the man who would only marry an inexperienced virgin.

The aftermath of many a marriage must have been bitter indeed. No wonder that sex has always been depreciated in Spain! They have spurned its subtleties and links with the psyche; they have turned away from it in disgust—a disgust greater than that professed by the hypocritical Puritans of England and America. When the Spaniard turns away in disgust, I believe that he is being sincere. Not so the Anglo-Saxon. The Spaniard, disappointed and disillusioned in his passions, either becomes a sensational convert, like the original Don Juan and his many successors, or the insatiable Don Juan portrayed in art and literature sinking ever lower in the life of a roué who at bottom is a woman-hater.

Man's fear of and dependence upon woman is very marked in Spain, as it is in all countries where sensuality is developed at the expense of the spirit. Is this one of the factors that has prevented these countries from progressing? The womanly woman is more of a danger to man than the emancipated woman and in Spain, where women have been—still are to a great extent—intolerant and narrow-minded, they impose their intransigence and meannesses upon their menfolk.

'When woman is ennobled, educated and emancipated, she automatically loses that mysterious spell with which she subordinates the virile spirit to her own ends,' wrote Dr. Marañon. 'Therefore I want women to rise up in revolt because I know that, when they triumph, men too will be completely emancipated.' There would seem to be some truth in this. I have often remarked that the women in orthodox Muslim countries (whose ancestral influence still permeates much of Spain) not only dominate the men at home, but subjugate them sensually.

In these homes, whatever the men may say outside, the woman triumphs. As soon as the woman goes out to work, man begins to free himself from her wiles and woman herself puts on a different face. But when this face becomes too detached, too severe, man may have to turn for his sensual satisfaction to the professionals of Venus.

Marriage and its subsequent responsibilities often transform a charming, spontaneous girl into a dominating matron, a house priestess with whom one would not dare to enjoy sexual relations. This has often occurred in Spain where women are passive, and frequently devoid of a sense of humour in their relations with their menfolk. The fiancée who used to banter archly with her *novio* is suddenly petrified into the commonly accepted 'ideal' of a spouse, and the laughter-loving Spaniard is presented with a fresh pretext for excursions into more yielding arms. 'Do you know,' enquired Martinez Sierra, 'why "bad women" often occupy part of the lives of men who are not at all bad in themselves? Simply because they know when to laugh.' The 'bad woman' is not just a 'sex machine', but a woman with whom a man can jest without having to censor his language or his thoughts.

I have mentioned the freedom of language that exists between the young—and even the not-so-young—of both sexes in Spain, but this freedom, which so many foreigners have commented upon with surprise, does not seem to apply today and certainly not to the wedded. Many Spanish husbands, especially in Castile and Andalusia, told me that they do not and could not talk freely upon intimate subjects in front of their wives. Perhaps they would not even want to. The prostitute and the boon companion at the tavern are his safety valves. It is not surprising that the tavern should be the meeting-place of the two tongue-looseners *par excellence*: alcohol and the prostitute. Virtuous Spanish women, like virtuous women everywhere, speak of the prostitute with disgust and contempt, but men are inclined to be not only tolerant, which is understandable, but sympathetic. Many men, in different parts of Spain, referred to them with genuine affection. Is the Spanish prostitute different, then, from her counterparts in other countries?

On the whole, I believe that she is. Apart from a few mercenary prostitutes and ministers' courtesans, Spain finds room for warm-hearted girls who are either too sensual for the national code, too poor to support themselves, or who, having transgressed once, have been rejected by bourgeois society and thrown out of their homes. This applies particularly to rigid Castile. The qualities, the national characteristics, come out even in these supposedly lowest of creatures. They are generous to the point of refusing money from lovers who happen to be out of work; they do not hurry their clients away; they sympathize with their clients' predicaments.

'And what are you in here for?' asked a prisoner during the Civil War of a woman who was sweeping up the path outside his cell. 'For being a whore,' she replied simply. 'Then come over here,' he said jocularly. Shaking her head, the self-confessed *puta* retorted: 'No, you can't do that here, but when I have finished sweeping, I shall come and give you a kiss between the bars.' (Incidentally, Spanish whores do not seem to object to kissing on the mouth to the same extent as their French and Anglo-Saxon colleagues.)

'I felt so sorry for the man I had last night,' a prostitute from a port in the north of Spain confided to me. 'He is a sea captain and newly married. I have known him for some time but nothing ever happened between us. He just liked my company and my jokes. But last night in his cabin, after dinner and a little more wine than usual, he succumbed. Immediately after, he thought of his wife and burst into tears. It was the first time he had been unfaithful to her. He threw himself on to his bunk and was quite inconsolable. I felt really sorry for him. I could quite understand how he felt. I slipped out very quietly and left him. He is such a nice person.'

Rigid as virtuous Spain may be on the question of women's purity, one does occasionally hear of exceptions which raise the eyebrows of even those people who think they know her well. A police inspector in Madrid told me of one case he knew personally. A young man, a supporter of Franco, chased by the Reds, took refuge in the apartment of the prostitute he used to consort with. She hid him in a cellar and looked after him all the time he was in danger. Suspected of harbouring an enemy, she was arrested and put to the wall by a firing squad. After a first shot in the air to intimidate her she was asked to reveal where she had hidden him but she refused point blank. To the credit of the firing squad, be it said that not one man could bring himself to fire at her. A few weeks later, the same performance was repeated by another squad. Still she refused to reveal her secret.

After the Civil War, when life returned to normal, the young man's mother sought her out and implored her to marry her son. 'He could never find a better wife,' she said. This lady came of a distinguished family but she did not hesitate to accept a 'common prostitute', who happened to be an uncommon woman. Or was she? One hears so many tales of devoted Spanish women who sacrificed their lives for their menfolk that one wonders whether this woman was such an exception. On the other hand, it may be argued that a Spanish woman loves no one more than her son and that the grateful Madrilenian mother looked upon the prostitute as her son's saviour, regardless of her calling, and was therefore prepared to sacrifice her dearest principles for his happiness as a mark of gratitude. That is possible.

But what of the Sevillan *señorito* who only a few years ago ravished a prostitute, had her educated in a Paris convent, and two years later introduced her to his aristocratic family as his legitimate wife? He married her in Paris and the family were presented with the *fait accompli*, which they accepted graciously. The new wife was charming, beautiful and polished. She is now one of the most respected members of the leading women's church organizations in Seville and nobody knows or, if they do, they have conveniently forgotten, that she was once the notorious 'Angelita' of the bordel of Rosalita la del Cura. (The latter was said to be the daughter of a village priest.) I was told that at least five prostitutes have married into the upper classes of Sevillan society in this century.

II

1. *From the* Rías *to the Mountains*

OUTSIDE France and Italy, most people's reactions to an interest in love as a serious subject of investigation is extremely mixed. I would not say that the Spaniards' reaction is the same as the English who, as I have described in *Love and the English*, treat the subject either as 'dirty' or a joke. The average Spanish attitude is severe or reserved. An embassy official to whom I wrote for introductions to people in Spain replied that in his opinion the subject was too 'frivolous'. The Catalan director of a cultural institute was more helpful. The Catalans, being nearer 'Europe', that is France, have the reputation of being broader-minded.

Surveys, results of questionnaires, sociological investigations, all these are available to a certain extent in France and England, but in Spain, where everything remains to be done, a tremendous vacuum confronted me. What could I do? Obviously, the first thing was to go and probe for myself. But how would I be received? And who could or would give me information? The two most reliable sources of information, it seemed to me, would be doctors and confessors, but would they talk to me?

What follows is an account of my 'search for love' in contemporary Spain. I do not presume to have covered all the ground—not even half of it—all I can hope to have brought back is a flavour, a very special flavour, different from that of France and England, a flavour which may soon disappear with the rest of what we consider as typically Spanish: the Cretan bullfight, the Italian serenade, the Iberian mantilla and the Andalusian *piropo*.

I decided to begin my travels in Galicia, for the good reason that, having already written one book about that fascinating region, I had excellent friends there, who were only too pleased to be able to help. The Gallegans, who have a Celtic and northern tenacity and loyalty, are among the few Spaniards—the Catalans excepted—who actually reply to letters and *do* things for their friends even when the latter are far away. The average Spaniard, by whom I mean the Spaniard of Castile and the southern Spaniard, is like the Oriental; he will welcome you with open arms, go to a great deal of trouble to be of assistance while you are on the spot and visible to the naked eye but, when this vision fades, only a catastrophe will shake him out of his mental lethargy. The vitality of the Spaniard is deceiving as well as exhausting; having spent himself talking, walking, gesticulating, smoking, he has no energy left for the things of the spirit and even less for writing to absent friends.

The overland journey to Galicia is tedious and involves two nights in trains. The first night in *wagons-lits* from Paris to Irun is noisy but tolerably comfortable; the second night, in a battered old train picked up at that most desolate of railway stations, Ventas de Baño, on its way from Barcelona to Vigo, is a nightmare. No sleepers, no *couchettes*, but plenty of talkative fellow-passengers, who are very useful to seekers after local information.

Ventas de Baño was a dead loss. The only person I could speak to there was the railway porter and he disappeared very quickly to attend to his little plot of land on the slope of a hill, from which he returned late in the afternoon, soaked to the skin—for there had been a rainstorm—when it was time to convey my luggage to the train bound for Vigo. Before he left me, lunching solitarily in the depressing railway *fonda*, he told me that he had five children to work for and that even his two sources of income, porterage and agriculture, could not suffice to bring them up properly. His wife worked too and the eldest daughter looked after the younger members of the family.

In most parts of Spain life is still so hard, and men have to work so long at so many varied jobs, that love is a luxury few can afford. For them, love *is* a 'frivolity' for which they have no time. The porter at Ventas de Baño was concerned lest he should lose a day's work and his family would go hungry. His lumbago was getting worse. Last winter he was laid up for a couple of weeks. Somebody had told him that wonderful pills were sold in England to cure rheumatism and lumbago. Was it true and would I send him some? With his tongue out he scrawled his name and address in my notebook. The raindrops fell slowly on to the floor of the *fonda* from his cap, and his worn jacket exuded a smell of wet fields and poultry dung.

The twenty-two-year-old girl from Bilbao who entered my compartment on the way to León had just spent two years in Belgium and she insisted on speaking to me in French with an

atrocious and highly comical Spanish accent, accompanied by
Spanish gestures. I asked her whether the men in that city were
handsome. She was short, but she raised herself on her toes,
threw her head back and lifted her right arm in a theatrical
gesture: '*Ah, sí, sí. Ils sont très guapos et très grands.*' She did
admit, however, that the men of her native province, Asturias,
were rather too fond of the bottle and of going off on their own
in gangs to spend the evening drinking with male companions.
'In the last few years, we have begun to go out to cafés to drink
with them,' she told me. Whether this will result in more interest
being taken in women by the men, or more interest in drinking by
the women, remains to be seen.

'I have a theory,' I said to her, 'that heavy drinkers make poor
lovers and that beer, in particular, is a drink that makes for poor
conversation. Perhaps it is the combination of northern characteristics plus beer that gives these uninteresting results. Wine-
drinkers like the French and the Andalusians are witty in speech
and in their courting.' The girl from Bilbao fixed her dark eyes
thoughtfully on my face and nodded gravely. 'It is true,' she
replied, 'our Asturian men are not very subtle in their conversation with women. But they say that the Andalusians talk a lot but
do nothing, so. . . ?' She raised her shoulders and eyebrows
interrogatively.

There was no dining-car on the train but at León a ten-
minute stop gave us time to rush across to the station *fonda* and
buy giant 'sandwiches' which are not really sandwiches at all but
crusty rolls cut in two and filled with greasy ham or strong
garlic sausage. Three men got into our compartment and watched
us eating. 'Would you like some?' we asked them, making an
offertory gesture of half a sandwich, as was expected of us. They
declined politely but asked me how much the sandwiches had
cost. I told them and they remarked that it was cheap. I agreed.
Thereafter I directed the conversation, with the utmost caution,
towards the object of my journey.

The introduction was facilitated by the most rustic in appearance of the three men, who told us that he was going to southern
France to help in the vineyards. 'It's good pay but as we can't
bring it back we spend it in France,' he said. 'I shall work in the
grape harvest for one week and spend the second week having a
good time in Paris.' I ascertained that he had a wife and two children, who never went on holiday. 'A man has to get away from

home sometimes,' he said with a half-apologetic, half-guilty look in our direction.

The other two men were employed on the national railways. They came from the mountains of León where ancient courtship customs are still to be found in isolated villages and they did not mind talking about them.

'Do you know about the mock marriages of Rosales?' asked one of the men. 'On the last night of the year, the night of St. Sylvester, the young people get together and two lists of names are drawn up, one for the boys and one for the girls. Then the names are cut into separate strips, mixed up in two bowls and called out—that's to say, each boy in turn chooses a strip from the girls' basin. The couples brought together in this way are elected sweethearts for a whole year. Oh, it doesn't mean anything serious—just that they are supposed to dance together on New Year's day, they can joke together a little more freely than with others, and the boy has to give her a present for Epiphany. . . . It's true though,' he added, 'that these mock engagements often result in a real wedding.' 'And it's also true,' interrupted his companion, 'that they can and do result in broken engagements, because when a boy who is already engaged gets a mock *novia*, the real one becomes jealous and there's a row. I've known it to happen many a time.'

'There's a funny belief in Rincon de Olivedes, near Logroño,' said the first man, scratching his nose thoughtfully. 'I worked there once and I was invited to a First Communion party. At church the children are separated and stand before the altar, boys on the right and girls on the left. When they are about to receive the sacrament, the priest's server calls on a boy and a girl to kneel at the altar; he doesn't call them in any special order, just at random. This is called a *suerte* and it is said that the little couples who kneel together like this will later be joined in matrimony. But I don't know whether it really leads to it or not. It might have done in the old days, when most marriages were decided by parents who wanted to increase their children's inheritance. Maybe they pressed a few coins into the server's hands before the ceremony so the *suerte* looked like being a question of chance when it was really pre-arranged. Like that the children would get used to the idea and not go roving when they grew up.'

'Yes, I suppose that many of these mock courtship and wedding customs were a form of rebellion on the part of the young,' said the other man, 'and now that there's no more need for them, they are dying out. I've heard of a mock wedding ceremony that's played like a game by boys and girls somewhere near La Coruña —I forget where exactly. The young folk build an imaginary church out of acacia branches, one of them plays the role of priest and the others caper about pretending to be devils and turning the pages of his breviary as he recites the marriage service. Everything is turned topsy-turvy. When the "priest" asks the "bridegroom" whether he accepts the "bride" for his wife, he answers "Yes, *señor cura,* I'm quite agreeable, but only for a little time," and so it goes on.'

The girl from Bilbao looked shocked. 'That doesn't sound very proper,' she remarked. 'I'm sure the priests don't approve—do they know that that goes on?' she asked. The men exchanged amused glances. 'Village priests are tolerant in Galicia,' said the first. 'Oh, very,' said the second, winking significantly. Do you know that popular refrain: 'When the carnation is born it is called *claveliño.* In the same way the priest's children call him *señor tío* (uncle). (This curious form of quatrain, with the vague and not always clear connexion between the first and second verses, is also found in the Far East, especially in Indonesia.)

'The town priests are more rigid,' said the man who was going to the grape harvest. 'They wouldn't approve of the mountain people's way of courting in the mountains of León.' We encouraged him to tell us more and he began to describe the local 'bundling' custom, which seems to be peculiar to people of Celtic or Iberian strain. In any case, it is a development which could not have taken place in a warm climate!

'Where I come from,' said the rustic, 'it's the custom for unmarried girls, once they reach the age of fifteen, to bring their beds down to the ground floor.' The girl from Bilbao opened her eyes wide. 'This is so she can receive her suitors. She wraps herself in the top sheet and when her suitor comes he lies on the bed beside her, with the blankets covering both of them. The girl remains undressed but the boy keeps all his clothes on.' 'And then what happens?' asked one of the other men, after a pause. 'Nothing,' replied the rustic casually. 'They talk.' 'How very extraordinary!' exclaimed the girl from Bilbao. 'You are not pulling our leg?' 'Of course not,' he said indignantly. 'It's quite a well-known custom—at least, I thought it was.' 'Not round our way,' said the girl from Bilbao primly. 'Your province isn't all that innocent,' teased one of the other men. 'If you lived in the country you'd soon find that out. In the summer months when the girls are sent up to look after the cattle, they receive their suitors in their little mountain huts. The girl sits on the bed, even lies on it, and very often girl and boy spend the night together. The first suitor to arrive and be welcomed leaves his gun outside—a warning to possible rivals.' 'I think I have heard sermons preached against that sort of thing,' mused the girl from Bilbao. 'I'm not surprised,' laughed the first man.

'I know of a similar custom near León but that one only applies to engaged couples. My grandmother told me about it once, I don't think it's kept up any more,' said the rustic. 'As soon as a couple are formally engaged, the girl opens her door to her *novio* when he comes courting and they talk together in a dark room; she lies on the bed and he sits beside her, wrapped in a blanket, with his arms resting on the bed.' 'That doesn't sound too good—restless hands can do a lot of damage,' remarked one of the men. The girl from Bilboa silenced him with a virginal frown.

'There are chaste customs too,' she observed. 'I know that until quite recently, in Trives, Asturias, on the eve of a wedding the mother-in-law used to wrap the bride in a sheet, put her to bed and sit the groom by her side. There, with a flagon of cider by his chair, he would spend the night watching over the bride by candlelight, in the presence of his mother.' 'That sounds more like a form of torture,' observed the rustic.

When the men went out to smoke and chat in the corridor, the girl from Bilbao leant over confidentially and whispered in my ear: 'An awful lot of philandering goes on, you know. We have a saying that goes: "Now that it's happened, it's happened, lass, don't worry; and since it's happened, God will set things right"— but He doesn't you know. And then what? Many's the girl that has had to set a straw doll on the bridal path.' 'I don't know that expression—could you explain it?' I asked her. The girl from Bilbao smiled enigmatically. 'Don't you? Oh well, that's got to do with another custom—a country custom. When a girl has had a child by a boy in another village from her own and he leaves her and marries someone else, the bridal pair may stumble across a rag or straw doll as they come out of church, and as they walk along together in procession they may find yet another doll in the middle of the path. The bride knows what *that* means—it's a reminder from the abandoned mother. . . . Many's the bride that has wept on the marriage night.'

'And what about the women? Are they always faithful?' I asked. 'I remember a popular song that laments for sailors because their wives have found other husbands in their absence. But perhaps that is mere calumny. I remember two sailors' wives I met in the coastal village of Corme in Galicia; they were anxious enough to see their captain husbands who had been away at sea for several weeks. The wives had travelled by bus from Muros, quite a distance, after having had word that their husbands, who were both on the same coaster, would be stopping at Corme where they would pick them up and take them to Bilbao. The two women were given the room opposite mine in the one and only *fonda*, where they snored loudly enough in their little twin beds to keep me awake until four o'clock in the morning, by which time the jolly sailors their husbands came marching up the street from the harbour arm in arm and singing at the top of their voices, in search of their spouses.

'When they reached the *fonda*, they began to bang and shake the front door. After a little while the proprietor, Señor Garrido, padded downstairs, unbolted the front door and let them into the wine-shop, where he had to use all his cunning (as he confided to me the next morning) to prevent the sailors from storming the stairs to go up to sleep with their wives. Patiently and firmly Señor Garrido explained that it would be quite impossible for them to exercise their conjugal rights, because the two wives were sharing the only room available. He therefore suggested that it would be better for them to return to their ship, after a convivial *copita* on the house, and return to take their wives aboard with them at a more reasonable hour. After three noisy rounds of white wine the sailors staggered down the street and Señor Garrido went back to his room.'

(A less fortunate seaman arrived home unexpectedly in the middle of the night to find his wife in bed with another man. Her bold Gallegan reaction was to sit up in bed and shout: 'All right, go and tell the whole village if you like!' Needless to say, he preferred to remain silent.)

'It must be difficult for the women whose husbands emigrate to South America and stay away for years at a time,' observed the girl from Bilbao. 'More women go nowadays, of course, and recently unmarried women have been emigrating too. I suppose that most of those that stay behind remain faithful but there are cases, of course. . . .'

Yes, there are cases. And who would blame the healthy, lusty women of Galicia for succumbing occasionally to temptation? Do their men remain faithful to them when they are away? The Vigoese writer, Alvarez Blázquez, told me that he had recovered an emigrant's notebook which his grandson has been on the point of throwing away. The book was an odd mixture of accounts and a terse diary starting from the time that the emigrant returned from Buenos Aires to his native village to find that his family had increased since his departure by one adulterous unit. The accounts revealed that he had saved a considerable sum, enough with which to buy land and a bigger farm and more livestock when he came back. But the pride in his achievements was shattered by the bitterness of the homecoming, a bitterness that grew instead of diminishing with the years, developing into a hatred of his wife that found expression in odd resentful comments inserted between the daily accounts which he kept doggedly until the day before he died. His unfaithful wife had died two years before him. It was characteristic of Gallegan peasant mentality that the ex-emigrant should have commented, after having entered his wife's death upon his ledger, that 'she even cheated me over the price of a cow, once'.

No soothing superstition seems to have been invented to explain away additions to the family in the husband's absence, as is the case in North Africa, where the useful theory of 'the sleeping child'—a child allegedly produced by the absent husband, lies dormant in the womb for one, two or more years. This face-saving device, while not always believed in, prevents malicious neighbourly comment.

At daybreak a little bunch of black-clad Gallegan peasants climbed into the train. They were accompanying two young relatives to Vigo to see them off overseas. The women were large, steatopygous as primitive goddesses, matriarchal, self-confident. Beside them, the men looked cowed and of secondary importance. The women stolidly contemplated the rain lashing against the windows. A mist rose from the *rías* out of which shadowy pine trees emerged as softly as in a Japanese print. The grain stores with thatched roofs, raised on stone columns, resembled Balinese house-temples and heightened the far-eastern atmosphere, but the temperature was northern.

The women had that calm, stoical attitude of mothers who have borne many children and achieve plenitude only when they are surrounded by the warm, living flesh of their progeny: sons especially. For them, the son is more important than the husband, and after him the grandson. The women live longer than their menfolk but widows seldom re-marry. They are wrapped up in their family affairs; sex, to them, is a youthful fever. It is not dignified for women to be interested in such things once they have married and youth is over.

These women make sacrifices and the men know it. The Gallegans have always honoured their women, and their women have always been freer than the rest of their countrymen. Only two years ago a statue representing 'the emigrant's wife' was put up in the little harbour of Pontevedra, facing the beautiful *ría* of that name. It was put up by the people, for the people. Few tourists ever see it, because it has been placed far from the town centre on a little promontory where the fishermen's cottages are bunched together protectively at the edge of the tides. The granite woman is dressed as a Gallegan peasant in a short skirt, with a scarf round her head. She gazes out to sea with a typical expression of courage, resignation and veiled sadness; a dove stretches its wings and prepares to take flight from her cupped hands. The sculptor has made no attempt to beautify or feminize the squat figure with thick calves and ankles. She is real, earthy and Gallegan, quite unlike the sinuous, dancing figure of the 'typical Spanish woman'—the flamenco dancer of the south in mantilla and flounces. The psychology is different too. In Galicia the 'typically Spanish' cult of virginity and female chastity is far from being as rigid and severe as in other parts of Spain. This laxity or natural way of looking at things, whichever one likes to call it, extends to the rural clergy who are far from being exemplary celibates. The increases *in absentia* of emigrants' families are often, rightly or wrongly, attributed to the village priest.

Although I could not find statistics on the subject, it is a well-known fact that the incidence of illegitimacy is fairly high in Galicia, but this relates to unmarried women rather than to wives whose husbands are overseas; moreover, the presence of illegitimate children does not hamper the woman's chances of marriage to another man, if and when she separates from the father of her child or children. A lapse from virginity does not prevent the woman from becoming a faithful and devoted wife.

For purely practical reasons, infidelity is not easy of achievement even in the case where temptation exists. In the country, where everybody knows one another, clandestine liaisons are out of the question. The watchful neighbours see to that. It is they, rather than the clergy, who are the real guardians of morals. And then, the average Gallegan peasant woman has so much hard work to do—she works like a *moujik* and looks like one too—that she has no time for sex as an extra-marital pastime. This mother of many children has enough to cope with in her own husband's demands. Marriage transforms her into the spiritual as well as the material centre of her home and family. She becomes a hearth goddess respected by all.

The Gallegan peasant woman who has had an illegitimate child is not chased from home as she probably would be in Castile. She is honoured as a mother and not, as in Castile, dishonoured as a woman. The concept of 'honour' as it is known and practised in the rest of Spain, where Islamic and Christian ideals have combined to attach such a great importance to purity of blood, has never appealed to the more rational and compassionate Gallegan soul.

The pride, independence and self-sufficiency of the Gallegan peasant woman is well illustrated by the following story, which was told to me in Santiago by a friend of a professor at the university. This professor had been brought up by his peasant mother. He was illegitimate, and his father was a *señorito* of an aristocratic family; the birth was no accident, but had been deliberately planned by the mother, who wished to have a son, a talented as well as a handsome son. Having observed the local *señorito* for some time, she decided that he was the very person to provide her with what she wanted. He was good-looking, upright, intelligent and well-mannered. Boldly—the Castilians would no doubt say immodestly—she went up to the *señorito* one day as he was riding through her parents' fields and put the proposition to him. It is a pity that the actual words of the dialogue have not been preserved. The peasant girl was well-built and handsome, and the *señorito* was happy to oblige her. The one, and only, experiment proved entirely satisfactory and the girl became pregnant.

A couple of months later, the *señorito*, who had enjoyed the experiment, came up to her suggesting a repetition of it. The peasant girl looked at him in astonishment. 'That would never

'An Offer' by Beguel

'A Romantic Suicide' by Alenzo

'The Soldier and the Lady' by Goya

'A Scene by the Manzanares' by Goya

'Horseback' by Sorolla

do,' she said, 'it would be immoral. I am going to have a child by you—that is what I wanted. I do not wish to commit a sin.' The *señorito*, amazed at her attitude, did not press his suit but, after thinking the matter over, asked her to marry him. Again he met with a refusal. 'It would not work,' said the peasant girl candidly. 'I am not educated. Our social status is different, there would be trouble between our families. No, it would not work and we should not be happy.' 'Then let me at least help to provide for our child,' he implored her. She shook her head. 'I can bring him up myself,' she retorted. And so she did. Her son was extremely attached to her; he recounted the tale of his unusual birth with pride and affection for the mother who had sacrificed so much for him. I doubt whether this would or could have happened in any other part of Spain.

The roughest and wildest-looking boys are greatly attached to their mothers, even those I saw in the reformatory school of Pontevedra (admirably directed by Señor Manuel Filgueïra González, who is very obviously liked and respected by all the boys, many of whom continue writing to him for years after they leave). These young delinquents or children in need of care are often very brutal when they first arrive, Señor Filgueïra told me. Their tendency to break things is catered for in a workshop allocated for this purpose—anything may be broken so long as it is mended by the boy who did the damage!

A ten-year-old boy had been placed in the school temporarily while his mother, a Castilian nurse, looked for work. He expressed such an intense hate for his mother that the director took him in hand and gently questioned him to find out the cause. Little by little it transpired that the mother had been sent away from her bourgeois home when she had her son—who was illegitimate. The child had heard about the scenes that had taken place between his mother and her parents before they were sent away, and his resentment, accentuated by his having been 'abandoned', as he thought, had made him turn against his mother. Señor Filgueïra explained to him the facts of life and Spanish society as simply as he could. Soon afterwards the boy's mother married one of her patients, who was prepared to recognize the child, and so the story had a happy ending for all concerned. The new father, by the way, was a Gallegan.

Another lad from a nearby village believed that his mother had denounced his delinquency to the police and had him sent to the reformatory school. He began to have fits and bouts of depression which disappeared after Filgueïra had assured him that his mother loved him and had not informed the police.

When we come to the bourgeoisie, the picture changes completely and we meet all the conventions and prejudices which are to be found in this class not only in Spain but in other countries as well, although in Spain perhaps more so.

In the questionnaire which I circulated among university students in Santiago,[1] I asked the boys whether or not they would marry a girl who was no longer a virgin. The replies varied but the 'doubtfuls' were in the majority. One sensed that they did not like the idea even though the most modern elements among them admitted that their attitude was a little old-fashioned. Typical answers were: 'Perhaps, if I was very much in love, I might marry her just the same'—'I wouldn't like it'—'It would be an impediment'—'If she had lost her virginity with *me*, then it would be all right and I would marry her'—'It depends on each individual case, one cannot decide beforehand'—'It is difficult to generalize, I could only make up my mind when confronted by an actual case.' A few of the younger boys, aged seventeen and eighteen, were cynical enough to doubt whether there were any virgins left and they implied that they would be presented with the *fait accompli* whether they liked it or not! A number of older boys replied that they would marry the girl and a student from Barcelona added: 'Why not? I am not an Arab!'

An eighteen-year-old student commented: 'Gabriel y Galán, may God forgive him, wrote: "Do you see that beautiful object which smells so badly? That is a young girl who has lost the virtue of modesty." When I heard an uncle of mine, who is a priest, recite that verse a few years ago I believed that an unmarried woman who had lost her virginity was an object of indignity. Now that I have begun to use my brain a little more, I think that my uncle stressed the two last lines of the verse somewhat unnecessarily.'

One still comes across men who like women to be 'pure', that

[1] I used questionnaires to save young people from the embarrassment of having to reply verbally to intimate questions, and to enable them to ponder over their answers. It was unfortunately impossible to obtain replies from a wide cross-section of the population, so that no attempt has been made in the following pages to draw up any of those intriguing charts, complete with carefully worked out percentages, that appear in solid sociological works.

is ignorant to the point of not knowing how babies are born. So it was with great glee that Don Federico told a friend of his that his wife, until after she was married, believed that babies emerged from the anal passage. He was delighted to be able to report this 'proof of his wife's innocence', as my friend put it. This man was an architect. Meeting him in the ordinary way, one would never have believed it possible that he could entertain such notions.

These phenomena are found in all provinces. 'I knew a Basque industrialist in Madrid,' said a friend of mine, 'young, newly wed, so obsessed by the notion of sin and with such a horror of the dangers of concupiscence, that he never had sexual intercourse with his wife before previously wrapping her up in a sheet, into which a hole was carefully cut for procreative purposes.' (This custom, incidentally, was practised in France until the nineteenth century.) One wonders what the wife thought of such a strange procedure. Could she have believed that it was normal?

Sexual education is far from being perfect anywhere, but in Spain, to date, the issue has been evaded with even more ostrich-like *naïveté* than elsewhere, although the problem exercises the imagination of a few doctors, teachers, and the younger generation of confessors.

Most of the students, who were asked about this in the questionnaire I circulated, replied that in their opinion their sexual education had been 'disastrous'. Most of the boys had learned the facts of life from other boys, some at the age of eight or nine, others as late as thirteen or fourteen. It is impossible to generalize from the variety of answers given to this question except to point out that quite a number of students aged from nineteen to twenty-two volunteered the information that they were virgins. This state of affairs exists also in Catalonia and Andalusia. The present generation is less obsessed and precocious about sex than their fathers were at their age, but nobody could explain why. On the other hand, two or three youngsters of fifteen admitted to having had intercourse with girl students of their own age; one of them added rather charmingly: 'I was initiated by a little dressmaker a few years older than myself. I must say that she was very sweet.' Two or three boys between eighteen and twenty had had recourse to prostitutes.

As for girls, their replies were on the whole shorter, more evasive, far more conventional, with a few notable exceptions. They said that their mothers had given them their sexual education at the age of twelve or thirteen; a few of them made the same sort of remarks as the boys—that it had been insufficient, that it was not clear enough, that it did not arm them sufficiently for their entry into the world and contacts with the masculine half of humanity. But the majority of the girls knew very little and were afraid to probe more deeply for fear of sinning against the eleventh commandment: 'Thou shalt not know nor take an interest in sex.'

University girl students with whom I spoke both in Galicia and in Catalonia admitted that their conventional upbringing was to blame for their ignorance and fear of the subject. Since their mothers had been brought up in the same way, the attitude had been perpetuated. (Circulating questionnaires in convent schools was sometimes accomplished on an almost clandestine basis. One girl was afraid that the Mother Superior would object to her filling in a questionnaire about love and sex, and she asked me to telephone her companions in another convent to make sure that the envelope left for them in the hall had actually reached them and not been confiscated. 'Why,' she said, 'when I received a telegram from my *novio* announcing his forthcoming visit to Santiago, the Mother Superior was shocked because he concluded with the word *abrazos* [embraces].')

'Most of the thoughtful girl students realize that there are sexual problems, that we don't know enough about them, and that these questions are discussed more openly in Europe,' said one girl student who had studied in Galicia and in Barcelona, 'but we don't do anything about it. We never reach any conclusions.' (It is remarkable how often the Spaniards refer to Europe as to another and quite different part of the world; in this they are partly right, of course, but one feels that they should begin to get out of this habit after so many centuries of mental isolation.)

'In any case,' added the girl student from Barcelona, 'there would not be much point in carrying our discussions further, for two good reasons: firstly, most girls want to marry and any form of sexual liberty would gravely prejudice their chances; secondly, the enormous pressure exercised by society, our family and religion, which culminates in the ideal of "feminine honour" and chastity, has a tremendous influence on our mental development.'

I had the temerity, since birth control and family planning are forbidden by the Catholic Church, to ask the students what they thought about it. All the girl students were horrified at the suggestion and declared that it was 'criminal' or 'inhuman'. Two of them thought that 'it might be a good thing for humanity so long as it did not interfere with the teachings of the church'. What are the teachings of the church? As far as I could gather, they have edged forward sufficiently to advocate, to a chosen few, the very fallible Ogino method. The inefficacy of this method is so obvious that in Madrid the children born in spite of these precautions are referred to familiarly as the *Oginitos* (a play on the diminutive for children, *hijitos*). One young doctor in Madrid told me that his confessor allowed him to use a sheath provided that it was pierced before use with a needle, so that it could not be said that the conception was being completely prevented, this being forbidden by the church!

Most of the male students were also against birth control as being contrary to religious principles, but a few agreed that it would be a good thing and that it was senseless to allow poor people to bring fourteen and more children into the world when they could not support them.

When these boys marry girls who have been brought up in convents, they will probably have to give in to their wives' ideas on the subject. Incidentally, it is difficult to determine just how 'religious' the students are. I was told that a questionnaire was circulated among them officially some two or three years ago; the results were so disturbing that they were never published. They revealed a good deal of cynicism and church-going merely for 'what people would say if they didn't' and the harm it might do them at the university, where ecclesiastical influence is predominant. On the other hand, I have met many genuinely pious young men all over Spain. At a hazardous guess, I would say that two-thirds of the youth are moving away from the church, although perhaps not ostensibly, while one-third remains constant and convinced.

As to the Ogino method being explained to a 'chosen few', I was told by a young woman who lives in Pontevedra, and who is married to a socially conscious young man, that her confessor told her about this method adding, 'Of course, it would not do to explain these things to the peasantry; they could not understand.' The young woman laughed as she told me this. 'Yet they are the women who would profit most by some form of birth control,' she said. We spoke in whispers in a café. A tired-looking woman was sitting at a nearby table with her husband and some friends.

'She is not yet forty, but you'd think she was fifty,' commented my friend. 'She's got some trouble with her womb. But she still goes on having a child every year. I do think she should change her confessor. I must tell her about mine, so he can advise her. I believe she takes vaginal douches of vinegar—that can't be very good, can it?' There are 'back-street abortionists' too, but who are we to cast stones? Our own glasshouse is too vulnerable!

One enlightened doctor did make a patient change her confessor. A smart young married woman came to him from Vigo, with her husband. They were 'modern', well-off, and had two lovely children. They had been blissfully happy until a few months before, when the wife began to develop neurotic symptoms, anxiety, insomnia, and a noticeable coldness in bed towards her husband. Until then, he assured the doctor, their relations had been entirely satisfactory. Little by little, in a series of talks with the doctor, the wife revealed that her sex life with her husband had been 'too pleasant, too exciting'. He had awakened her latent sensuality and she had plunged with zest and Gallegan vitality into the love-play to which he introduced her, apparently with skill and imagination.

Remembering her conventual upbringing all of a sudden, the young wife began to have doubts. Was it right that she should enjoy her sexual life as much? Was it not sinful—would the church not condemn such behaviour? In her perplexity, she consulted her confessor, an oldish man, who threw up his hands in horror. '*Dios mío!*' he exclaimed in sepulchral tones in the confessional. '*Dios mío!* My poor daughter, what have you been up to? Sexual intercourse is for the purpose of procreation, it is sinful to feel any pleasure in the carnal act,' etc. etc. All the old medieval ideas were trotted out until the poor woman promised to obey her spiritual director and wean herself from her husband's too ardent embraces—with the consequent breakdown in her health.

Very fortunately, the doctor knew of a more modern and liberal confessor and it was to him he sent her rather than attempt any cures of his own, which he knew would not have the desired effect upon the woman's religious conscience. I understand that the woman was completely cured and resumed her normal happy relations with her husband soon after. 'Too bad, isn't it,' remarked the doctor who told me this story, 'when they try to prevent you from having a little orgy with your own wife?'

Another and very different case, in which he sent a patient to a confessor, concerned a shrewd peasant from a fishing village in the northern *rías* of Galicia. Belief in magic and witchcraft is still very prevalent in these remote parts, especially among the women, and the men occasionally take advantage of it. One of the more current beliefs has to do with the *meigallo*. This mysterious 'thing' is vague enough to cover all sorts of contingencies. The *meigallo* can be an enchantment that provokes disease, a spell that makes people do things under a strange compulsion, an extension of the evil eye. And there are witches, known in many localities, who are capable not only of healing but also of casting a *meigallo* on those who have had the misfortune to offend them. Some witches are of an amorous disposition and they are capable of casting the kind of *meigallo* that brings men into their nets.

'This,' explained the anxious peasant woman who had come with her fisherman husband to consult the doctor, 'is what has happened in our case.' While his wife did all the talking, the man sat mute, with lowered eyes, twirling his cap in his hands. 'There is a woman in our village,' she said, 'who has cast a *meigallo* over my poor Juan.' 'Do you know who she is?' asked the doctor, trying to conceal a smile. 'O yes, of course I do!' said the woman eagerly. 'It is Mariquita. She has had her eye on my Juan for some time. Juan tried to avoid her and then she began to cast a *meigallo* over him, to make him go to her.' 'What were the symptoms?' asked the doctor gravely. The fisherman reddened. 'The symptoms? Oh, well he'd have bad headaches and then he'd say to me: "I know what it is, this is a *meigallo*. I have never suffered from headaches before." I gave him some aspirins but they did not do any good. "I feel Mariquita calling me," my husband said. "I feel a strange force telling me to go and see her. It is terrible—she has a very powerful *meigallo*." ' 'And what did you do?' asked the doctor, beginning to feel sympathetic towards the poor credulous woman. 'What could I do?' she said plaintively. 'My poor Juan was quite beside himself. I feared for his reason. These *meigallos* can be very dangerous. More than one man has been driven out of his mind because of them. I told him to go and see Mariquita and spend the night with her.' 'Did this happen often?' enquired the doctor. The fisherman stirred uncomfortably in his seat. 'Quite often; I hoped that it would pass,' replied the woman, 'but it has only grown worse. That is why I made up my mind to come and see you about it, doctor. The *meigallo* seems to have got hold of

Juan real bad. He can't shake it off. And we can't go on like this. After all, I am his wife and'—she looked up at the doctor anxiously —'do you think you will be able to help?'

The doctor sighed. 'I do not cure *meigallos*,' he said. 'The only person who can help you is a priest. And I suggest that your husband go now and confess to a priest whose name I will give you. Since he is not your local priest,' and he looked hard at the fisherman as he said this, 'Juan will find it easier to explain what has happened.' 'Why should that be?' the woman wanted to know. 'It is easier to talk to strangers,' said the doctor evasively. 'Juan will find it difficult to talk to any priest wherever he may be. He hasn't been to confession for a long time,' said the woman, looking at her husband reproachfully. The fisherman hung his head. 'I think he should make up for lost time and go now, before you take the bus home. Will you do that, Juan?' The fisherman raised his head slightly and nodded. 'I am sorry you couldn't cure him of his *meigallo*,' said the woman sadly as they went out; 'but Juan did warn me before we came. "Doctors don't know anything about *meigallos*," he said.' The doctor smiled.

At the beginning of the century, the magistrate Nicolas Tenorio described dances that took place in the summer under the light of the full moon in a village called Viana del Bocho, but these have now disappeared. They were a curious survival of the belief in the moon's amorous influences. The young people danced together to the accompaniment of tambourines and *conchas*, and sang a love lament, with their faces raised towards the moon. The dance and song ended with the ullulation, the 'hu, hu, hu,' of northern peoples, and lasted until dawn. 'Come out moon; come out, moon, come out from behind the clouds,' they would sing, 'so that those who have loved and forgotten may fall in love again.' The influence of the moon on procreation is still believed in all over Spain, from Galicia to Andalusia. It is better to conceive when the moon is waxing if you want a male child and when it is waning if you want a female child. The same belief applies to the mating of animals and is observed by many farmers.

The following *copla* with its popular association of love and fire, probably refers to a love charm:

Meu Manuel, meu Manuliño
meu Manuel feits de cera;

> quen me dera ser o lume
> que o meu Manuel derretera.

('My Manuel, my Manuel, my Manuel made of wax, if I could only be the fire capable of melting him!' The melting of wax effigies named after the loved one was supposed to be an infallible method of reducing their resistance to a lover's attractions.)

Very probably a more usual method was to employ physical force, after due warning, as in the next popular refrain: 'Marujita, Marujita, you of the yellow skirt, if I meet you on my path it won't be any use your saying "I don't want to".'

The old medieval symptoms of lovers are recalled in many a popular song: 'I lay down to sleep, to the sound of running water, and the water told me: "He who loves does not sleep."—We have five senses and we need all of them, but we lose all five as soon as we fall in love.'

From medieval times to the present day, Gallegan love lyrics have been closely connected with nature, and the crudest description of love-making, earthy though it may be, has a naïve charm:

> Lembráste miña neniña
> de aquela noite de vrán?
> Ti contabas as estrelas
> i eu as herbiñas do chán.

(Do you remember, my lass, that night in summer? You counted the stars and I the blades of grass. . . .)

As elsewhere in Spain, St. Anthony is the 'marrying saint' *par excellence*, the saint who is appealed to to find everything from lost objects to new sweethearts. When he refuses to comply, he is punished. In the village of Forcaray, in Galicia, St. Anthony's statue has to be guarded carefully to defend him from disappointed village girls who put him out in the rain or tie a rope round his neck when he is slow in finding them a *novio*. When he does find them one, the triumphant *novias* wind their sweethearts' ties round the saint's neck. One morning he was found draped with no less than seven ties! In this village it is believed that the death of a rival *novia* can be brought about by treading on her dress during a High Mass or a procession.[1]

[1] Information supplied by Srta. Chelo Mariño Bobillo, Santiago de Compostela.

I was surprised to learn how very circumspect most engaged couples are. At first I was inclined to believe that the young people were misleading me when they assured me that *novios* never kissed on the mouth but only on the cheek, but this was repeated many times, in different parts of Spain, and confirmed by adults who had no reason to want to delude me. Affectionate kisses are permitted between *novios,* and then only on the cheek, but passionate kisses are strictly forbidden. These are sinful and lead to perdition. As a doctor told me in Barcelona, 'We have a saying that a kiss on the mouth is equal to half a child!'[1] There is a grain of truth in this belief, especially so in the case of ardent young Spaniards, with whom the transition from a kiss on the mouth to less innocent demonstrations of ardour may be swifter and more difficult to control than in their northern counterparts. One of the greatest difficulties confronting young wooers in England and elsewhere consists in just this, and the first question they ask harassed and uncertain grown-ups is: 'How far can we go?' The Spaniards believe, probably rightly and certainly very wisely, that it is better not to set light to the gunpowder and to abstain from the fatal first step, the kiss on the mouth.

'Don't you ever really kiss your *novia?*' I asked a thirty-two-year-old psychiatrist, whom I had always seen accompanied by a dark, intense-looking but rather severe young lady. He laughed and shook his head. 'Believe it or not, but she won't let me,' he said. 'Of course I should like to kiss her, but it would upset her whole code and I respect her too much to insist. We still expect women to be chaste, really, even though from a rational point of view, we might disagree with the theory.' He had been engaged to this girl for three years.

Engagements often last a long time in Spain for economic reasons; it is not at all rare to hear of young people having been engaged for four, five or six years or even more. The repression that this implies must have a bad effect upon their subsequent marital relations, but on this point it is extremely difficult to obtain precise information. On the other hand, since it is estimated that even in England, where relations between the sexes are so much freer, a large majority of husbands do not give their wives satisfaction, one cannot be dogmatic and declare that the Spanish system is worse.

[1] In England, until quite recently, innocent lasses believed that a kiss on the mouth would produce a *whole* child!

One could say, perhaps, that Spanish women are brought up to exercise a great deal more self-control than their northern sisters, but at the price of what? I heard from *novios*, doctors and girls themselves that they resort to self-abuse, as happens in many convents among the nuns. (I have heard some pathetic accounts from convent-visiting doctors, but there is no place for them in a book about love.)

The strict segregation of the sexes leads to a certain amount of latent or active Lesbianism. The fact that girls are brought up in each other's company and go everywhere in pairs, coupled with the intense interest taken in the human physique, in the importance of being *guapa*, pretty, accentuates the tendency. Even in the quiet, outwardly demure little town of Pontevedra, I was astonished, when I assisted at the sessions of the juvenile court, by the cases of Lesbianism and incitement to Lesbianism which had been discovered and which according to the local magistrate had attained the proportions of a 'public scandal'.

There has also been an unaccountable increase in homosexuality, usually confined to the capital and to Andalusia where it has flourished since Arab times. It seems to correspond to the prevailing moral climate, which has also produced *gamberros*, the equivalent of 'teddy-boys'. It must be said at once, however, that until now this development has not reached the importance and the sadistic violence of the more industrialized countries of the west. Whether the epidemic will spread to Spain remains to be seen. Young men in Spain do seem to have more time for lounging about with their hands in their pockets, but their pockets are usually empty; they have no money to spend on luxuries and with which to become independent of their parents. As a rule women do not go out to work and family life is stronger, or appears to be so on the surface.

Village *gamberros* are dealt with pretty effectively. It is easier to do so in a smaller community. One young *gamberro* who took his revenge on a girl who refused to become his sweetheart by writing obscenities about her on the doors of forty houses in the village, was obliged, by the local judge, to repaint the doors at his own expense in the colour selected by the owners. True to Spanish advocacy of stern measures, one reader wrote to a national paper suggesting that all *gamberros* should be branded on the forehead with the letter G. The editor did not agree with him.

Have ideas about love changed much? Are the new generation's ideas on the subject very different from those of their parents?—I asked in my questionnaire. The majority of the boys believed that although in essence love is the same, 'for it is eternal', nevertheless its expression has changed, become freer, 'more liberal, more modern'. A few added: 'More human, too; there is more companionship than there used to be in our parents' time.' A little less than half expressed the view that it was still the same. One student thought it had become too materialistic, another believed that the clergy busied themselves too much in the subject and a third thought that 'now we love too much with our heads'. One student was convinced that there is too much emphasis on sex, and three said that they didn't know; it was impossible to know what their parents had thought when they were their age.

The majority of the girls thought that their ideas about love were the same as those of their parents; only a few expressed the opinion that there is now more choice, more freedom from parents' influence, and that relations are on the whole less conventional and more personal. One girl, no doubt reflecting her confessor's views, said that there was too much emphasis on sex and that love 'isn't valued as it used to be'.

When I asked them whether, in their opinion, there are sufficient facilities for meeting and making the acquaintance of young people of the opposite sex, the answers varied. There seemed to be a general consensus that facilities do exist but the more thoughtful students expressed the view that in spite of this relationships tend to be on a superficial level. 'There are facilities, but the time-table is pretty rigid,' said one student.

It is an observable fact that the time-table for sweethearts' meetings *is* fixed; in a university town like Santiago, they are to be seen between say one and two in the afternoon and seven and ten o'clock at night. They meet in cafés, in the streets, walk together in the public gardens, sit on benches watching the birds in the aviary. When dusk approaches they hold hands and arms, but on the whole they are decorous. The more daring know of secluded lovers' meeting places such as the pine woods a little way outside the town, and here indeed one may sing about 'counting the stars and the blades of grass. . . .'.

Spanish parents are aware of the existence of *novios* but until the relationship is serious and their progeny of age to talk about marriage, they take no notice whatsoever and pretend they do not know what is happening under their noses. They would not dream of inviting the young men home. A twenty-year-old girl student, engaged to a young man doing his military service in North Africa, assured me that her parents knew nothing of her engagement, officially, and that they would be informed only upon his return. He had never seen her parents or her home. A doctor in Barcelona remarked, when his twenty-year-old son left the room where we were talking: 'He's gone out to see his *novia*—but I don't want to know anything about it for a long time yet. He can't marry at his age.' Perhaps a European father might have added: 'He has time to change his mind,' but not a Spanish father. There are changes in *novios* among the very young students but as soon as a relationship becomes more or less formal, although the parents are supposed not to know, the girl's reputation is at stake and it isn't easy for the young man to break off relations. Nor would it be easy for the girl to find another *novio*, however 'pure' she may be.

Young people are certainly freer than they used to be, although customs vary from place to place. They are obviously much freer in every sense of the word wherever there is money enough to spare for a motor-scooter. This occurs mostly in the towns, and although one young bourgeoise Madrilenian told me that it wasn't really 'done' for a girl to go off with a boy on his motor-scooter, the pastime is becoming popular. In Seville, a shocked gentleman told me that when he returns from his farm in the country on Sunday nights he lowers his headlamps 'so as not to see all the goings-on at the side of the road, beside the motor-scooters at rest'. But a young Madrilenian assured me that 'girls usually stop before the last ditch because they know that they could never get married if they "had an accident". Foreign girls are easier,' he said, 'and they are prepared to share expenses; Spanish girls still expect the boys to foot all the bills.'

Both boys and girls were inclined to believe that they still do not get to know each other at a deep level. 'There is no real friendship,' said one, and this opinion was voiced by many others. 'The girl's religious upbringing makes it difficult,' said another. 'They are on the defensive all the time.' One young cynic of seventeen said: 'We have all the facilities we want—more than enough to get bored very quickly.'

The girls believe that they have enough facilities. One of them thought 'too many'.

Asked whether they believed in pre-marital chastity, all the girls agreed that this is essential, and nearly all the boys thought that it is necessary for the girls but not so much for men. Those who did not attach importance to the virginity of their future wives logically replied that they believed both girls and boys should have some experience before marriage. One boy thought that pre-marital experience might lead to recriminations after marriage and another thought that to repress girls only leads to their having to resort to masturbation.

The boys were on the whole more broad-minded and tolerant than the girls, even on behalf of the girls, but this occurs in other countries too. Whether or not they remain as tolerant when they come up against the problem on a personal basis is difficult to assess. This is a case where male pride and jealousy tend to assert themselves. Pride is more important than the jealousy factor in the Spanish male, who seems to have changed a good deal in this respect. I was told by the police that *crimes passionnels* (which are not reported in the Press) are fairly infrequent at the present time. They occur, but not at the rate which one would expect from an allegedly passionate people. And although it is still legal for a man to kill his wife and/or her lover when he catches them *in flagrante*, this is a facility of which advantage rarely appears to be taken.

Curiously enough, jealousy seems to have emigrated overseas. The South Americans have preserved these old-fashioned defects, according to what I was told by a psychiatrist in Madrid. He and his assistants were horrified, during a discussion with a group of psychiatrists from Latin American states, to discover that these gentlemen approved of the law allowing a man to assassinate his wife's lover. 'We are more civilized than that,' observed the Spaniards smugly.

On the importance of love in one's life, the girls, as was to be expected, were unanimous, where the boys were not, in allotting it a place of honour. The most subdued reply was: 'It is very important for the relative happiness we can hope to attain in this life.' Only one girl believed that: 'Some people haven't experienced it and therefore can't know,' and a third believed that: 'Only a great intellectual or religious vocation can fill a life devoid of human love.' All the others said that love was very important.

The majority of the boys agreed that it is of 'great importance' and one went as far as to exclaim: 'What a naïve question! What would life be without it?' One opined that it is 'not as important as spirituality', another that 'our whole Christian and western civilization is based upon it', a third that 'love is a liberation from loneliness and can be a man's salvation', a fourth that 'it is the basis of life and humanity'. The more moderate believed that 'love is quite important for one's personal happiness', or 'important, but not everything in life'; several thought that love is of 'relative importance', and one young cynic, the same seventeen-year-old who replied in blasé vein to all the questions, confessed that it 'didn't prevent him from sleeping'. Another admitted to being 'too proud, too egotistical to find love important'.

Is love spoken about between students of both sexes, I wanted to know: a little, a lot, seriously or in jest? About ninety per cent. of the boys said that love is a subject that is discussed infrequently and when it is, in jest. Of the girls, sixty per cent. said that it is spoken about in jest, the rest thought that it is spoken about quite a lot and some were of the opinion that it is spoken about a little, but seriously. One of the more intelligent girl students said that it is talked about quite a lot but that it is veiled behind a bantering attitude. Two or three disappointed girls remarked ruefully that the boys tend to talk about love as a sport or pastime. One male student believed that: 'It is the best pastime between both students and non-students.' Another boy said it is difficult to talk about it with girls because of their religious upbringing and another, more traditional, said that the subject is too intimate and should not be talked about in public.

It would seem that on the whole the young people of Spain are not very different in this respect from those of other European countries. It may be that in their case the 'jesting' period goes on a little longer, since the economic situation does not permit them to marry as early as they do, say in England. The girls, of course, marry younger and it was said in many universities, from Santiago to Seville, that they frequent the faculties in search of *novios* rather than knowledge. This is not peculiar to Spain, and it would hardly be fair to point an accusing finger when only recently an article in an English newspaper affirmed that fifty per cent. of our English girls go to universities for husband-catching purposes.

Since the Spaniards are such starers I was interested to discover whether they believed in love at first sight. I was a little surprised to find from their answers to this question that about ninety per cent. of the boys and of the girls do not believe that this is possible. There was no difference on this point between the boys and the girls, which reveals their typical and fundamental lack of woolly romantic notions. 'Love at first sight is an old-fashioned idea,' said one boy contemptuously. 'It is a purely literary concept,' said another. Another boy remarked with perspicacity that in his opinion what is usually termed 'love at first sight' is in reality a 'presentiment of love'. Most boys and girls were firm in the belief that a sudden physical attraction is possible, but that this is not real love. Several boys and girls added, 'Love only comes with knowledge of the person concerned.'

Immediately after the question on love at first sight, I asked whether the boys and girls had an ideal man or woman. It was not surprising that all those, with one or two exceptions, who had expressed a belief in love at first sight replied in the affirmative to the second question. The two were linked. The girls differed on this point. They seemed to have more of a fixed ideal than the boys, but in their case the ideal was more mental than physical, whereas those boys who said they had an ideal were thinking almost exclusively in physical terms. A boy would say, for instance: 'I have not got an ideal—but perhaps a certain expression of the eyes moves me in a special sort of way,' or, 'I thought I had an ideal, but when I fell in love it was with quite a different type of girl.'

The third question, related to the previous one, referred to the qualities sought for in their future partner; whereas physical attractiveness ranked fairly high in nearly all the boys' answers, it very seldom entered into the girls' lists and when it did, it came very low down. This, again, is a fairly general state of affairs. The male attaches more importance to vital statistics than the female. But beauty did not come first on the boys' list except in about ten per cent. of the answers. It usually ranked third or fourth, after 'femininity, simplicity and modesty', three high-ranking qualities in ninety per cent. of the replies.

Goodness and understanding came first in many replies. Fidelity was only mentioned once. Few Spaniards believe that their wives will be unfaithful to them. Intelligence, alas for the emancipated minority, came very low on the list indeed. One young man said he would prefer his wife to be naïve, 'in fact almost silly'. This reminded me of a Navarrese friend who, speaking of a mutual feminine acquaintance, exclaimed spontaneously: 'Isn't she delightful? She is so silly—that's how I like women to be!'

One young student of seventeen wanted his future wife to have a lot of *savoir-fer* [*sic*] and another, more modestly, hoped that she would be patient with his faults. Several mentioned the Spanish quality called *angel*, which is a mixture of tenderness and *simpatía* This ubiquitous word *simpatía*, as everybody who has been in Spain for any length of time knows so well, is considered very important both in men and women. Not to be *simpático* is a grave defect. It is a complex quality composed of amiability, easygoingness, cheerfulness, kindness, generosity—a very Spanish mixture.

On the whole, the girls demand a lot more from their men than the men demand of them. Their lists of desired qualities were impressive. There were slight variations according to status. The students rate intelligence and cultural superiority pretty high, the office worker's first requirement is that her *novio* should be very much in love with her and also that he should have a 'lot of personality'. She evidently wants her future husband to be very much above her mentally. She also wants him to be 'religious'. The Catalan girls want even more from their men than the Gallegans, and they insist that 'he must be a hard worker and ambitious'. These girls seem to have a more matter-of-fact attitude towards the realities of married life, although the Gallegans cannot be accused of being ultra-romantic. Here are the requirements of three fairly typical middle-of-the-road Catalan girls who want their *novio* to be:

1	2	3
religious	in love with me	in love with me
refined	very superior to me	a lot of personality
cultured	a lot of personality	a hard worker
fond of children	a hard worker	*simpático*
rather romantic	*simpático*	understanding
very affectionate	not ugly but not too	decided, a lot of initi-
sincere	handsome	ative
rather proud	understanding	a good Christian
a hard worker	a good Christian	cheerful
above all, religious	at least seven years older than me	

Few girls mentioned 'fidelity' among the required qualities. Would they mention it more frequently after marriage, one wonders? Unfortunately, I was unable to compare as it proved more difficult to obtain replies to questionnaires from married couples.

Manliness, personality, nobility of character, were frequently mentioned by the girls. Nobility of character seemed to me to be a typically Spanish requirement. It is clearly allied with the desire for a man to have 'a little pride', a watered-down version of the traditional Spanish haughtiness which is found as much in the peasantry as in the aristocracy. Most Spanish girls want their *novios* to be affectionate with them, but slightly haughty and aloof towards everybody else. This trait does not apply to the Gallegans as much as to the Castilians, Catalans and Andalusians.

When it came to describing the faults that boys and girls find in one another, the answers were hard-hitting and also, curiously enough, very similar.

The girls find that on the whole boys are boastful, presumptuous, not 'educated' enough (by this they mean ill-behaved), superficial, cynical, lacking in intellectual curiosity, frivolous, vain, too imbued with a sense of *amor proprio*. To this a few girls added: 'They have little understanding of women, little respect for them and no sense of responsibility.' 'Their favourite sport,' added another, 'is to add yet another girl's name to their endless list of conquests.' Several mentioned 'lack of delicacy', one thought boys are 'quite absurd' and 'they want girls to do everything for them', while an extremist dismissed them as 'drunkards, womanizers, badly brought-up and shameless'.

When we turn to the boys, we find that they too consider the girls to be superficial, lacking in intellectual curiosity and understanding of masculine character. 'They think very little and have tiny minds.'—'They are envious, vain, ambitious, mercenary and domineering.'—'They are not idealistic enough.'—'They are too preoccupied with getting a sweetheart or husband.'—'They don't take enough interest in social questions, they are selfish and *petites bourgeoises*.'—'They haven't enough personality to stand up for their opinions in their family circle.'—'They have no idea of life, men or themselves; all this is due to their bad, conventual education.'—'They are too interested in the cinema and badly digested modern ways.'—'They are madcaps when they are let loose from convent schools.'—'They bore me,' said the misogynist. 'I only notice their enchantments,' exclaimed the idealist.

It is difficult to come to any conclusion, but it would seem that both parties put on an act in each other's presence. One wonders, too, whether the boys are being sincere when they complain of the girls' lack of interest in topical subjects and lack of education. The few girls who have achieved brilliant academic results complained of the boys' envy and coldness towards them. One or two bright girls who had taken degrees and written theses admitted with a blush that they would not pursue their investigations after they were married. It appeared to me that the Spanish male, who needs even more admiration and reassurance than his counterpart elsewhere, would be very disturbed indeed were his womenfolk to become his intellectual equals.

On the question of the importance of the economic and social status in marriage, answers varied to such a degree that it is difficult to generalize. One did infer, however, that the question of economic status was of importance, particularly to the students' families, and that the question of social status appeared to them to be less important. Young people in Spain are still dependent on their parents to a great degree and many of them do not marry young because of this. In the north in particular, many conflicts result from the economic favouritism displayed towards the eldest son at the expense of the others; on the other hand, many heirs have to support their parents at the expense of their personal happiness.

One would have to live in the country for a long time and have access to many hitherto reserved sources of information before being in a position to make any sweeping generalizations about people's love-life. There is no doubt, however, that it varies to a considerable degree between localities, and between town, port and country. The ports of Vigo and La Coruña, for instance, are obviously more sophisticated, more 'Europeanized' than the quiet little inland towns and scattered villages. In the ports, you can buy contraceptives, if you know where to go for them, and you may frequent rendezvous houses, or *casas de cita*. The younger generation of the bourgeoisie in these towns is less restrained. An engaged couple consulted a doctor recently on the subject of the *novia*'s fertility. They had had sexual relations but as no pregnancy had occurred the young man was worried as he very much wished to have children; he was prepared to break off the engagement if the doctor found that his *novia* was sterile. They both went to the consultation together. 'This would never have happened in Castile,' said the doctor, who had practised in both provinces. He also remarked that the Gallegan peasant girls, unlike their counterparts in Castile, are not in the least bit shy of genital examinations.

Here are some more problems I was told about in Galicia. In the busy, pleasant port of La Coruña, a young and very 'modern' girl puffed nervously at her cigarette as she spoke to me about her *novio*. She was in her mid-twenties, worked in a fashion shop and had had several affairs. 'Up to now,' she said, 'I have had the reputation of being easy. It didn't worry me until I met and fell in love with Miguel. He's marvellous. I know I would be very happy with him; he loves me, but he knows about my past and he cannot believe that I shall be faithful to him. How can I convince him? Mere words, mere demonstrations of affection won't do. He wants some proof. But what? I don't know, and nor does he. But we cannot get married until he feels sure of me. Sometimes I think he never will. I don't know what would become of me if he lost confidence completely and refused to marry me. Then I do believe I would take the downward path for good.'

I should not be surprised if this is a common problem among the so-called emancipated young women of Spain who go too far and then come up against the double standard of morality which is unavoidable not only because of the value attached to woman's chastity but because of the conviction that once she has lost it she loses all her principles. If a woman gives herself, it means that she has loved, whereas if a man 'has fun' it is considered only as 'fun' and not as anything necessarily involving deep sentiments. For a girl, much more is at stake than virginity *per se*.

'What have your friends advised you to do?' I asked the worried *novia*. 'The most experienced woman I know,' she said, 'has suggested that I should use the same methods of seduction that I practised on other men, in other words, try and retain him by the senses until he realizes that I love him above all spiritually.' 'Is that not a contradiction in terms?' I ventured. The *novia* smiled. 'Perhaps it is,' she agreed, 'I must say that it repels me to have to resort to any tricks. With my present *novio*, I feel unusually reserved. But maybe the end justifies the means.'

In Pontevedra, a youngish man of thirty told me that not all the problems were on the women's side. 'Take my case,' he said. 'It may sound silly and romantic—that sort of thing is supposed to be out of date—but I have been in love with a married woman for five years and I cannot get her out of my system. As the French say, she is "under my skin". She does not respond to my love; in fact she has told me very definitely that she is happy with her husband and nothing will make her be unfaithful to him. But I still continue to be obsessed by her. If I happen to see her in the morning when I go to my work, I am unhinged for the rest of the day. I should go overseas, I know. I have relatives in South America; they have offered me a good job out there. But somehow I cannot tear myself away from here, where she is. Maybe one day I shall take my confessor's advice and take the plunge, but so far I have not had the courage.'

'Gallegan women may be tender-hearted,' I remarked to a lawyer in Vigo, 'although the peasant women look so formidable and masculine that it is hard to believe they would ever melt, but what about the men? I have just been speaking to a romantic in Pontevedra, but are they not in the minority? Most of the men look pretty tough. And in the bourgeois families I know I have not noticed any particular tenderness on the part of husbands. In fact, they seem to be on the tyrannical side. One of your colleagues, who is all charm with the ladies, behaves like a sultan in his own house. "Bring me this, give me another helping of that," he commands his wife in imperious tones. He is quite unaware of his behaviour and when I commented upon it to him he looked quite hurt. "Do I really behave like a sultan? It has never occurred to me," he said in injured tones.

'So many wives seem to be taken for granted,' I said. 'All the interesting conversations take place in a separate part of the room; the men tend to congregate together, and the women gradually creep down towards the end of the table to talk about trivialities. They do not seem to take an active part in any other but domestic and family life.'

'Few women are educated enough,' the lawyer replied, puffing at his cigar. He was a rotund and amiable man who loved the good things of life as well as those of the spirit, gastronomy as well as poetry, Eros as much as Diana. 'When I see a pretty woman,' he admitted, 'I do not feel inclined to talk politics or philosophy with her. She stirs me profoundly—but *not* in the head.'

In his professional capacity he deals with many separation cases. There is no divorce in Spain and a judicial separation is all that a woman can hope for when she is so badly treated that she cannot put up with her husband in the spirit of resignation and obedience expected of her. 'Some women remain so attached to even an exceptionally bad husband that they hesitate to separate from him,' said the lawyer, rummaging among his papers. 'Take this case,' he said, opening a file. 'Here is a woman who has been married nine years. She has two children. Her husband works at the docks. He beats her regularly; recently he punched her so hard that she fell and broke two ribs. Moreover, it is difficult to believe this but she told me herself, she keeps the stick with which he beats her and presents it to him upon his demand! You would not think it could be possible, but there it is. I have advised her, and her family have advised her, to obtain a judicial separation. She came to consult me about the steps to be taken but she cannot make up her mind. Not after nine years, at the rate of four or five beatings a week! Do you know what she says? "Maybe one day he will realize all the sacrifices I have made for him, Señor, and then it might be bad for the children," as if the children weren't living in an inferno at home! It is quite incomprehensible. Can it be true that some women *like* to be beaten?'

Although I was assured that jealousy has disappeared from the Spanish husband's character, I could not help but remark that this is far from being the case with the women, who keep a very close eye upon their spouses, not, I would add, without some justification.

'Men are inclined to roam,' said a young wife from Pontevedra. 'One has to watch them with the servants. I would certainly never have a pretty one around in the house. I know of too many cases where it has proved fatal to domestic felicity for the wife.'

'We are not as Don Juanesque as we used to be,' said a middle-aged bourgeois of Santiago. 'I think we have improved in that respect. Only a few years ago I would have thought myself obliged to pay court to every attractive woman I met. I realize now that that is rather foolish and unnecessary.' It did not escape me, however, that there was still a glint in his eye and a tentatively hopeful expression on his face which I did my utmost to dissipate. 'All the men of my age are the same,' he added with a sigh. But I also heard a twenty-three-year-old student admit: 'When foreign girls come to Santiago, they expect us to behave like Don Juans, so we do!'

'My *novio* is twenty years old, like me,' said a pretty Gallegan girl. 'We love each other very much and he is always very considerate with me. But after he has been with me, I have heard that he sometimes goes out with another girl who is supposed to be rather easy. When I questioned him about it, he said that any man who really wants to be a man cannot always hang on to the same woman, and that if he went out with another girl it was simply because she amuses him more than I do. I didn't think that was right, though, and I wrote to a magazine for advice.' 'And what did they reply?' I asked, with curiosity. 'I had a very stern letter back which I have shown to my *novio*,' said the girl. 'He didn't like it at all. He was furious with me because I wrote. As a matter of fact, I am on the point of breaking with him. I think I made a mistake to behave so naïvely. But I have had no experience of men, so how could I know? My mother says men are all the same, but I do not believe her.

'The man who replies to problems in the paper I wrote to addressed himself more to my *novio* than to me. That's why my *novio* was so wild. He wrote, "Look, young man, what you are doing is not manly at all, although you may think it is because of the false but widespread assumption that Don Juanism is a sign of virility. It is not manly to 'collect women', but it is manly to know how to love and make one woman really and truly happy. That is what counts, although we are often inclined to forget it (and you can see from what I write that I am not exculpating myself). And it is far worse to make a public display of your infidelity and then try to convince your *novia* that that is the right thing to do. If you feel you cannot be faithful to one woman, well then don't go and propose to give your name to an innocent girl who knows nothing about base instincts." I'll show you the letter if you like,' she took it out of her handbag with a triumphal gesture. The letter was signed, *José de Juanes*. 'And what is the name of the paper?' I asked her when I had read the letter. 'It's a weekly,' she said, *'España Semanal*. My *novio* reads it because of the articles on science and medicine, and I read it for the fashion and problem pages.' 'Don José sounds sensible and warmhearted,' I reflected. 'I must look him up when I go to Madrid.'

Abroad, we think of the fiery Spanish woman, the seductive Spanish woman, as an Andalusian flamenco dancer with flashing

eyes and curved hips. In hard fact, however, it is not the Andalusian woman who is feared in Spain. *She* is not the temptress who
attracts the men and upsets the women; it is the Gallegan woman
they are afraid of, the northern woman with her more subtle wiles
and fascination. This was a surprise to me, but there is no doubt
about it. The fact was confirmed by men and women in all parts
of Spain.

'Yes, it is true, they have powers over men,' said a Sevillan
woman reluctantly, with a snap of her fan. 'Why should it be so?
How can one analyse charm? We too are supposed to have charm.
Foreigners like us very much,' and she resumed her fanning, 'for
our vivacity, our *sal*. But our own men—it is strange how they
fall for these women of the north. I do not think they are as
beautiful as we are. I believe that we have more delicate limbs,
tinier waists, better features, more brilliant eyes. What is it then?
Perhaps it is because of the contrast, they fall for their gentler
charm.'

'We may be more vivacious,' said another and older Andalusian woman, 'but so are our men. And sometimes we exhaust one
another with our mutual vivacity. That is when we start to
quarrel and to fight. Sheer nerves. Tension. Excitement. But the
Gallegan women are more clever. They have spirit, a lot of spirit,
but they know when to hide it and when to appear to be soft and
tender. That is how they trap our men. By their sweetness, their
soft, caressing ways and caressing looks. Have you noticed how
an Andalusian woman looks at a man? She looks at him with the
boldness of a man. There is a challenge in her gaze, and pride.
She provokes him to a duel. Look at our flamenco dances. Are
they not duels, danced duels? How the man has to stamp and fight
and exhaust himself to disarm his partner! She is protecting herself, putting a high price on her honour and her femininity. Just as
she does in life. She provokes him and then slips away. She is full
of fire and yet of restraint. Is it not enough to make a man mad?
Or look for satisfaction in other quarters? Your Gallegan woman
goes about her conquests in a different key. She takes her time.
She spins her net slowly and methodically. She is quiet and
cautious and flattering. Yes, she knows how to flatter men better
than we do. And to make them feel good. We want our men to
bend the knee to us. The Gallegan woman appears—appears, I
say—to bend to the man.'

'A Gallegan friend of mine,' I remarked, 'has described the

Gallegan woman as being essentially a mother, maternal in gesture even when she is only a *novia*, whereas in the rest of Spain the woman is a heroine, a Calderonian heroine of her honour.' 'There is a lot of truth in that,' replied the Andalusian lady. 'That is how God has made us.' 'Perhaps the excitement of the chase is enough for you?' I suggested. 'You stimulate and provoke a man and then you have no qualms about leaving him all on fire. That is how a woman displays cruelty in love. The sadism is not one-sided.'

'That is our only form of revenge,' she answered quietly, fixing her large dark eyes on me. 'It may be that the Gallegan women are fonder of men. Yes, perhaps they are. It is known that they are more *generous* to them,' she said with a malicious smile.

By this she meant what we have already seen: the Gallegan woman, at least the woman of the people, is less inhibited in her sexual behaviour than the Castilian or the Andalusian. As my Gallegan friend said to me: 'The Gallegan woman's behaviour is spontaneously natural and feminine, perhaps intensified by the deep and vital atmosphere of the pagan life of the soil. As you know, with us an unmarried mother is not repudiated. In Galicia the man is conquered by the woman. In the rest of Spain, *he* is the conqueror, the *conquistador*.'

The tenderness of the Gallegan woman does not proceed from weakness. On the contrary, she is at least as strong-minded and independent as the rest of her countrywomen, if not more, and she certainly works harder. Most foreigners have observed that the average Spanish woman, from whatever province she may be, appears to have more character, is more masculine, than the man. Could it be that the women, who conserve their sexual strength and lead a more sexually restrained life than the men, are stronger for this very reason? Or is it because the Spanish mother broods too much over her sons and makes them effeminate? On the other hand, is the prolonged dependence upon both parents a lethargy-inducing factor, one that makes for infantilism and hysteria?

The Spanish family is said to be closely integrated. It gives an appearance of being solid, if by that we mean passive obedience to the head of the family and a fear of breaking away from it and leading one's own life, which is largely due to the economic situation. But what are the results? Lack of independence in the sons, lack of individual judgments and of initiative, lack of stimulus. There does not appear to me to be a greater degree of confidence between father and sons than anywhere else. Nor is home life very rich, with its continual economic preoccupations (many heads of families are obliged to take two or three separate jobs to make ends meet and they have little time left to be with their family), its incessant feminine chatter in lieu of conversation, its lack of books (they are very expensive) and the Spaniard's congenital dislike of intellectual pursuits.

The centre of the home, in spite of café life and the men's casino or club (to which women are beginning to go more frequently than before) is the mother; the mother is the pivot, affectionate and harsh in turn, generous of embraces and buffets, alternatively tearful or excessively gay—woman, in fact, unstable, primeval, but warm, warm as the womb and irresistible. This may not—indeed, cannot—be true of all families, but in the main I believe it is a fairly accurate picture which may account for the average Spaniard's Don Juanism and mental apathy.

2. *Love in the North*

'WHEN I go to Covadonga,' says a popular Asturian *copla*, 'I go to see my sweetheart; if they do not give me a bed I shall sleep in hers.' The gay defiance of this song and its pretence at freedom from convention may apply to the goings-on in the *barracas* during the summer months, but they do not correspond to the bourgeois mentality of the towns. Nevertheless, I was told by Don José, who runs the Answers to Correspondence column in *España Semanal*, that the most complicated love problems he has had to deal with in all his fifteen years' experience come from the Asturias and the north of Spain.

Why should this be so? One simple reason may be that the Asturians seem to read and write more than the people in the other provinces and so their problems come to light more frequently. (I have already referred to the average Spaniard's laziness in this respect. It exasperated even saints like Teresa, who often alludes in her letters to her correspondents' lack of epistolary energy. 'Had I as much leisure as you,' she wrote to Don Ramirez in Toledo, 'I should not be as tardy in writing as you are,' and to Don Diego Ortiz, also of Toledo, she said: 'It would not be a waste of time if you wrote to me often.' To Mother Mary of St. Joseph, the Prioress of Seville, of whom she was extremely fond, she exclaimed petulantly: 'You delay so long in writing that I lose my temper.') Yet there are still medieval traits and customs extant even in modern towns like, say, Gijón, from where a young man wrote to a newspaper to enquire whether a verbal promise of marriage made before a holy image could be considered as valid. Quite a few young couples apparently do this still all over Spain. It is a survival of the oral promises that gave the church so much trouble until as late as the nineteenth century. *Apalabrarse* was the expression used for this private ritual. The Archbishop of Santiago de Compostela wrote in 1828: 'It has been found that the majority of the legates of the Archbishopric are convinced that a simple promise of matrimony by word of mouth constitutes a regular marriage,' and he goes on to complain of 'the multitude of young girls who have been seduced by these oral promises and lent themselves to illicit relations believing, like their families, that they were legally authorized to do so'.

Incidentally, the young man who made the enquiry about a betrothal before an image also wanted to know whether or not one can believe in the horoscopes published by the Press.

I came across another case of filial dependence upon parents in the north, a young man of thirty who had been engaged to a girl for eight years. Was this to be explained by economic difficulties, as most of the other cases I had been told about? He nodded sadly. 'I have often thought seriously about getting married during these eight years,' he said, 'but my parents don't like the idea. They refuse to help me, although they could well afford to. I work in the family business and they prefer to keep me on a small salary, smaller than they would pay anyone from outside, and I have to work exceptionally long hours. It's quite a problem, I don't know what I should do about it. I suppose I must take a decision one way or the other and either marry my *novia* or leave her and devote my life to my parents.' 'But surely,' I could not help exclaiming, 'you should know after eight years whether or not you love your *novia*? Would you seriously think of leaving her now?' The young man looked worried. 'It is a problem,' he repeated.

The young Basque businessman of twenty-six who appeared to be prosperous and independent of parents had another problem to contend with—an older mistress whom he was on the point of discarding after she had set him up in life and he had found a young and 'innocent' *novia*. His problem, as he explained to me over coffee in the local *casino*, was twofold. 'I've had this liaison ever since I was in my teens,' he said. 'I feel like a false Pygmalion. You see, my mistress has done so much for me. She has practically brought me up and given me the material means to get on in life. I wouldn't be where I am now if it had not been for her. She has always been very sensible about our relationship. She has never pretended that it could last. I was the one who thought it might once, until I met Carmen, my *novia*. As a matter of fact, my mistress has always advised me to look out for a *novia* and to marry and settle down and have a family. Well, now I have followed her advice but I haven't dared tell her about it yet. I believe she guesses something. Women are intuitive about that sort of thing, aren't they? Lately, I have seen her crying all by herself. I shall have to tell her and I suppose I had better tell my *novia* about it too or else she's bound to find out. Tricky, isn't it?'

In nearby Navarre, I met yet another young man with parental and economic troubles, of whom there are so many in Spain. 'We are two brothers,' he told me. 'My parents treat the elder brother as the sole heir; they have given him a good education and are helping him in his medical career, whereas I was sent to a primary school and have to be content with a subordinate position in a small country post office with no prospects whatsoever and hardly enough money to marry on. My parents could help me a little if they wished. It does not seem fair, does it?'

'Why don't you demand your rights—or why don't you go somewhere else for a living?' I asked him. The young man smiled as he sipped his Coca-Cola. It suddenly occurred to me that he could ill afford to spend his hard-earned money, even on soft drinks, and I felt embarrassed. But there was nothing I could do about it. It would have been a terrible insult to offer to pay my share. It had been a struggle even with the feminine interviewees and café waiters will not be bribed. 'You are a stranger, are you not?' they would say when I made surreptitious attempts to pay while my friends were not looking. 'In that case, it is the custom of the country for *us* to pay—not you.'

Tradition! And it was tradition that made the young man opposite me smile so uncertainly. 'You suggest that I should speak up, or leave? That is very reasonable,' he said, 'but it is difficult, more difficult than you think. It is easy for you who are accustomed to rebel against your parents, and to lead your own lives. Besides, you have more opportunities. Here, you must not only have diplomas but you must know the right people. That is all important. What would be the use of my going to another town where I am unknown and have no connexions? I would lead the same or perhaps an even worse kind of garret existence.'

In Europe we have had—and are still going through—a crisis in authority, but in Spain, almost a century behind the times, authority is still unquestioned (publicly), and furthermore there are three thick layers of it: political, religious and domestic. Dictator, priest and father-patriarch. The censorship affects love too. Not long ago a woman poet had one of her love poems completely distorted and turned into religious channels by the censorship. A novelist was called up and rebuked for the 'realism' of one of his love-scenes. 'At least,' the censor told him, 'you should have made your lovers say their prayers before putting them to bed.'[1] We have seen that many Spaniards do actually put this precept into practice. A prayer before an image of the Virgin often precedes love-making and condones it in the simple, pagan eyes of the lovers—at least in those of the girl. But men, too, invoke the Deity in cases which hardly seem to call for divine intervention. Doctor González Lafora relates a curious case which he dealt with in the twenties.[2]

His patient, a wealthy bachelor of thirty-four, lived with his brothers and sisters, all of them unmarried. Apart from his house he had a studio, or what used to be known as a *garçonnière* in France, and in Spain with disarming frankness *á picadero*, where he received his lady-friends. The latter, invited on the pretext of admiring his *objets d'art*, were nearly all friends of his sisters or wives of friends. He was in the habit of seducing two or three of them at a time and this involved him in the most extraordinary complications. 'Sometimes,' he told the doctor, 'they meet on the stairs and I have to be very ingenious to prevent them from confiding in one another and finding me out. They all realize that I want them for a few moments only and that I am mocking them, yet when I make a fresh appointment they never fail to turn up.'

One day he fell in love with a charming, well-bred girl with whom he had amorous relations for seven years, although he was not faithful to her during that time. When the girl's parents wished to arrange a 'good match', her lover advised her to accept. She did so and went away to live abroad with her husband. A year later, she returned to Spain and sought out her Don Juan, anxious to resume their relations. They met several times in a *casa de cita* but, to his intense disappointment, Don Juan was impotent—he could not make love to her any more, but he remained normal with other women. The only woman he failed with was the woman who aroused him emotionally.

The woman went away again and, to forget her, Don Juan threw himself into his old life of pleasure. One of his mistresses, the wife of an intimate friend, became pregnant by him. After the birth of the child she was sad and preoccupied. The child reminded her constantly of her transgression. Don Juan, however,

[1] Spanish writers and intellectuals have recently sent a petition to the Government asking for censorship regulations to be relaxed.
[2] Dr. González Lafora: *Don Juan, los milagros, y otros ensayos* (1927).

developed a parental love for the child and at the same time his love for the mother was fortified by her romantic melancholy; he fell in love with her and gave up all his other mistresses to devote himself to the mother of his child. Together they visited theatres and cinemas, weeping copiously at the tragic scenes. Their relationship had become spiritualized. One day a sudden fear assailed Don Juan. 'I wonder whether I could still make love to her or whether I would be a failure as I was with my other mistress?' The thought worried him so much that he decided to make an experiment and arranged for a clandestine rendezvous with his mistress in an understanding friend's house. The result may be imagined: it was a total failure. He was as impotent with this last mistress he had loved as with the first.

In the end, Don Juan exposed his problem to the doctor: 'Doctor,' he said, 'you must cure me; you are my last hope. I have offered up candles and I have prayed to all my favourite saints so that they may help me to satisfy my desires, but they have not answered my prayers.'

Here, writes Dr. Lafora, is the true Spanish Don Juan, who remembers God and His saints when he is in need of them, not to be saved in another life, as was the case of the legendary hero of that name, but to be saved on this earth. This kind of Don Juan does not hesitate to accept God as an accomplice in his immorality.

In the beautiful but austere province of Navarre, where there seem to be more convents than anywhere else in Spain, I found no traces of Don Juanism and an atmosphere which would delight the purest of Puritans. 'It is indeed very difficult to sin here,' admitted a young Navarrese businessman, whose own life was exemplary. 'People get to know everything,' he added as an afterthought. 'And people talk.' That most efficient of morality stabilizers, the thought of 'What will the neighbours say?' works even better in Navarre than in the rest of Spain, if that were possible. The moral and clerical atmosphere of the little capital, Pamplona, has hardly changed since Unamuno commented so acidly in his *Ruta del Aventurero*: 'From the top to the bottom of Pamplonese society, from the highest stratum to the lowest, I found the whole place poisoned by clerical alkaloid. It oozed out of every corner and there was hardly one Pamplonese in the town who did not possess deposits of this penetrating substance in his family. One drop in the eye is enough to infect you for ever. All the water of the river Arga would not have been sufficient to dissolve the vast quantities of cleritoxin and clerigalic acid produced by the town.'

The Navarrese woman keeps strictly to her place—the home. She is the housewife, mother and regulator of sentiments. As Manuel Iribarren writes, 'Although she now goes to the university when she is young, wins diplomas and assumes positions of responsibility in private and public enterprises, her real goal and objective is to reign in her own house. It is when she marries that she fulfils her personality.'[1]

In the not so remote past a girl was allowed by law, the local *fuero*, to refuse two of the suitors presented to her by her parents, but she was obliged to submit to their authority when they presented her with a third one. Young people used to meet at fairs or fiestas, once their marriage had been agreed upon by their respective parents. This first meeting, *a vistas* as it was called, allowed the boys and girls to see but not to speak to each other, and as the girl was nearly always accompanied by a relative, sister or cousin, there were frequent confusions. 'It is surprising,' observes Manuel Iribarren, 'that these marriages, in which personal selection hardly entered at all, should have given such excellent results.' He would no doubt agree with Dr. Johnson who was of the opinion that: 'Most marriages would in general be as happy, and often more so, if they were all made by the Lord Chancellor upon a due consideration of the characters and circumstances, without the parties having any choice in the matter.'

The popular refrain: 'Marry lass, according to your own taste; don't take anybody else's into account, for if you go to hell, your parents won't be able to get you out of it,' is now supposed to be followed by the majority of modern Navarrese girls. I have my doubts. Parents, relatives, well-meaning friends and priests all put their fingers in the marriage pie. The parish priest is a matrimonial agency unto himself, in Navarre as elsewhere. 'The fundamentally religious education which the woman receives in Navarre from the moment she is born,' writes Señor Iribarren, 'tends to reproduce the strong woman of the Scriptures. She is not jealous by temperament or education. She rarely commits adultery. And she occupies an irreplaceable position at home and at church.'

[1] Manuel Iribarren: *Navarra.*

She cannot even bathe with her husband in the swimming pool of the fashionable tennis club in Pamplona. There are two pools, one for each sex, modestly surrounded by an impenetrable box hedge. A man of the *pueblo* confided to me that this was perhaps a wise precaution because, 'We Spaniards are always eager to sin against the ninth commandment. We like our wives, but most of us covet our neighbours' wives even more!'

The women of the valleys at the foot of the Pyrenees are sturdier than their urban sisters and they stick up more for their rights. Collective action, however, seems to have been confined to trivial matters. A copiously documented instance concerns the long-drawn-out battle between the men and women of the valley of Roncal over the vexed question of mantillas versus the traditional valley costume. The record of the men's gradual defeat is locked up in a chest in the village of Uztarróz among other valley council minutes.

The trouble started when the valley council decreed that henceforth the Roncalese would not be permitted to wear any other than traditional dress on feast days and for church services—that is, the men were to put on capes and ruffs and the women the valley headdress and apron. In addition, 'Those spinsters who, through human frailty, have fallen into temptation and sinned against the sixth commandment,' were to make themselves conspicuous by wearing a white linen cloth upon their heads, to distinguish them from married women and virgins. This was intended to embarrass them and to serve as a warning to others, but it probably brought them more customers.

The valley women wanted to wear fashionable mantillas in church and they were furious at having to continue to wear the outmoded valley dress. Although a fine of eight *reales* was imposed upon mantilla-wearers, scant notice was taken of the council's injunctions. The women resisted by invoking specious pretexts such as that ever-exploitable feminine mystery, the state of their health. When they were fined, they had the effrontery to submit the matter to the Royal Council of Pamplona. This was a crafty move, because they knew that their menfolk disliked to have valley affairs discussed in the capital.

The startled council yielded to the extent of emphasizing that, 'These sartorial injunctions are to be enforced according to the discretion of the valley mayors who are to take the ladies' health into consideration,' but they parried further feminine thrusts by adding: 'Any persons who may be thinking of taking up the matter with the Royal Council of Pamplona must submit their petition beforehand to the council of this valley.'

The matter did not end there. The obstinate womenfolk actually began to stop attending High Mass and Vespers on feast days so as not to have to wear the traditional *tocado* on their stubborn little heads. Twenty-one rebels were to be found in the village of Roncal alone. Eighteen were fined and persuaded to behave more submissively in the future but three obstinate women, Juana Burugoni, Lucia Recari and Augustina Ederra, refused to pay and were bundled into prison.

From prison the rebels continued the good fight and appointed lawyers to defend them before the Royal Council of Pamplona. The valley lawyer argued weakly on behalf of the valley council that, 'The mantilla is an expensive luxury and our sterile soil cannot pay for such extravagances on the part of our womenfolk.'

La Burugoni's lawyer declared that in his opinion the Roncalese headdress forced women to appear in public with bare faces; this, he thought, was brazen and bound to provoke blushes, especially among the virgins. Moreover, it would be more to the point—if the valley was really as poor as their lawyer had made it out to be —to forbid the use of velvet, silk fringes and silver hooks and eyes that some of the womenfolk displayed. . . .

Finally, the Tribunal of the Royal Council of Pamplona authorized Lucia Recari to wear a mantilla in view of 'the medical information submitted by doctors Lucea and Romeo, who have certified that the said Lucia cannot move her head because of the tumour on her neck'. This was the beginning of the end. The hamlets of the valley of Roncal now began to disagree among themselves. The representatives of Burgui were liberal enough to suggest that the women should be allowed to wear what suited them best. The conservatives of Roncal fought on, but in vain. That was why, in the summer of 1955, I had to rely upon the parish priest of Garde, Don Marcelino, to find me the one and only Roncelesa of the valley, Señorita Boj, who possessed a complete traditional costume. She wore a scarlet capulet over her head, for the *tocado* that had caused so much trouble has entirely disappeared, like the Basque *tocado* which the church objected to because of its too obvious resemblance to a phallus.

What went on behind the religious façade is recalled by a popular verse from the plains: 'You earn only three *duros* a month and yet you wear silk stockings? Either you get on very well with the master or you steal from your mistress.'

In the mountains, Basque songs are heard, plaintive and lyrical, with the eternal accent on absence, separation, and the love of the native soil peculiar to emigrant peoples. Romantics are found among them, and Manuel Iribarren relates the story of a young Navarrese who exchanged verbal promises with his *novia* before leaving to make his fortune overseas. When he returned a few years later, wealthy and hopeful, he found that the girl had been married off by her parents. He built himself a sumptuous house opposite hers and lived in it, unmarried and morose, until the end of his days.

One of my friends, Luis, was a well-known singer of melancholy Basque songs. 'You should see him at a *despedida*,' I was told. 'When everybody else is roaring drunk, Luis goes and sits by himself in a corner to sing his confounded Basque songs.' (*Despedidas* are bachelor parties, mostly drinking bouts, in honour of a boon companion about to enter into holy matrimony.)

Barcelona: modern, industrialized, better laid out and with a far greater splash of fountains in its square than the capital, Madrid. Barcelona: the town that is nearer to Europe and European influence than any other in Spain. Barcelona: a city which shared its troubadours with France in the Middle Ages, and where fifteenth-century ladies behaved with the gay abandon of Parisiennes, as one is told by Francesch Eximenio: 'Our court and elegant ladies wish to resemble the French; they wear tight corsets, dance and drink all day, kiss men in public, speak of love and lovers, and jest with young men.'

Young ladies may copy Parisian fashions and hair-styles in Barcelona, and even outdo the Parisiennes, but there the resemblance ends. Apart from a small, flashy minority of bourgeoises, the average Catalan girl is level-headed and prudishly brought up. The group of Gallegan students to whom I spoke in Barcelona were distinctly averse to Catalan girls. 'They are less affectionate than our Gallegan girls—they are too independent—they believe they can get along without men—they are too tall, they have big feet and they don't like *piropos*.' (I am inclined to agree with the nineteenth-century traveller Henry Inglis, who found that 'there is more witchery hid in the eyes of an Andalusian than perhaps in all the separate charms of a woman of Barcelona'.)

Talking to Catalan girls, I learned that they preferred their own Catalan boys, who are 'more intelligent, more modern, more polished than the Gallegans'. Given half an economic and solid chance, your Catalan girl would become as self-sufficient and overpowering as an American woman executive. Catalan men, too, are 'tall, with big feet and independent' and they are more go-ahead than the rest of their countrymen. They are also more austere than the 'typical Spaniard' of Castile and Andalusia, and less decorative. They have not got the same lively gift of repartee. Their language strikes one as hard. The atmosphere of Barcelona, too, is hard and businesslike. People are much more sensible than in other parts of Spain, they hurry more and they are tolerably efficient. They read and publish more books. It is only when you see the boys and girls holding hands and dancing a *sardana* after High Mass outside the cathedral on a Sunday morning that you begin to find them *simpáticos*. But they are reliable and helpful.

I arrived at the worst possible moment for arranging interviews—on the eve of the feast of St. John, when the town was empty of taxis, the surrounding countryside was ablaze with bonfires, and most of the population were taking two or three days' vacation. In spite of this handicap, the few people to whom I had introductions sprang into action and made appointments right and left, going to endless personal trouble over my strange and unprecedented request. It is true that they had been alerted by cautious preliminary letters, for I had begun to realize that it was too much of a shock to present myself with an introductory visiting card from a mutual friend and plunge straight into my subject without warning. As soon as the word 'love' was pronounced, I felt my interlocutor wrapping himself in an invisible Spanish cape and becoming more and more impenetrable as I continued with my discourse. By writing careful, explanatory letters beforehand, the first astonished reactions were over by the time I confronted the recipients and they had had more time to think. Not that that always helped much, because it was becoming more and more obvious to me that the Spaniard does very little thinking about love and personal relationships.

These remarks do not apply to the doctors whom I was fortunate to be able to interview and who had given a good deal of thought to the question, especially in so far as it concerns the younger generation. As I have already mentioned, I had decided before I left England that doctors and confessors would be my most reliable sources of information. Confessors were a little more difficult. Not only was there the secret of the confessional to be considered; I had also to reckon with the possibility of suspicion in view of the fact that I was a heretic with criminal views about birth control, and their cogmatic slant which makes it difficult for them to view problems objectively. Some of the younger confessors, particularly those of the Order of St. Felipe Neri, are making an effort to put a higher value on human love than they have done so far, and a Jesuit magazine recently carried a frank article on the scientific facts of sex and personality by the eminent Dr. Juan Rof Carballo. But the psychiatrist I talked with outside Barcelona had had obstacles put in his path when he wanted to circulate a questionnaire among young people on the subject which interested me. Nevertheless, things were improving, he said, and many associations and Catholic study groups were asking him to give them talks on sex education, preparation for marriage, and similar subjects.

'Some of them need it,' he added. 'I have known about eight cases of wives who knew absolutely nothing about sex-life when they were married. Most of the marriages ended in a judicial separation. But the men need to be educated too. I can tell you from my experience that most Spanish men are 'elementary' and brutal in the bedroom. Their initiation to sex? Very often it takes place with servants from Galicia and Andalusia. Young people have more freedom nowadays—far more than in my day—but they are not allowed out alone at night. As soon as a boy and girl are seen together the word *novios* is used and this puts a sexual spoke in the wheel of friendship.

'Many Spaniards are like precocious boys of fourteen,' continued the doctor. 'At bottom, they are very timid. Does that surprise you? We have a reputation abroad for being bold and audacious. Don Juans, in fact. But the Don Juan type is timid too. He only goes for the women he can feel sure of and his intuition in that respect is pretty acute. He does not know how to *woo* a woman; he sweeps her off her feet.

'Long engagements? Yes, we have plenty of them here too. We are not so different from the rest of Spain, although we are supposed to be more "European". Not in the emotional sphere. We are still bound by convention, religious upbringing and tradition. It's a bit different in the working class. There is a lot of ignorance, poverty and scepticism among them. But their morals are modelled on those of the bourgeoise. They are more rigid than you might think. Unmarried mothers? Oh yes, we are as severe as in Castile—especially in the middle classes. A girl who transgresses usually has to follow the profession of a prostitute. Many of them are quite decent girls, and affectionate like most Spanish pros. They have children and are excellent mothers. They are doing good business at the moment with the Americans. The Americans come here on leave, even from France. They find our girls warmer, less mercenary than the French.'

'Barcelona is not the whole of Catalonia,' observed a poet who lived in a pleasant village a few miles outside Barcelona. I found him helping to decorate the street which was to be followed by the local Corpus Christi procession the next day. It was one of those charming communal affairs of which we have lost the secret, and with it the fun and neighbourliness, in our drab industrial west. The narrow uphill street was a mass of colour, a pattern of flowers and geometrical designs carefully and artistically worked out in coloured powders, pebbles, flowers and berries.

'Barcelona is not the whole of Catalonia,' repeated the poet, putting a handful of berries into his pocket as he prepared to offer me a glass of Benedictine in his apartment facing the mountains. He lived alone with a simple-looking housekeeper. A marriage had been arranged for him twelve years before by his confessor, but it had not worked. The girl was much younger than he was and she had left him.

The poet is popular with the young generation. 'We discuss most subjects here,' he said, looking round at his books and pictures, 'with the exception of love. I do not know why it is, but we never talk about that. We Spaniards have not written much about it either. Most of our artists have painted religious subjects better than human ones with the exception of Velazquez and Goya. We oscillate between heaven and hell. Perhaps less so in Catalonia. Yes, much less so because we are practical too.' (I learned afterwards that the poet was wealthy. The money comes, not from his poems but from a lucrative little sweetshop round the corner. Yes, the Catalans are a practical people.)

In the Mas archives in Barcelona, a picture of a bearded female saint upon a crucifix attracted my attention. The girl in charge of the files looked over my shoulder and smiled. 'That is St. Liberata,' she said, 'the saint to whom married women used to appeal against their husbands. Her cult has been forbidden.'

This is the androgynous saint known as St. Uncumber in England and St. Debarras in France. She was probably born in Portugal where, according to legend, her father the king had betrothed her to the heathen king of Sicily. The saint prayed to be made ugly so that a marriage would be impossible; soon afterwards she began to grow a beard which grew faster every time it was cut off on her father's orders. Finally, he had her crucified. As she was dying, the saint heard a voice from heaven telling her that she would be the mother of all who were heavy of heart. Women have since interpreted this celestial message in its widest sense, believing that it allowed them to petition the saint to rid them of bad husbands.

Another curious example of ambiguous devotion to saints is mentioned by Dr. González Lafora[1] in his allusion to the Virgen de los Dolores of Toledo, who is still appealed to by Toledan girls. This image is to be found in the Street of the Pins, *la calle de los Alfileres*. Legend says that a girl whose lover was sent away from the town bid him adieu in this street. Every time she passed through it she was so overcome by emotion that she felt like fainting. To prevent this from happening, she pricked herself with a pin. One day the Virgen de los Dolores appeared to her and said: 'I too have suffered. Have patience. All will be well.' A few days later the lover re-appeared and the pair were happily married. Since then the Virgen de los Dolores has become the patron of Toledan lovers who, when they pass before her image, drop a pin in a nearby groove in the wall accompanied by a petition. It is said that an average of between twenty to thirty pins a week are cast before the Toledan image during the winter months but that the quantity increases to between two and three hundred in the month of May. There are black-headed pins among the white. According to one writer, this indicates the girl's preference for a dark sweetheart, but Dr. González believes that they stand for the desired death of a *novio* or husband—perhaps one who has been unfaithful—or of a relative who is ill and in such pain that his release is prayed for. 'They pray to the image,' he writes, 'to execute the crime which they dare not commit themselves.'

Pins—objects made of steel—evidently represent a magnet, or the power of attraction. English brides used to distribute pins among their bridesmaids after the wedding and this was supposed to procure them a husband within the year. In Andalusia, a 'sweet-

[1] Dr. González Lafora: *Don Juan, los milagros, y otros ensayos.*

heart-divining' game is played with a pair of scissors, and in Madrid pins are thrown in the holy water font in front of an image of St. Anthony.

May is the sweetheart's month in most European countries, when nature bursts into life and birds trill courtship songs. We still have May queens but these festivities are tame compared with the lovely rituals preserved in so many parts of Spain.

Does the devil get into one's body in the month of May? So it would seem, according to a Gallegan song reserved for this day and the custom of boy dancers making jokes to 'get the May out of people's bodies'. In one coastal village, Adam and Eve represent the king and queen of the May. 'May has come, we sing of love and the girls are dressed with flowers,' goes a popular refrain.

3. Love in Castile

In Castile, religious Castile, the first songs of May-day morning are addressed to the Queen of Heaven, Mary. In the villages near Cuenca, they begin on the night of 30th April, when the rival groups of married men and unmarried boys meet to sing a May song to the Holy Virgin. The songs are simple; they compare the Virgin to a white butterfly, to a divine dove, and end by asking her blessing on the festivities. The groups then separate and the boys go off to serenade the unmarried girls.

If the girl in front of whose house they stop happens to have a *novio* they introduce his name into the song; if she has no *novio* they bring in the name of the boy in the group who, in the opinion of the 'corporal', or group leader, is best suited to her. The song celebrates love and the fertility of the fields: 'May has come blessing the corn and the barley . . . your broad forehead is a field of battle where king Cupid has planted his flag. . . .' A description of the girl follows, down to her dress and shoes, and her defects are glossed over: 'She is very tiny, but well made,' they sing to a short girl. Each household contributes a few pesetas towards the expenses of next day's banquet and dance in the public square. The mayor opens the dance, accompanied by his councillors dressed up in their Sunday best and wearing the stately ceremonial *expression de circonstance* which the most rustic Spaniard is capable of assuming.

The courtship ritual of the people of Serrano, one of the few ever to have been described in detail,[1] is astonishingly complex. Not that rustic sweethearts are eloquent. Their method of proposing, according to Señor Iglesias, is down to earth and conducted along materialistic lines like the following: 'Look here, *chaha*, if you aren't yet involved with anybody and would like to live with me, I've got a vine at X and some olive trees over at Y and I'm not a bad proposition for any girl. With your property and mine we'd be able to make quite a lot. What do you say?'

[1] Lorenzo González Iglesias: *El Protocolo del Amor Serrano* (Madrid, 1947).

Once this initial and not very romantic declaration is over, the courtship proceeds according to a protocol worthy of a medieval Court of Love. The sweetheart is declared *novio formal* and he is expected to make gifts to his *novia* on specific dates. The presents, too, follow a well-defined pattern. At carnival time, for instance, he is expected to give her half a calf and on the day of St. John a special kind of cake, half of which she is supposed to return to him in the afternoon; at Christmas come the traditional gifts of cod, cheese and marzipan sweets; and this is only an infinitesimal part of all that goes on between the courtship and the actual wedding.

In Lagartera, near Toledo, the wedding costumes have retained their primitive, barbaric splendour and the grave, beautiful ceremony of the paternal benediction is still carried on with patriarchal Spanish dignity. Even here, in rigorous Castile, it may happen that the bride is pregnant at the time of the wedding ceremony. In this case, the fact is tacitly announced to the community by the carrying of a special bouquet before the bridal procession.

The hardness and inflexibility of the Castilian landscape are reflected in their love-life. As the air-conditioned *Talgo* swayed over the unending plains of golden stubble, I looked upon dusty roads and crumbling castles and remembered Unamuno's reflections on the amorous life of these people:[1]

'It is not the ardent and tormented love of Abelard, nor the refinement of the Provençal troubadours. . . . The *Lovers of Teruel* of Tirso are sober in the expression of their tenderness even though they die of love. Jimena, in the *Mocedades del Cid,* is so little feminine and erotic that she prefers to have her love appreciated rather than her beauty. And this same Jimena . . . admires the wildness of her lover. As the popular proverb goes, "Man and bear, the uglier the better." And even more so when he is brutal. Celia in *El Condenada por Desconfiado* loved Enrico, who ill-treated her, because he was *brave*.

'In love too a dissociative element appears for it is gross rather than sensual, austere and dutiful rather than sentimental; either the passing satisfaction of the appetites or the duties of the home. . . . The casuistics of adultery are not a Spanish trait, nor has the *amie* ever become an institution. Outside matrimony, love resembles that of a fighting cock or of a Don Juan Tenorio, but never that of a Werther. . . .

[1] M. de Unamuno: *En Torno al Casticismo* (Madrid, 1916).

'We have neither a Marquis de Sade, a Manon Lescaut nor a Marguerite Gautier. Jealousy in the Calderonian theatre reflects offended honour and jealous lovers kill without a kiss, unlike Othello. Love with refinement, and in matrimony, grave and sober. The woman, the mother, does not appear in our national theatre; she is hidden in the holy of holies of the hearth.'

Castile: Vast plains, passive and eternal as the desert, with cinnamon-coloured villages pressed tightly round a vigilant church; villages in which life is as enclosed and intense as that of a concentration camp and love follows the pattern reproduced in Lorca's plays. For example *The Blood Wedding*, with the archetypal Spanish mother who likes men to be lusty. 'Your grandfather left a son at every corner,' she says proudly. For her, procreation and fecundity are the object of married sexual love. We must engender life in bed, in the fields. But a woman must not have a lover. Women are valued only for their sons.

In *Yerma*, the wife is convinced that her husband does not 'put his will to having children'. She is barren, but she married only to have children. Finally, she kills her husband. *Yerma* is, of course, treated by Lorca as a classical theme. The 'motherhood yearning' and desire to kill the blamed husband is not confined to Spain.

In *The House of Bernarda Alba* a mother gives her son money to go after the visiting girls. The men carry a loose woman away to the olive groves and insult another, burying her child at the wayside. One young man, the most eligible son, is marked off for the plain elder daughter and is in love with the youngest, who is determined to be his mistress if she cannot be his wife. Servants and sisters spy on one another. Neighbours eavesdrop. . . . Lorca shows woman eternally submitted to man; a sexual servitude in which joy and freedom of choice never enter. Sex is portrayed as a dark prison, a prison of which the gaolers are cruel, cruel as secret police.

José Mora Guarnido writes in his book on Lorca:[1] 'In the villages and towns of Spain, woman's fate, in spite of all that popular literature has said to the contrary, has been bitter and unhappy. Especially in the middle and upper classes, where a woman's destiny depended on the amount of her dowry. Marriage for love was a rare occurrence, except in the poor classes. Pretty

[1] José Mora Guarnido: *Federico García Lorca y su mundo* (Losada, 1948).

girls of the middle class withered sadly upon their balconies waiting for the gallant who rarely came to see them. These gallants were to be seen near the coaches of ugly girls with rich parents. Doña Vicenta, Lorca's mother, often remarked upon these injustices that account for the gravity and sadness of so many women of Granada.' The prototypes for Bernarda Alba and her daughters were a family whom Lorca knew as a child in Andalusia. They fascinated him so much that he used to hide himself in the dried-up well at the bottom of their garden to observe their comings and goings.

In Castile, I came across several cases of extreme feminine modesty. In Saragossa, a girl of twenty-four told me that she could not bring herself to be affectionate with her *novio*. After their marriage, she would go to her room, desperate at the thought that she loved him so much and did not dare express her feelings. 'I devour his photograph with kisses,' she said.

In Valladolid, a young woman of twenty-eight admitted that she was unable to retain her *novios* because she did not know how to behave with them, believing that a girl should never show her feelings even when she is in love. Castile is not the only province in Spain where one hears of similar cases. A girl in Bilbao, where relations are supposed to be freer, admitted that she had been so prim with her *novio* that he had got tired of her and left her.

In the villages, the people have their own rough and ready moral code. Until quite recently, they were very much opposed to the re-marriage of widowers, and even more so of widows. S. L. Bensusan relates in his *Home Life in Spain*, that the villagers of Doqueira, incensed at the marriage of a widow with her lover of many years' standing, decided to give them a *cencerrada* (the Spanish equivalent of the French charivari and English rough music) upon their wedding night, even though the widow was quite popular with everybody.

'On the night when Doña Dolores was re-wedded, Doqueira's youth, armed with tin cans, kettles, whistles and every noise-producing instrument they could think of, serenaded the lovers' farm a little way beyond the village, and shouted extremely ribald verses taught by the local rhyme-maker and sung to a *jota*. Though the lover and the buxom lady of his choice were doubtless considerably disturbed and not a little vexed, they were wise enough to take no offence at the interruption. In fact, before the score or more of village roisterers had sung their indecent rhymes half a dozen times over, the lover's headman, Pablo, made his way from the kitchen with a big pitcher of wine which was handed round to the serenaders and the *guardia civil* who had accompanied them in the interests of law and order. The little timely gift changed the whole mood of the company; the offensive verses were dropped, the *jota* resumed its proper words, the only shouts were those of *olé!* and the small company straggled back under the stars to mud huts and well-earned repose.'

Gerald Brenan says that in the south of Spain he has come across *cencerradas* quite recently in small towns and isolated villages. There the villagers indulge in warnings to the parties concerned and in horn-blowing 'which wore down the nerves of the engaged persons and the *pregones* finished them off. On at least two occasions when I was in the village a couple who had had their banns announced in church broke down and decided that they could not go through with it. Widows in particular so dreaded the publicity that they rarely re-married; instead, if they came from poor families and had no position to keep up, they simply went to live with their man.'[1] The proud and susceptible Andalusians do not seem to be able to 'face the music' with the same equanimity as their more northern countrymen.

Leonard Williams, correspondent of *The Times* in Spain at the beginning of this century, points out that in 1765 Charles III attempted to suppress *cencerradas* by imposing a fine of a hundred dollars and four years' imprisonment, not only on the performers upon kettles, pots and frying-pans, but also on those who bore them company. This had no effect whatsoever. Williams also describes a ludicrous incident which occurred in Seville. A barber who had organized and led many *cencerradas* in his younger days decided to re-marry. 'No sooner had the wedding night arrived than his former victims, to the number of I dare not say how many hundreds blockaded half his *barrio* with a gigantic *cencerrada* of retaliation. The civil guards were needed to maintain order and assuage the lacerated feelings of the newly wedded pair. Nor was the least of the fun of the fair the humourous poem relative to the event, published by Felípe Pérez y González in *El Liberal*, and aptly titled "The Barber of Seville".'

On the other hand, a Basque charivari which took place in 1950 ended with one man being killed and two wounded, according to

[1] Gerald Brenan: *South from Granada* (Hamish Hamilton, 1957).

Violet Alford.[1] This was provoked by an affair between two married people.

To conclude with Castile: even this austere province is changing slowly. I met a young man in Cuenca, which is far from being a modern city, who had fallen in love with a foreign girl and was determined to marry her, although she had told him she was illegitimate. I asked him whether his parents knew about this and he shook his head. 'I have thought it over very carefully,' he told me, 'and I have decided that it would be better not to. It wouldn't go down at all well, not here in Spain, in the bourgeoisie. My fiancée has adopted the Catholic faith in order to be able to marry me. My parents are satisfied. So am I. Let sleeping dogs lie.'

Are the Castilian peasants as austere as they are made out to be? A doctor told me that in the village where he was born, girls and boys between the ages of fourteen and sixteen indulged in sexual play behind the haystacks. A lady doctor from the same province had never heard of this pre-marital play and contended that in her village morals were typically 'Castilian and severe', closer to the national way of Spanish love-life described by Dr. Gregorio Marañon as, 'monogamic, austere to the point of mysticism, in a home filled by numerous progeny conceived almost without sin, in which the bedroom is as rigorous and dignified as a monastic cell'.

According to the earliest writers of epics, the love that bound the members of a Castilian family was profound. The Cid's sadness at having to part from his wife and daughters was said to be as 'painful as the tearing of nails from the flesh'. Could anguish be better described in one short sentence?

[1] Violet Alford: *Singing of the Travels* (1956).

4. Love in the South

SMALL satin-shiny black bulls wandering among pink oleanders by the side of purple streams: that is the image that stands out from my ten-hour journey by *Taf* from Madrid to Seville.

The first tourists of the season had already arrived and the second-class hotel to which I had been recommended was full. After a long search by taxi, we dived into one of the less elegant quarters. One street was so narrow that my driver feared he could not take his car up to the luminous hotel sign that glittered in the centre of it. Obligingly he stopped and went on foot to find out if there was any accommodation; he returned soon afterwards announcing triumphantly that this time we were lucky. 'But you'd better go and see whether you like the room,' he said, as an after-thought. Fearing the worst, that is a *Bohème*-like attic, I went to investigate.

The proprietor, in carpet slippers, was seated in the patio reading the bullfighting page of the local newspaper. Taurine and flamenco-dancer posters lined the walls. The wicker chairs were painted in bright blue and yellow. A taciturn young man showed me up to an enormous double room, in which a crucifix of conventual size dominated twin iron bedsteads. The walls were high, white-washed and ascetic. 'It is rather large,' I murmured, 'for one person.' 'For one person?' he echoed. 'Oh, those taxi-drivers! What liars they are! He told us it was for two young ladies.'

On our way downstairs, the young man leaned over the banisters and shouted angrily to the proprietor: 'She is alone.' The proprietor looked up from his paper and eyed me discreetly up and down. He was an elderly, white-haired Andalusian gentle-man, slow-moving, courteous and grave. A current of sympathy sprang between us. 'The *señorita* can stay in No. 21 tonight,' he said quietly. 'Later, we shall see.' He bowed to me, without the flicker of a smile. I thanked him and went out to hail the taxi. 'The *mozo* will do that,' exclaimed the proprietor, Don Alfonso. The taxi-driver, pleased with the success of his little stratagem, nodded good night and grinned cheekily at the *mozo*. Don Alfonso accompanied me to the nearest restaurant, for his own dining-room was closed, and solemnly recommended me to the manager.

I should have moved out after a couple of days. By European standards my third-class hotel (for so it was officially and very appropriately rated) had little to recommend it. The mattress was thin and lumpy, the rug beside my bed was so threadbare and filthy that I hid it and replaced it by one of my own towels; the wardrobe door had a tendency to squeak open when one was least expecting it, and the food, though plentiful, was and could only be appreciated by the hotel clientele of local farmers, third-rate commercial travellers, and a sprinkling of impecunious foreign students.

I stayed on, however, to the astonishment of the bourgeois Sevillans whom I encountered later and who occasionally escorted me back to my poster-filled patio. Why did I stay? For one thing, the street, being narrow, was cool and traffic-free (nowadays Seville is as infested by noisy malodorous traffic as any other modern city). The better types of hotel are usually provided with space for cars to sweep up at full blast. And only in a third-rate hotel could I unashamedly order *churros* for breakfast every morning, especially bought for me by the maid-of-all-work, Maria, together with the latest gossip. She was married to Juan, the young man who had showed me to my room on the first night, and who changed into a waiter in the daytime. They were both vaguely related to Don Alfonso, who sat in an armchair on the pavement, dandling their baby, when Maria and Juan were busy with their respective chores.

After two days, I was part of the family. Don Alfonso would hail me from a distance as I came up the street for lunch: 'There are two ever such fat envelopes for you from Madrid.' In the evening, when I ran up the street late for dinner, he would urge me, 'Do not run so fast, Señorita, there will always be some dinner left for you, and if the dining-room should be closed, I shall have food sent up to your room.'

Maria and Juan were typical of so many young Spanish couples of the working class who never stop from dawn to midnight in order to make a bare living. Many of them realize that conditions are better abroad. Maria made discreet enquiries. A young Sevillan taxi-driver told me he was soon going to join his brother in London. 'His *novia* has just gone over,' he said. 'They will both

'The Wedding Present' by Vazquez

Wedding costumes and procession at Lagartera

Paternal benediction, Lagartera

Fiesta de San Antonio, Madrid

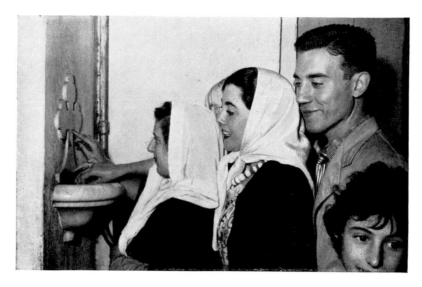

Dropping pins in the holy water font

Serenading at the *feria*

work there and save money. You can't do that here.' Fewer and
fewer young Sevillans spend their days and nights composing
coplas and strumming guitars for the benefit of tourists in search
of local colour. They too want to travel for a change.

'But Seville is so smiling, so gay! Look how the people amuse
themselves at the *feria*—see how they enjoy the drama of their
Holy Week,' objected a regular English visitor. 'Do you know
that even in one of their revolutions—I think it was in the
twenties, not the last one—they brought out their beloved image
of the Virgen de la Macarena in the annual procession, coiffed
with a Phrygian bonnet! Nothing ever changes here.' 'As you
said yourself, that was in the last revolution but one,' I remarked.
'And after every revolution more and more of the old beliefs are
lost, and more reality sets in. Many of the clichés about Spain
and the Spaniards are no longer valid. I only hope the testing
time will not be too violent, too reactionary.' A Spanish friend
disagreed with me. 'Our nature has not changed,' he said sadly.
'I cannot foresee a change without violence, cruelty and bloodshed.
I see no signs of tolerance, of rationalism, except in a minority.'

'Much of the façade,' said a well-known doctor, 'is pure
hypocrisy.' We had been talking about the religious brotherhoods. That morning I had seen the Corpus Christi procession
and the famous dance of the *Seises* at the cathedral. 'Do not forget,'
the doctor reminded me, 'that the cathedral was built on the site
of a temple to Venus. It seems to have given people the dancing
itch. Nobody has ever been able to prevent the Sevillans from
dancing in their cathedral. Archbishop Segura tried to suppress
the *Seises*. Now he has gone, the *Seises* have bobbed up again.'

'The members of the brotherhoods were very solemn,' I
remarked. 'The children too were grave and fervent. On the other
hand some of the middle-aged men looked a trifle weary. I saw
my hotel proprietor among them, Don Alfonso.' I laughed at the
recollection. Don Alfonso in his best suit, carrying a large
banner, was the very embodiment of a Spanish hidalgo. He had
noticed me, too, sitting in the front row of the sun-drenched
chairs in the Plaza San Francisco and he had bowed with his usual
native elegance, but he watched narrowly to see the effect he
produced. He must have been gratified by my nod of smiling
approval. A few hours later, back in his fume-filled kitchen, his
white head emerging from the hatch as he surveyed the guests at
lunch, chewing fillets of beef that must have come from the local

bull-ring, he was sombre and taciturn. It was only on my last day that in a sudden burst of confidence he showed me some photographs of himself at various points of his career, which had included fighting during the Civil War—on the wrong side, so far as my own personal sympathies were concerned.

'The brotherhoods?' said the doctor disparagingly. 'Ah well, you in England have your men's clubs.'

'They are not on a comparable level,' I protested.

'No, indeed. Not at all. But the basic idea is similar: to get away from the women. Of course, one can get away from them by going to the casino, by drinking and gambling and so on. But if one wants to do it respectably, without hurting their feelings and get kudos from it as well, other stratagems must be resorted to. In England, men read and discuss politics. Here, it is difficult to discuss politics and men don't read. Religion is the answer. Brotherhoods. They meet regularly and it becomes a kind of harmless secret society.'

'I thought that the members of religious brotherhoods were supposed to be very pious and have a clean—by that I mean a virtuous—record,' I remarked. The doctor laughed outright. 'If that were the case, the brotherhoods would hardly have any members at all,' he said. 'Most of them, and I know all about their private lives, have a *querida* [mistress] in some private apartment.' 'How very nineteenth-century!' I exclaimed. The doctor nodded. 'Yes, quite. Perhaps the younger generation will be different. Their fathers are still very Oriental on the whole. It is a point of honour with them to have a mistress. We do so many things in Spain in the name of honour—but then people do strange things in other countries in the name of liberty.' He shrugged his shoulders.

'Is Andalusia very different—from an amorous point of view— from the rest of the peninsula?' I asked him. 'I think there is a common basis, a common way of looking at life and love in Spain which is the result of our racial and social mould,' he said, 'but with certain traits peculiar to specific provinces. You have spoken to me about Galicia. Yes, I am inclined to agree. That part of Spain is very different. The Celtic-Iberian elements have not been diluted, the Moors did not settle there. I myself am from Extremadura. There are slight differences between us and the Andalusians—not many. The trouble is that such a lot of nonsense has been written, especially by foreigners, about Andalusia.'

'Are the women as passionate as one is led to believe?' 'You mean the Carmen myth?' said the doctor. 'It is a myth; or a hoax. No, the average Andalusian woman is passive, tolerant of her husband's escapades, without a will of her own. She is very faithful. The few cases of adultery that occur here rarely have Andalusians as their protagonists. The Andalusian wife is above all a mother. She consoles herself with her children—of which, as you know, she has many. One wife I know, well-to-do and bourgeoise, has fourteen children and she tells me she has supped with her husband perhaps one hundred times in the seventeen years they have been married. He goes off at night with his male —and probably female—companions, and comes home so late that she cannot stay up for him. As they are rich, they have two cooks. One for the wife and another for the husband. That is an extreme case, I admit, but I could quote many more along the same lines. Women are victims.'

'As in Lorca's plays,' I observed. 'But then, is Spain not a country of victims? Animals are the victims of man, culminating in the great national bull sacrifice; women are the victims of men, although I would qualify this by adding that they are nearly always the willing victims. They rear their menfolk, they spoil them, and they accustom them from childhood to have a different set of values and morals from those of the womenfolk. The women are much to blame for this state of affairs which many of them deplore in late life. And so for man himself—he is Unamuno's victim of a "tragic sense of life", of his national-religious beliefs. These are trebly potent. Spain has inherited three major, patriarchal religions: those of Israel, Christianity and Mohammedanism: the avenging God, the fear of hell, the fatalism of the Orient . . . what a heritage! Can one wonder that his mind is tortured, his sense of doom so deeply ingrained?'

'No more than anywhere else. You have contemporary philosophers and historians in Europe,' the doctor reminded me, 'who also believe in man's doom. I have just been reading Professor Niebuhr's *Nations and Empires*.'

'I doubt whether this view is shared by the masses,' I retorted. 'Whereas here in Spain the sense of doom and of tragedy *is* a thing of the masses. It springs from beneath, from the very soil which the people tread.'

'They certainly believe in the influence of the soil,' said the doctor. 'The gipsies say that their inspiration, which is called the *duende*, springs from the soles of the feet upwards all over their body.'

This led us to talk about the curious Spanish foot fetishism, which I have already referred to. 'Does that come from a continuity of belief too?' I wondered. 'It is a trait I have found in North Africa and among many Arab friends. Is that detail part of the heritage of Islam?' 'It would be difficult to determine,' smiled the doctor, who then went on to quote Andalusian *coplas* on the subject of footsteps. 'They are nearly all connected with jealousy,' he remarked; 'and jealousy is much more developed in the Arab south than it is in the north, although even here it has almost disappeared:

> I shall tear up the stones in your street
> And cover them with sand
> To see the footprints
> Of those who prowl near your *reja*.

> If I knew which stones
> My love steps upon in the street,
> I would turn them upside down
> So that nobody could tread upon them.

'The popular muse,' said the doctor, 'is wise enough to realize that jealousy is usually a great exaggeration. This is well expressed and more concisely than in an elaborate speech, in the following *copla*:

> Jealousy and the waves of the sea
> Give one the impression
> That they are mountains.
> But they are only foam.

'Reverting to the subject of Spanish mothers,' the doctor continued, 'it would be an error to suppose that their spoiling is disinterested. The Spaniard is possessive, and I know of many cases of ferocious maternal possessiveness. May I illustrate the point by quoting to you what an Asturian mother once said to me. Her candour was unbelievable. She was a widow, she told me, with a married son aged twenty-eight. She brought him up, launched him in a lucrative business, and lived in the same house as the son, her daughter-in-law and their two children.

' "I have a domineering character," she admitted, "and I have imposed my will on my son to the point of meddling in his married life. I like him to spoil me and look after me as he used to do when he was single. On Christmas Eve I make him sit with me before allowing him to join his wife and children in their apartment. When he demurs, I remind him of the sacrifices I made to educate him.

' "My daughter-in-law is unhappy, because she has no authority in the house. But I don't care. The only thing I want is to prevent my son from leaving me. But many mothers are like me. It is only natural. . . ."

'There are many mothers like her,' said the doctor, 'only they do not express themselves quite so crudely. Others I have known justified their selfishness by stressing their "great affection" for their children. I do not deny that similar cases are to be found outside Spain, but then victims are usually daughters. In our country, sons are less independent, less virile, and afraid to assert themselves.'

'What about the younger generation?' I asked him. 'They are freer,' he replied. 'They are becoming very Europeanized— at least outwardly. This is not always to the good. I regret to see the word "sexy" making its appearance in our Press. I prefer the Spanish *sal*, which is more subtle. I do not believe that foreign influences have ever improved the Spaniards. They are not critical enough to separate the grain from the chaff.'

He repeated what I had already heard in other provinces: 'The duenna has disappeared, but you will find no young people out at night by themselves. As you know, we have official *vigilantes* equipped with field-glasses, to enforce decorum in our parks and on our beaches. Real companionship between the sexes is still a long way off. But people do want to know more about sex and I give lectures all over the province. I have been invited to lecture at the University of Salamanca, too. Ecclesiastics are beginning to realize that they must move with the times. But sex is still the "big black giant". Of all the mortal sins, the Spaniards have elected to pounce upon that of fornication to the near exclusion of all the others.' 'That is not peculiar to Spain,' I replied, 'it is widespread in patriarchal societies, and since most societies are patriarchal——' 'Man's desire to dominate engulfs woman,' concluded the doctor, 'and forces her to see sex as he does: as a means of conquest and submission, instead of the fusion it should be.'

'One always thinks of love in Andalusia as a charming duet,' I observed as I prepared to leave. 'I realize that it is a false picture, bequeathed to us by the Romantics, but still—the duet did exist at one time, did it not—between the guitar-playing lover on the one hand and the dark beauty behind her *reja*?' 'Never,' said the doctor. 'It has never been a duet; only a solo. The active male and the passive female. Picturesque? Certainly. And more musical than elsewhere. Young men's *rondas* are part of the national ritual, from the rustic tunes of the villages to the more polished performances of the towns. But music is ephemeral and love sung to somebody else's words and tunes is even more transient. The birds sing during the courtship season, then the concert is over. I fear that the same thing often occurs with young people. To serenade a girl was the "done thing", part of the process of growing up to be a man. Just as it was—and is—the "done thing" later on in life to be a Don Juan and to be able to boast of one's conquests.'

Although the Carmen myth had been exploded, I could not help paying a visit to her old tobacco factory in a private game of make-believe. I braced myself against possible disappointment by indulging beforehand in a *batida* (a kind of iced sundae) at the luxury hotel next door. The immense patio of this hotel is overlooked by several storeys of bedroom windows and galleries. The grey stone and the iron-wrought lanterns give it the appearance of a *plazuela*. Beneath the palms, old American ladies and a cripple in a wheel-chair sipped drinks and spoke in well-bred whispers. The *batida* cost five times more than in the elegant tea-room *La Española*, near my hotel, and smut from the chimneys fell constantly into the patio, forcing me to a hasty retreat.

Carmen's tobacco factory, now the Faculty of Letters of the University of Seville, was practically empty. The last students were passing the last examination before the summer vacation.

The Dean received me courteously but he was horrified when I submitted my questionnaire and asked whether I could distribute them among the students. He ran his fingers nervously through his grey hair and regretted that I had come so late in the year. 'Nearly all the students have left,' he explained. Hurriedly, he passed me to the newly appointed Professor of Ethnology. Our footsteps echoed up the marble staircase. I could not even begin to imagine the *cigarreras* with their babies and coloured shawls, the dense atmosphere, the friendly noise and chatter. The atmosphere itself seemed to have been disinfected and all the old plebeian smells replaced by the one pervading, almost universal chalk-leather-sweat smell of pedagogy.

The Professor of Ethnology knew more about the American Indians than about the Spaniards. I suppose that this was to be expected. He did admit, however, that it was time somebody undertook local investigations as the province was full of still uncollected folk material, He would put some of his students to work on it next year. So far they had never undertaken any kind of field work.

I asked the Dean and the Professor of Ethnology whether there were many girl students at the Faculty. 'Quite a lot,' they said, 'but at least half of them only come here to find a *novio*.'

In parks and public places, young couples are decorous, as in other parts of Spain. They walk together arm in arm or hand in hand but they never kiss. Their behaviour in private is another matter, and the roadside scenes at week-ends when the more modern elements of society go off to the country on motor-scooters have already been referred to.

The mixture of decorum and freedom which has astonished so many foreign travellers for so many centuries is still in evidence. I was invited to give a talk at a local Association for Employees, a religious foundation which caters mainly for the educational needs of young people from the lower middle class. It was a warm day and I was wearing a sleeveless, but not *décolletée* dress. As I was to dine outside the town after my talk, and the evenings were inclined to be chilly, I took a stole with me.

The head of the association, a gay little Spanish spinster, received me with a few of her colleagues in a Victorian drawing-room. We sipped orangeade, nibbled biscuits, and I chatted with the English teacher, a pretty brunette with a Murillo-like face. The atmosphere was genial yet semi-conventual. Before we went upstairs to the lecture-room, the head took me aside and asked me in a coaxing, confidential whisper whether I would mind putting my stole round my shoulders while I gave my talk. The atmosphere, in the closely filled smallish room was almost unbearably hot, even without a mohair stole. The head, realizing this, picked up a large black fan and fanned me assiduously during the whole hour that my talk lasted, a feat of which I would have been incapable, but her flexible little wrists rose to the occasion and never for a moment did she betray any signs of weariness. 'You must have been very warm,' she whispered afterwards, with an apologetic smile.

My talk was about foreign parts and I wondered whether my audience would be interested. One hears and sees so much of the poor education given in Spain, and of the people's intellectual apathy. Perhaps it was because I did not adopt the average Spanish lecturer's pompous and pedantic style, but spoke in the only kind of Spanish I knew, which is simple and conversational, that my audience was warm, sympathetic and bubbling over with questions. Rarely have I felt such a flow from an audience as in that stuffy, crowded classroom in Seville.

With characteristic Spanish spontaneity, the head looked round when questions were over and asked me whether I would like one of the girls to dance a *Sevillana* for me. I welcomed the suggestion but there was no orchestra and the gramophone was out of order. Two girls got up and a small space was cleared for them in the centre of the room. The rest began to sing and clap. I had expected a pleasant but amateurish performance by *jeunes filles bien élevées*, since that is what they were supposed to be, but as soon as my eyes alighted on the smaller and younger of the two girls, I began to have doubts. She had the fiery, laughing eyes of a gipsy, the swarthy complexion with an apricot tinge unknown to European races, the tight, lithe body of a Salome. And she danced—how she danced—with true Andalusian *sal* and gipsy fervour! Here was the *duende*, rising not so much from her feet as from her swaying hips. The decorous head of the establishment, who had been so insistent about my covering my arms with a stole, and the rest of her staff looked on with obviously chaste pleasure. An extraordinary spectacle. I turned to the English teacher; 'What a gipsy!' I murmured. She nodded and smiled faintly. 'You are right—she is a gipsy from Triana,' she replied.

The famous and overwritten district of Triana, across the Guadalquivir, has practically been obliterated by blocks of modern flats which surround it from every angle. The gipsy cabaret, with its pretence at a gipsy encampment and sprinkling of genuine gipsies on the programme, is engulfed between two miniature skyscrapers. Outside, rows of coaches from travel agencies disgorge foreign passengers nightly, on a 'See Seville by Night' tour. The best gipsies have gone abroad. They are in great demand for film work. And most of them have intermarried with non-gipsies. Triana is disappointing.

Spanish ethnographers have never wanted to appear interested either in gipsies or in Andalusians. This is the least studied part of Spain. Spanish scholars dig into the classical past. To them any-thing Roman, Greek or Arabic is worthy of study—everything except the fascinating peoples of the south.

'Manuel could have told you a lot about them,' said my friend, the Sevillan Poet. 'He abducted a gipsy girl, there was an awful row about it, and he had to go to prison. But that was over twenty years ago. Things have calmed down since then. Manuel was really fond of the gipsies and he wrote a book about them. I forget what it was called. Oh, it's out of print now. I could write to him and find out whether he's got a copy left. Of course, the chances are that he won't reply.' My friend was right. Manuel never did reply.

The Poet walked with me up and down the shady alleys of the gardens of the Alcázar, from time to time bending to break off a twig of *albahaca*, the love plant dedicated to Krishna and brought to Spain from India by some unknown Arab botanist of the Golden Age of Andalusia. To present a woman with *albahaca* is a love-token. In some villages, he told me, it is the custom for the girls to present their *novios* with a pot of this sweet-smelling herb. The Poet, who described himself as a middle-aged Don Juan, occasionally offered a sprig to the attractive young foreign visitors who thronged the gardens. Sad and grave as he appeared to be on his Andalusian surface, he never overlooked an attractive female.

Being a poet, he had sung of love, but he was at a loss to talk about it in prose. A subtle change came over him when the subject was introduced. The average Spaniard, when brought down to earth from his favourite state of nebulousness and hyperbole in praise of Woman, becomes wary or perplexed. He is wary because the subject is attached to real persons and so his natural reserve comes into play, he is perplexed because he has rarely taken the trouble to analyse his sentiments—on this score or on any other.

The middle-aged Don Juan could not talk about his private life, of course, but he related a number of experiences under the guise of 'things he had been told by his friends'. He did not attempt to conceal the errors of his youth. He was quite frank about *them*. He had reached the age of repentance, combined with satiety, which overwhelms so many Spaniards—men and women

—who feel that they are no longer admissible to the Garden of Love. (One occasionally comes across letters written to newspapers and magazines by women who sign themselves 'Mary Magdalene', in which they admit they have led a loose life but intend to reform, and ask for advice on the best way of doing this so as to convince people of their sincerity. One young man wrote to say that he had fallen in love with a prostitute who wished to mend her ways but was not sure what to do; he was firmly advised by the editor to go ahead and marry her.)

'The younger generation is not as obsessed by sex as we were in my time,' reflected the Poet, with a side-glance at a blonde Scandinavian tourist sketching on a nearby bench. 'Just imagine, I had a mistress when I was seventeen. Isn't it dreadful? I was initiated by a woman several years older than myself. That is a fairly common occurrence. Eve still offers the apple. As for sex, I learned about that from the other boys at the village school I went to when I was six years old. We used to play a game with the buns given to us during the mid-morning break. We divided them into "male" and "female" buns and stuck pens into the female ones. Quite realistic.' 'Doctor X told me that country lads aren't so precocious in several matters as the town boys,' I remarked. The Poet looked dubious. 'I don't know what happens nowadays, but we certainly were precocious in my young days,' he said.

'I think,' he continued, 'that the atmosphere is healthier today. When I was a child I could go—and did go—to low-down, vulgar cabarets where for a peseta or two we watched the most obscene spectacles ever devised. There is none of that sort of thing available nowadays. Just as well.'

'And the bordels have been closed,' I added. 'Has that made for a lot of sordid underground traffic?' The Poet refused to commit himself. 'Possibly,' he said cautiously. 'I wouldn't know. I am past all that now. I am growing old.' I smiled disbelievingly. 'Is it true, all they say about the Spanish woman's *recato*, modesty?' I asked him. He hesitated before replying: 'I believe it is, from what my friends have told me. A Spanish woman preserves a certain amount of modesty even when she is married, even during the most intimate moments. Ruben Darío (who married a Sevillan waitress—a loyal girl who always refused to admit that he drank too much and was too fond of women) always used to say that one should choose a Spanish woman for one's wife and a Parisienne for one's mistress.' 'Obviously, the prostitutes must be very different,' I said, wondering whether his reaction would be similar to that of other Spaniards I had spoken with on this subject. 'Oh, yes, of course. Once our women let themselves go, they are all right. And very generous.' He then proceeded to tell me a story that matched the many others I had heard about the open-handedness of Spanish prostitutes.

'Pierre, a French artist friend of mine, fell for a lovely dancer in Seville—that was a few years ago now. She was half-gipsy and "engaged" to a taxi-cab driver called Jorge. She was very aloof with Pierre. She only gave in to him when she felt like it, she said. Pierre had to woo her for some time before she agreed to become his mistress. One day she told him over dinner that he had better clear out of Seville because Jorge was after his blood. "And he means business—he is very quick with his knife," she said. Pierre was so infatuated with the girl that he persuaded her to go away with him. They went to Madrid but the gipsy didn't care for it at all. She pined for her native Seville and became a bit of an embarrassment because she would tap her heels in a wild *Sevillana* every night before going to bed. The other hotel guests complained. Pierre told me afterwards that he believed his gipsy was fonder of dancing than of bedroom games, and I can quite believe it. I am sure that most flamenco dancers get more fun from their dancing than from love-making. Well, to cut a long and tedious story short, Pierre got a bit fed-up; he had to return to Paris anyway, and as his gipsy was obviously a bit tired of him too, he bought her a ticket to return to Seville. And he slipped a few bank notes in an envelope. She was overjoyed at the sight of the railway ticket but as for the bank notes she tore them up in a rage. "What do you take me for?" she shouted. Pierre was furious to see his precious bank notes in pieces, I can tell you. He wasn't doing so well at the time. But he admired her Spanish pride. Anyway, he dined out on the story for many a night after his return to Paris. Until, about six weeks later, he received a badly spelled note from her, posted from Seville, asking him to send her money—for the same amount which she had so cheerfully torn up! Since then, Pierre says he has given up trying to understand the Spaniards.'

We got on to the subject of repentance. 'I have known a couple of bordel owners,' said the Poet, 'who repented through their daughters, whom they brought up very strictly and then clapped into a convent. There was Rosalita la del Cura, for instance, who received guests in her ante-chamber with the elegance of a great lady. In this private ante-chamber of hers one never discussed "business". And this was the only place where one could mention her daughter. She used to tell me, with great pride, that she was bringing her up to be as "pure as crystal" and a nun. The girl didn't know anything about her mother's profession. Later on, Rosalita la del Cura gave up her "social" life and became the portress at her daughter's convent. When the Civil War came and the Reds threatened the inmates of the convents, Rosalita hid all the nuns, one by one, in private houses and hiding-holes. It became her great mission in life, and one for which she risked her life, to protect the nuns from being "soiled by men". Curious anticlimax, don't you think, for an ex-bordel keeper?'

'It goes to show,' I remarked, 'that however impure a Spaniard may be, there usually comes a time in his or her life when the deeply rooted, national respect for what they call "purity", carnal purity, overwhelms them. This is a country of Magdalenes and repentant Don Juans as well as of gay sinners. Surely their horror of the flesh has been greater than that of any other European country! Could there be anything more nauseating, more terrifying than the picture of decomposed flesh painted by Valdés Leal, and commissioned by the repentant Don Juan—the Señor de Mañara? On the other hand, it is only a natural reaction, a forced reaction, from the Spaniards' adoration of physical charms. Ever since the days of Cervantes, and probably before, physical attraction—and physical attraction only—has been the reason for love. And that is still true today. I know of no other country where beauty is worshipped to the same extent.'

The Poet turned to me with a puzzled smile. 'Is that so? I would have thought it was fairly general,' he said. I shook my head. 'Not to the same extent, no. In Spain, even three-year-olds playing together in the park will remark upon one another's physical assets. I have often seen toddlers patting each other's plump cheeks and saying admiringly: "*Qué guapita eres!* [How pretty you are!]" Physical attractiveness is the great criterion. It affects men and women more deeply than in other countries, with the possible exception of Italy, and all classes of society. At a recent dinner-party in Madrid, a Spanish duchess spent over half an hour arguing whether the daughter of countess so-and-so was *guapa* or not. The girl was dissected by every guest at the table, male and female, in a form of mental strip-tease.

'One may argue, of course, that heads must be very empty if

they are filled with such trivialities—but to a Spaniard, beauty is
not trivial, it is a *raison d'être*. When the reaction sets in with
satiety and middle age, there is a revolt—an almost sadistic revolt
against the flesh and a pleasure in mutilation. Never has the
human form been so mutilated, even by her artists, as in Spain.
Perhaps that is why torture has never been considered quite so
terrible as elsewhere. To the Spaniard, there is a *reason*, a justifi-
able moral reason, for it.'

'I suppose,' smiled the Poet, 'that in a country where so many
people are beautiful, and you must admit that Andalusia is full
of very handsome people, the fight against sensuality has been
particularly difficult. We have a legacy of sensuality that dates
from Moorish days and perhaps from long before their time. Yes,
long before, the dancers of Cádiz were appreciated in Rome
centuries before the Arab invasion, precisely for their sensual
qualities. Our religion condemns the flesh, but the Creator has
given us such beautiful flesh! It is all very difficult.'

Even your Don Juans, unlike the Don Juans of other countries, have been essentially religious,' I said. 'Why did Tirso de
Molina insist upon this aspect? Historically, in the sixteenth
century, the questions of predestination and free will were being
ardently disputed between the Jesuits and the Dominicans. Tirso
sided with the former, he believed that whatever a man's life had
been, if he repented in the end, his soul could be saved. . . . Your
Don Juan was the great seeker of illusions; was he ever convinced
of their reality? I do not think so. He knew, he repeated that he
was mocking, playing a game, acting a part. Your Spanish lover
is above all an actor; I do not believe that he is really taken in by
his role any more than the woman is—or was.'

'Remember,' said the Poet, 'that the main stream of my countrymen has been very little affected by theories. The masses have
remained realistic, untouched by preoccupations with illusions.
Reality is tragedy enough for them; living, existing, finding
enough to eat. Come to my village, to my farm, and you will find
a very simple reality there, and a gay mockery of beliefs. There
are still more peasants than bourgeois in Spain.'

'Is life more lax in the country?' The Poet smiled. 'They are
taught to be conventional,' he said, 'but even so, certain things
go on behind teacher's back. Elopements, for instance; the intellectuals call them "Iberian rapts" because they are said to be a
survival of archaic rites. They are quite proper. The fiancé takes

the girl to his parents' house and she is as well guarded there as she would be in her own house. The marriage is eventually celebrated and then the young people are allowed to cohabit. The advantage of this method is: economy. It does away with the costly paraphernalia of a bourgeois wedding which the peasants can ill afford.'

'And virginity?' I asked, changing the subject, 'is it as strictly upheld as in the towns?' 'In theory,' said the Poet, 'but accidents occur. The peasants are usually quite philosophical about it. There was a case not long ago on my own farm. My headman came to me one morning in a state of agitation. I had just got back from Seville and wondered what dreadful accident had happened in my absence. "It's about Mercedes," he blurted out at last. Mercedes is his daughter. An attractive girl. I've known her since she was so high and if circumstances had been different, well, I might have been tempted. Anyway, I have always taken an avuncular interest in her and I rather think, without being presumptuous, that she was well disposed towards me.' The middle-aged Don Juan smiled enigmatically and stroked the carnation in his buttonhole.

'"What I am about to say will be a blow for you, Señor," said my headman. "It has been a terrible blow for us. I never would have believed it, never. . . ." "What has happened?" I asked him sharply. For a moment I thought that Mercedes had been carried off in an "Iberian rapt". My headman reddened; he really was upset. "I've told her," he said, "I've told her that you would be very, very angry. The fact is, Señor—my Mercedes is pregnant."

'I was astonished. She had been going round, I knew, with a young man from a neighbour's farm. They were *novios*, but discreetly so, as is usual with us. I was astounded, not so much by the fact itself, but that it had been able to take place at all, for Mercedes was very closely watched. "Well, Antonio," I said gently, "these things happen, you know. We must be tolerant. After all, they were *novios*, were they not?" Antonio nodded. "The Señor is not too angry, then? I must apologize, though. It never should have happened—not on your farm." I tried to conceal a smile. "We must arrange for the wedding to take place as soon as possible," I said. My headman gulped. "That is very kind of you, Señor. Yes, indeed we must, but Mercedes will have to wear a pleated skirt. I am so sorry about that, Señor, so very sorry." I must explain,' interrupted the Poet, seeing the puzzled expression on my face, 'that a girl who has had pre-marital relations with her *novio* is obliged to wear a pleated skirt at the wedding.' I remembered the bouquets of Lagartera and realized that this public recognition of conventional transgression seems to be an unwritten law among the peasantry. How embarrassing it must be for the couple concerned!

' "Send Mercedes along to have a talk with me," I said to my headman. "I want her to see that I am not angry, although I shall have to be a little severe with her at first. But what is done is done. Ah well, never mind, Antonio, you will have a grandchild a little earlier than you expected, that is all!"

'Eventually, Mercedes came and tapped at my door. I had never seen her looking so rosy, so modest, so maidenly, so maddeningly tempting. I also noticed, since I had been told about it, that she was a little plumper than she should have been at her age. I soon put her at her ease and said that I wanted her to have a fine wedding. Then, with pretended severity, I added: "But, Mercedes, tell me something: you are very well chaperoned by your parents. I know that they are religious, God-fearing people; how could it have happened? How did you manage to commit this transgression?" Mercedes blushed. "Well, Señor, it was like this: José and I arranged to meet beside the well at the top of the maize field every evening at eight o'clock. I resisted his advances for a long time, Señor, really I did. But then, one evening—it was later than usual, and there was such a strong smell of pennyroyal in the field that . . . something came over me and I seemed to lose consciousness. It was the fault of the pennyroyal, Señor, I assure you." I have been wondering ever since,' said the Poet, 'whether there is something in what she says and whether pennyroyal has ever been considered to be an aphrodisiac! If you find out anything about this plant when you get back to England, do please let me know.'[1]

At night, we wandered through the village, which was situated some way from the Poet's farm. He showed me the heavily white-washed house with the tiny patio where he had lived as a boy, and looked up and down the narrow, unpaved street with affection. 'This is the street in which I saw, for the first and last time in my life, an Andalusian *pantasma*. I don't know whether people still believe in them. Perhaps they do. My nurse, Carmen, told me about them. I must have been about seven years old and I was very impressionable. I shall always remember how she stole

[1] In England, pennyroyal is a traditional abortive.

quietly out of bed one night—she slept with me—and took up a position by the window. I woke up, startled, and whispered: "What is the matter, Carmen?" but she silenced me with an imperious gesture and continued to peer out of the window. She was evidently waiting for something, somebody to pass—but what? I felt my heart beating wildly against my breast. The sense of expectancy was almost unbearable. After a few minutes, I could stand it no longer and I too crept out of bed and stood shivering beside Carmen. "What is it, Carmen? Do tell me!" I implored.

'Carmen took her large black eyes off the street for an instant and said in a low, dramatic voice: "We are going to see a *pantasma*! If you are frightened, go back to bed. Because, if you should scream or show signs of fear, goodness knows what the *pantasma* will do to you."

'Curiosity overcame fear. "I shall not scream," I said bravely. "Then stay here and watch. It will be coming along any moment now," said Carmen, resuming her watchful position. A few seconds later, she started and pointed excitedly to the end of the street, which was in total darkness. I leaned forward and gasped. For there, gliding swiftly towards us, was a tall figure in white, bearing a light on its head. Before it reached the level of our house, I rushed back to my bed, pulled the clothes over my head and refused to look up again until I felt Carmen's warm body snuggling down beside me. In an access of terror, I flung my arms round her neck and pressed myself tightly against her firm breast. I remember to this day how very firm her breasts were; her nipples were so hard as to be almost painful. For a long time afterwards, I believed that women's breasts were held up by a bone in the centre!

'I also wondered how it was that Carmen should have known when the *pantasma* was due to pass the house. I suspect that she was acting as a sentinel on behalf of a friend and that the *pantasma* was a lover on his way to a clandestine rendezvous. The belief in *pantasmas* was so strong that nobody would have ventured to follow his course. To see one was considered to be unlucky, but the sceptical minority took advantage of the commonly held belief.'

'The Andalusians don't seem to have such a complicated love-life as the northerners,' Don José de Juanes told me when I saw him in Madrid. 'At least, I don't get so many letters from them as I do from the north.' Is this because they are lazier about writing letters, more reserved and subjected to parental control, or more cowed and submissive? Here is a batch of love problems which would seem to prove that their affairs do not differ so very much from those of the rest of their countrymen.

One *novio* admits that he is typically Andalusian and mistrustful of his *novia*. He is nevertheless 'madly in love' with her and although she had never given him any cause for suspicion, he feels he must have a proof of her love. 'What kind of test can I submit her to so that I can be completely certain of her love?' he asks.

A girl writes that her *novio* does not allow her to go out with her friends when he cannot accompany them but he goes out to drink and dance with his friends whenever he feels like it. To justify himself, he says that *novios* have certain rights which cannot be shared by *novias* and that men can do what they like because they are men and the woman must stay at home because she is a woman. The poor girl had heard this so often that she has begun to believe and obey him, in the belief that this is as it should be. 'If you do obey him,' replied Don José with a directness which would dismay his English counterparts, 'you will prove yourself to be as dull as slimming bread. You would condemn yourself to a life of perpetual slavery—you could never be happy with a man like that.'

Another girl brings up the curious and typically Spanish problem of betrothal promises made before an image. 'My *novio* had to leave our town. Before he left, in a moment of doubt, he asked me to promise him before an image never to abandon him. I was not sure whether I loved him enough to marry him but I agreed to make this promise to pacify him. Now I wonder whether it would be a sin to tell him that I do not love him enough to go through with it?'

And to prove that girls can be as vain as boys, a girl from Córdoba confesses: 'I love my *novio* very much, but I like boys to like me and I become coquettish when I walk in the street. This makes my *novio* furious. He is going away on his military service and I don't know whether I shall be able to keep faithful to him during his absence.'

A young man from Extremadura complains that his *novia* was unable to wait for him during his absence in another city, yet he cannot forget her. A girl whose *novio* is doing his military service wonders whether he will be faithful to her, as her mother keeps on telling her that all men are bad. 'She even says that of my father,' writes the girl, 'but that is not true, I know. He lives for her and for us, and never goes out to meet his friends. Yet she says he is faithless. Should I believe her when she tells me that my *novio* is being disloyal to me?'

A young man from Seville is in a turmoil. He knew a girl for eleven years, and became her *novio* for five. 'I had to break off relations, because her parents objected to the life of a libertine which I was then leading. Since then our respective parents arranged for us to meet and become engaged to other partners. The inevitable has happened. We have met again and realize that we are still deeply in love. I am in despair. What can I do with my present *novia*? My first one has quarrelled and broken with hers.' . . .

Overheard on the platform of Seville's railway station, waiting for the air-conditioned *Taf* to leave for Madrid—from one young man to another: 'The best present that a woman can give a man is a sleepless night.' From a Don Juanesque type to an attractive blonde, as he bid her *buen viaje*: 'Good-bye for now, marvel, child, woman who smells of corn, angel from the waist up, devil from the waist down, don't forget to send me a telegram as soon as you arrive in Madrid!' Charming Andalusia! Who would ever hear the like on a *British* railway platform?

5. In Madrid

THE *Taf* arrived in Madrid about ten o'clock at night, just in time for us to think about dinner, indeed almost too early by the average Spanish standard, but there was some delay before we could all get taxis. My taxi-driver, coaxed into the station by my porter, told me candidly that he was feeling bored and not at all inclined to pick up another fare. It was a condescension to take me at all.

We rattled uphill and through a mass of narrow streets to the Hotel Inglés in the Calle de Echagaray, once fashionable, now rather out-of-date, but friendly, comfortable, clean, and with an excellent cuisine, all for a pound a day, and conveniently situated near the Puerta del Sol and the main thoroughfares. Taxis curse one another as they endeavour to pass through the noisy throng of young men who fill the street from end to end every evening, after their visits to the *tascas* (cheap cafés) with which the street is amply provided. It is only a step to the modern, decorous Calle San Jerónimo, but here one might be in the provinces with their prickly smells of sizzling oil and *chorizos*, chirping canaries, loud chatter, strains of song and sad cries of lottery vendors seated in dim doorways. I was not surprised when a policeman informed me that the street was well-known to him and his colleagues.

In the middle of all this chaos, the Hotel Inglés, true to its name, stands respectably aloof and dignified. Its clients are mostly Spanish bourgeois, and include residents like the spinster whom I always met early in the morning, prayer-book in hand, black veil over her permanent wave, on her way to Mass. There is no possibility of arranging a romantic assignation in the Hotel Inglés. Each floor is vigilantly guarded by a small army of chambermaids, posted at strategic intervals along the labyrinthine corridors, who sit and gossip and closely observe the goings in and out of clients from morning until late at night. Like most Spanish chambermaids, they are maternal, slightly domineering and extremely voluble.

Since the lounge was always full of unashamedly eager eaves-
droppers, I took to interviewing people in the nearby Plaza Santa
Ana. Miss Sackville-West's Spanish grandmother, the dancer
Pepita, passed here, and my Sevillan poet's artist friend lunched
here with his gipsy mistress. It must have been Bohemian at one
time. Now it is bourgeois, with occasional incongruously rustic
incursions by *botijo*-laden donkeys led by wrinkled old men. A
large modern store occupies one side of the square and cafés line
the other sides; but the square itself, small, compact and shrubby,
is so closely filled with tables, chairs and benches that one can
both observe and participate in local life.

The Plaza Santa Ana is a family square, intimate and friendly.
Children play, solitary ladies sip *horchata* while they wait for their
novios or husbands, young mothers, gaudy as tarts, are chaperoned
by sallow-faced mothers in black, and the only bawdy asides one
hears issue from the lips of the irrepressible shoeblacks, who
inhabit a corner of their own; but even they, after a few days of
insolent *piropos*, begin to treat one with the respect due to a
regular.

My only interviewee who attracted attention to the point of
blocking half of the tiny square and interrupting the children's
games, was Carmen, the gipsy from Seville. I had to come back
to Madrid to be able to speak to a true gipsy. I had not found any
tame ones in Seville. Carmen was different. She came at the insist-
ence of one of my Spanish cousins, a journalist with a heart of
gold who is constantly dragging people out of sloughs of despond
although he earns just enough to enable him to eat.

When I told Victor that I wanted to interview a gipsy, he got
to work at once. Five minutes later, my telephone rang and he
enquired gaily: 'Do you still want a gipsy? Because if you do I've
got one here now. She's singing on my landing.'

That was the trouble with Carmen. Ever since she won the first
prize in a *saeta* singing competition in Seville, of which she
permanently carries a commemorative set of photographs in her
shabby leather handbag, she feels that she must sing on every
possible and impossible occasion. It has become both her mission
in life and her means of living. She had given up trading in
Andalusia to try her fortune in Madrid, where she had some half-
gipsy relatives, who happened to be the porters of Victor's block.
The porters told Carmen that my cousin Victor knew a lot of
cinema people and as soon as she heard this Carmen rushed up to

serenade him on his landing. 'She has a very powerful voice—
you'll have to restrain her,' Victor warned me on the telephone.

Carmen drank a coffee with me in the Plaza Santa Ana and
began to tell me the story of her life. She worked herself up to such
an emotional pitch at the recollection of her orphaned childhood
and fiery stepmother, that the tears began to roll and her ample
bosom heaved with sobs. At this point she had interested only our
immediate neighbours and the waiters, but when she burst into a
saeta, in no time a crowd gathered round us. Carmen went on
talking to me as if nothing had happened. She did not even seem
to notice the crowd who, after a few puzzled stares, reluctantly
began to disperse.

'Shall I sing you another one?' asked Carmen through her
tears. 'I have an extensive repertoire.' 'I am sure you have, that
was very nice,' I said soothingly, 'but maybe we could arrange a
saeta evening at my cousin Victor's—that would be better than
here.' 'Ah, your cousin Victor!' shrieked Carmen, raising her
eyeballs and her hands in a Greco-like attitude of ecstasy. 'Your
cousin Victor! He is a saint! I love him as if he were my own
brother. Did I tell you that he got me an interview with a film
director and that I have been engaged for his next film? Your
cousin Victor is——' I tried to interrupt her gipsy flow of
gratitude and bring the conversation round, as tactfully as I could,
to the subject which interested me. It was a difficult task.

Carmen dived into her handbag and drew out a miscellaneous
collection of photographs, used railway tickets, identity papers
and faded letters. 'This is me singing a *saeta* before the Mayor of
Seville. It was broadcast,' she told me triumphantly. I picked up
the photograph of a round-faced, whiskered gentleman of about
forty. 'Who is he?' I enquired. Carmen's chin quivered and tears
began to flow again. 'That is my poor husband—he died ten years
ago. He was very good to me,' she said. 'What a life I have had!
Ah, Señorita, what a life!' Her tears fell thick and fast.

Being now a little hardened to Carmen's outbursts, I insisted
upon knowing more about her marriage and courtship. She
shrugged her shoulders as if such things were unimportant
trivialities. 'Oh, we courted in the old-fashioned gipsy way,'
she said. 'That's all gone now. We're all good Christians, married
to Andalusians and settled down. It was quite simple. Nothing to
it, really. My husband saw me, looked at me, and I looked at him,
and we knew we were meant for one another. Then we met a few

more times. And then he asked me to run away with him. You know the film *Maria de la O?* Well, it was just like that. Mind you,' and here she leaned over with a ferocious expression and clutched my arm, 'he never touched me, no, not even touched me, until we were married. I stayed with his parents, in their home. That was the way it used to be. Now it's all changed.' 'Are the men jealous?' I asked her. Carmen's eyes lit up in amusement. 'They won't allow you to look at another man,' she said. 'But the men?' 'The men,' said Carmen sententiously, 'are the same as all other men. Chastity is a woman's virtue.'

'Did they sing at your wedding?' I pursued relentlessly. Carmen's eyes filled with tears again; she had a positively eighteenth-century facility for crying at will. 'Of course they sang,' she said. 'It was the custom then for singers to improvise *coplas* about the bride and groom, bringing in all they knew about their characters and their lives. I remember what they sang about me and the sad life I had led until then—yes, I can remember it as if it were yesterday. "We know very well, Carmen," they sang "that you had a lonely childhood. You did not know what it was to have a mother's love. Now you have found a good husband and he will look after you and you will know what love is. We wish you happiness, Carmen, for so far your life has been sad."

'The day after the wedding, we sat on a sort of dais. Behind us hung the wedding sheet—you know what I mean, Señorita?—and they sang us a *copla* about the three red roses on the white field. The fewer the spots of blood on the sheet the gentler the bridegroom was supposed to be and so a special *copla* was sung in his praise. Ah yes, my Fernando was a very good husband to me!'

On the other hand, a friend who knew a wealthy gipsy matador told me that the latter referred to his children scattered over Andalusia as casually as if they were rabbits. Most of them, however, appeared to belong to one woman, whom he seemed to consider as his wife. 'Why don't you buy a house for them all?' he was asked one day. 'I have thought of it,' replied the *gitano*, 'but as soon as people know I want to buy one, they put the price up to about three times its value and that puts me off.'

This time I did not try to check Carmen as she raised her voice and sang the wedding *copla*, the *coplas* that are sung no more, now that life is becoming conventional and uniform.

Well, not quite. Spain is one of the few remaining countries which has not yet been sucked up into the amorphous mass of dull people who have forgotten their folk tales and customs and sense of seasonal rhythm. Madrid, the capital, preserves at least two gay courtship customs; the student *tuna* and the *novio*-seeking feast of San Antonio la Florida.

The students still go serenading, in the heart of Madrid, beneath the new blocks of flats in the Calle de Ayala. Quite recently, my aunt wrote and told me: 'The *tuna* came again last night to serenade one of the pretty girl students who live opposite me. There were about forty or fifty boys, dressed in black, with tight trousers, black stockings and shiny patent-leather shoes. Their black capes are tied at the shoulder with a bunch of multi-coloured ribbons and they play tambourines, bandurias and guitars decorated with ribbons. They sing a mixture of songs, some classical, some modern, but all of them have something to do with love. The girls whom they are serenading come out on to their balcony and after a while, provided they know them of course, they are invited up for liqueurs and biscuits. It is all very gay and youthful.'

As for the fiesta of San Antonio la Florida, which takes place in the month of June and was painted by Goya, this is frequented by Madrilenian midinettes who go there to drop pins in the holy water font and ask the saint to send them a *novio*. They put on their prettiest clothes and this is one of the rare occasions upon which one can still see the traditional mantilla.

The boys go to serenade the girls and perhaps find a *novia*. More than one marriage has resulted from these gay encounters under the auspices of the amiable saint, whose abode is close to the house where Goya lived. (If you happen to be in Madrid at that time and are interested in rustic pottery as much or more than in rustic sweethearts, you will find some beautiful specimens at the fiesta of San Antonio. A dainty miniature *botijo* and an exquisite vase, executed in delicate shades of pink, green and yellow, smile up at me as I write and remind me, every time I look at them, of a sunny, dusty day in June and the laughing girls and guitar-playing boys.)

'That pin-dropping business is just a superstition, nobody really believes in it,' sniffed the sophisticated young lady whom I met in an art gallery later on in the day. I was telling her how much I had enjoyed the fiesta. 'But it is so pretty—so gay!' I exclaimed. She immediately relented. The word 'pretty' has a magical effect in Spain. 'Yes, it is pretty,' she agreed with a smile.

Having an hour to spare before an appointment with my useful informant Don José de Juanes, I decided to go for a ride in the tube, to test the tube-going male's gallantry. Alas, it is no better than ours—it is worse, for the young men are the first to make a rush for the few available seats. How quickly they forgot the *piropos* reserved for street-level!

If there is a lack of gallantry in the tube, there is an excess of it in certain cafés along the avenues leading to the Puerta del Sol. I went into one to while away the last few minutes before my appointment and found myself in a network of pros of all hues. Every one of the new hair dyes seemed to have been experimented upon, from the palest ash blonde to the fiercest mahogany. Under the dye and the heavy paint, many of the girls were extremely beautiful. Nor were their expressions as hard and sulky as those of our native pros. I observed their behaviour with the male clients. They preserved the sweetness of manner, the attractive without being meretricious smiles of the average Spanish woman. A woman is what a man wants her to be; a bawdy Englishman will look for a bawdy pro., but a Spaniard seems to require more grace.

'Oh, but most of them are so vain and stupid!' a Madrilenian friend exclaimed. 'Love of luxury has always been one of our chief defects and that is what pushes many of our girls out on to the streets.' 'Things are not very different at home,' I observed.

'If the girls are vain, the men love to show off,' smiled Don José, the 'problem letter' man who has dealt with Spanish love difficulties for fifteen years and has a background of over three hundred thousand letters to draw information from. 'There is still a Don Juan type among us. You will see him frequently in the cafés of Madrid because he needs an audience. He must be able to show off his new conquests to his envious and not so successful rivals. He wants them to look up as he goes into the café with his striking partner and follow their triumphal passage to the far end. He never sits near the entrance where he would not be noticed; he looks for a long passage and a throng of admirers. His partner dresses more and more provocatively as time goes on. Should the wife find out—*adiós!*—she will be quickly dropped, for if he cannot 'produce' a mistress in public then she is no more use to him. Pride and *amor propio* have more to do with it than *amor*—but that is the hallmark of a Don Juan.'

Although the sale of contraceptives is officially banned, there is a flourishing black market. 'In one pharmacy I went to, I was told that they are not available in Spain,' complained a young Englishman in Madrid. 'Then you must have gone to the wrong place,' said his Spanish companion. 'Let me give you the address of one whose proprietor is more broad-minded.'

'Are they really safe?' asked a Spanish bourgeoise who works in a Ministry. 'Because I know a lot of women who would risk having a love affair if they could be sure.'

Barcelona is a fairly easy market. When I was there I overheard a Catalan vendor confide to a friend: 'I know I could make more money than I do at markets and fairs. I should do like the others. They all sell these articles nowadays and some of my regular clients ask for them too. But I refuse to sell articles that go against my moral principles.'

Don José takes his work very seriously. His answers to problems are extensive, sensible and human. At the same time he does not hesitate to advise young people in a style which would appear peremptory to an Anglo-Saxon. His condensed replies to letters, which fill a column of his paper, abound with terse remarks like the following: 'You should give up that boy—he is no good for you'—'Choose the other girl—she would suit you better', and so on.

Don José encourages his correspondents to go to see him and discuss their problems in further detail when they happen to pass through the capital. And they do. In the absence of Marriage Guidance Counsellors and others of their kind in Spain, Don José seems to be fulfilling their objectives single-handed.

It would seem, from conversations I had with people who move in many circles, from police officers to doctors and journalists, that there are few suicides in Spain and that these are mostly confined to women. There had been a case recently. Of course, it never appeared in the Press, since the subject is taboo. A girl whose *novio* had become the gigolo of a rich American woman staying at one of Madrid's leading hotels had discovered his infidelity and thrown herself out of the window.

I was told that in Madrid between forty and fifty per cent. of the girls are no longer virgins by the age of twenty-five. On the other hand, there are cases of women, married women, who are either frigid or refuse to consummate their marriage—one woman refused her husband for two years. Another woman's only fear on her wedding-night was that her husband might disarrange her coiffure—surely an extreme case of vanity.

It is hardly surprising to learn that the Oedipus complex seems to be strongly marked in Spain where the family unit is so compact. I was shown several extraordinary letters dealing with cases of incest beside which our recent theatrical plays on the theme seem positively tame. It is a pity that Spanish dramatists are not allowed a free rein, for their country is so rich in human drama of every description.

Undoubtedly, some of the themes might be too intense and too alien for Anglo-Saxon audiences. The theme of vengeance, for instance. The following case occurred in Galicia, although it savours of Castile. A married woman complained to me about her husband. She seemed to have grounds for actively disliking him, since he ill-treats her and is a drunkard. She has to go out to work to support him. 'I feel like taking a lover!' she exclaimed. 'I hate my husband. I should like him to be all alone in the world, and desperately ill so that he would be forced to get on his knees and beg me to take him in. I should like to see him grovelling in misery.' Until then, I had believed that a similar attitude described in one of my Spanish friend's novels was an exaggeration.

It is inevitable that the many cases of happy love and happily married life should not come to light with the same frequency as love-problems, but I was given several charming examples of domestic felicity and deep sentiment: a young couple of twenty-eight who have been married for eight years and still go about hand in hand; a young wife of thirty-five who is dying of cancer and tried to hide the fact from her husband, but realized that he knew when she woke up one night and found him weeping silently and passing his hand over her forehead, without touching her; two old peasants from the Canaries, married since the ages of twelve and thirteen respectively, now aged one hundred and three and one hundred and four, who decided to go on a cruise because the husband had always promised his wife that one day he would take her travelling!

For a foreign woman, one of the Spaniard's most annoying traits and one which makes travelling in Spain obnoxious (although less so than in Italy) is his 'ocular activity' coupled with the irritating custom of addressing personal remarks to women, known as *piropos*. I have already alluded to this in passing; if I had extended myself on the subject, the space devoted to it would have become excessive and tedious. I had come across the habit in Castile and in Andalusia, but not in Galicia or in Cataluña. In the latter province, most *piropos* are addressed to one by immigrant Andalusians.

Ocular activity is, however, quite intense; though less in Galicia than in the other provinces. As Richard Wright observed,[1] 'If the Spanish woman stares at you, the Spanish man all but converts the streets and cafés of Spanish cities and towns into bedrooms. For all I know Spanish women may even consider this crude kind of bug-eyed wonder as a compliment to the feminine half of the human race ... but I cannot conceive of any French, American or Englishwoman of any maturity whatsoever revelling in these adolescent and cannibalistic devourings with the irises and pupils.'

'Don't you think *piropos* are barbarous?' enquired an Argentinian artist who has lived in Madrid for years. 'What effrontery for a man in the street to address personal remarks to an unknown woman!' I agreed with him, but when I brought up the subject before a group of young doctors of both sexes in a Madrid hospital, national pride raised its head and the until then detached, scientific discussion degenerated into violent monologues and protests. 'Good gracious!' exclaimed the doctor in charge, raising his hands to his head, 'I have never seen my assistants in this state before. It proves that a discussion of national sex characteristics in the presence of a foreigner arouses the most violent passions!' And he leaned back and smiled at the unusual spectacle.

I was interested to observe that the staunchest defenders of the *piropo* were the Andalusians, male and female. A lady doctor from Córdoba simply could not understand my attitude. 'But *piropos* are a homage to feminine beauty—what is wrong with that?' she exclaimed indignantly. 'Is it a compliment,' I retorted acidly, 'to hear a common shoeblack in the Plaza Santa Ana shout as you pass by: "Beautiful creature! Let me buy one of those new foam mattresses so that we may sleep together comfortably!" ' The assistants rocked with laughter. 'I agree it is an impertinence,' said a woman doctor from Madrid who was known among her colleagues as 'the foreigner' because she was a feminist and favoured modern ways.

[1] Richard Wright: *Pagan Spain* (The Bodley Head, 1960).

'And you, Fernando,' said the doctor in charge, addressing himself to a handsome young doctor from Madrid, 'do you address *piropos* to the ladies?' The answer was significant: 'No, I do not—not any longer. I am in love with my *novia* and I have stopped making *piropos*.' The young doctor from Granada was less sure of himself. 'I used to, but not now—I think it's because I don't dare to any more" he said, adding quickly, 'but you must admit that many of the women one sees in the streets go about *pidiendo guerra* [asking for war].' I thought of the tarty young mothers I had seen in the Plaza Santa Ana and others who brazenly admit that they deck themselves out ready for the fray and are anxious to 'collect' as many *piropos* as possible in the day. As long as women are vain and men are gallant, there will be *piropos* in Spain.

'You wouldn't believe how vain our women can be,' said a young Cordoban. 'A girl I know—and she is very pretty too—simply cannot bear to meet another pretty girl in the street—one who might be considered to be prettier than she is. She gets quite hysterical about it and goes back home weeping frantically.' 'That, *amigo mío*, is a pathological case', laughed one of the doctors present.

A couple of anti-*piropo* articles had appeared recently in the Spanish Press, one written by a priest and the other by a lay writer: 'There is no justification for the *piropo* which is merely an excuse to meddle with women,' wrote the priest. The lay writer observed that in 'the old days' the *piropo* was often quite charming and witty, whereas now it has degenerated and is the mark of the unlettered who confuse virility with *gamberrismo* or teddy-boy-ism. He admits that for every pleasant *piropo* one hears nowadays, more then a hundred are vulgar and dirty. He cannot understand how it is that 'a man who is so respectful and jealous with his womenfolk at home would behave in the street as if he were suffering from an attack of sexual hysteria.

'For the Spaniard, it would seem that there are only two types of women: his mother, wife and sisters, who are "saints", and the rest, of which he has an entirely different conception. He does not seem to understand that a generalization of this theory would be offensive in the extreme.'

The writer also attacks Spanish women for not reacting more vigorously. 'Of course, it is difficult to protest; a box on the ear would be the best answer but it implies an instantaneous reaction which does not come naturally to the average Spanish woman.' I tried to answer back once myself one day in Seville and informed my *piropeador* that in my opinion he 'lacked education', which is quite an insult in Spain. He only laughed and replied: 'I cannot understand why you should object. I was only telling you pleasant things. If you had been lame or deformed and I had commented on that, it would be different.' It was useless to pursue the conversation. The only thing that can be said in favour of the *piropo* is that it is preferable to the wolf-whistles imported from the barbarous west, which one does not hear in Spain.

* * *

'Well,' said the retired art historian whom I had met in Madrid at the beginning of my travels, 'have you come to any conclusions about love and the Spanish?'

'I would prefer to call them "impressions",' I replied guardedly. 'What has struck me most is the contrast that exists between the various provinces of Spain, particularly between the north and the south. In Andalusia, land of guitars, scented nights and moonlight serenades, love resembles the gay patterns of Iberian vases; it is flamboyant, highly decorative and superficial. The picturesque courtship ritual was a masculine diversion, a form of virgin-worship at a secular level which enabled the man to display his poetic and musical gifts. The woman was, and has remained, passive and reserved. But behind the façade lies a profound sense of disillusionment, shared by men and women alike. They equate love with beauty, and they are fully aware that beauty is evanescent. Religion emphasizes this innate tendency to belittle human values. Typical of this attitude was a young Sevillan woman's remark: "It is difficult to find a human ideal. Christ is the perfect ideal." Although there is less bigotry in the north of Spain, most Spanish women are stamped by a conventional education which greatly inhibits their relationships with the opposite sex.'

'Andalusia is still very backward,' said the art historian, 'but our northern women, as you say, are more emancipated; more respect is shown to them by the men and there is more equality between the sexes—haven't you found that?'

'To a limited extent,' I replied, 'but there is still not enough respect shown to women as human beings. It is curious that in those countries where the cult of the Virgin Mary predominates, women's status should be so low.'

'She is respected as a mother.'

'And treated as a second-rate citizen by the State and by her husband, especially in the convention-riddled middle class! I have not found much companionship between the sexes.'

'The general lack of education accounts for that. There is a very different spirit among the younger, university-educated generation.'

'Granted, for a minority. But there is more to it than the lack of a liberal education. I believe that it is much more difficult for a Spaniard to be completely in love than, say, an Englishman or a Frenchman, because of his temperament. The average Spaniard is too proud, too self-centred and too intolerant to be able to fuse his personality with that of another human being. He is an individualist and a lover of the monologue. He does not understand or approve of a dialogue—a characteristic which does not make living with him (or her) easy.'

'And that goes for politics as well as home life!' said the art historian. 'But I think you are a little hard on us. We have intense lovers, and romantic ones too. Do not forget, though, that we are reserved and unused to revealing our intimate sentiments.'

'I realize that,' I said, 'and it has surprised me to find that on the whole people have responded readily to my indiscreet questioning on the subject of love. I would not have believed it possible.'

'You see,' concluded the art historian, 'even we are changing—slowly perhaps, but changing nevertheless. My only hope is that in our approximation to the more modern countries of Europe we shall stop before we reach the stage that you are in now, with your vast number of divorces, broken homes, and juvenile delinquents!'

Index

Index